THE NATURALIST'S GUIDE TO THE

ATLANTIC SEASHORE

Beach Ecology from the
Gulf of Maine to Cape Hatteras

SCOTT W. SHUMWAY

FALCONGUIDES ®

GUILFORD, CONNECTICUT
HELENA, MONTANA

Text design by Mary Ballachino
Map created by M.A. Dubé © Rowman & Littlefield

Library of Congress Cataloging-in-Publication Data

Shumway, Scott.
   The naturalist's guide to the Atlantic seashore : beach ecology from the Gulf of Maine to Cape Hatteras / Scott Shumway. -- 1st ed.

     p. cm.
    ISBN: 978-0-7627-4237-0 Includes
    bibliographical references.
    1. Seashore ecology—Atlantic Coast (U.S.) I. Title.
    QH541.5.S35S527 2008
    578.769'90974--dc22

                                                                    2007042831

Printed in Huizhou, Guangdong, PRC, China

Distributed by NATIONAL BOOK NETWORK

CONTENTS

Acknowledgments iv

About the Author v

Preface vi

Map viii

Introduction 1

The Coastline: Where the Ocean Meets the Land 11

Food Chains and the Forgotten Plankton 25

Rocky Shores 37

Sandy Beaches 73

Sand Dunes 97

Estuaries 109

Salt Marshes 135

Tidal Flats 159

Seagrass Meadows 177

The Open Ocean 185

The Beach in Winter 203

Afterword 215

References 216

Index 224

ACKNOWLEDGMENTS

Many people reviewed drafts of chapters, including Tim Barker, Barbara Brennessel, Frank Caruso, Debi Cato, Geoff Collins, Ben Eck, Ann Hadley, Paul Jivoff, Garry Kessler, Heidi Leighton, Sheila McPharlin, Marianne Moore, Bob Morris, Dan Murray, Harry Newell, Bryan Oakley, Carol Shumway, Anne Reid, Rick Wahle, and Patricia Brady Wilhelm. Their efforts are greatly appreciated and greatly improved the book. I thank my editors—Patrick Straub, Erin Turner, and Meghan Hiller— for all of their help in guiding me through this project.

I thank all those people who explored habitats with me or made it possible to visit interesting places, including Barbara Brennessel, Mark Devoto, Lois Grossman, Paul Jivoff, Garry Kessler, John Kricher, Heidi Leighton, Jim Morin, Nick Picariello, Dennis and Gail Preston, Anne Reid, and Don Young. Ben Cooper gathered the Cooper family together for vacations on Cape Cod, Nantucket, and Hilton Head. He read drafts of several chapters, but sadly, he passed away before the book was published.

Thank you to Don Anderson, JoAnn Burkholder, Craig Cato, Dennis Donohue, Jason Goldstein, Paul Hargraves, Andy Howard, Garry Kessler, Bart Krishnamoorthy, Blair Nikula, Sandra Shumway, Greg Skomal, Bob Steneck, Tim Voorheis, and Rick Wahle for sharing their photographs. I thank Jim Carlton for providing access to his library.

Faculty scholarship awards, a Patricia Higgins Arnold '66 and Christopher B. Arnold Faculty Enrichment Award, and a sabbatical from Wheaton College provided opportunities for writing, reading, exploring, and photographing.

I thank my colleagues John Kricher and Barbara Brennessel for their constant support and encouragement. Anne Reid and Garry Kessler deserve special thanks for their reviews, photographs, advice, and companionship. I am deeply indebted to Ken Davignon for his patience and sage Photoshop advice.

My interest in nature has been fueled by the opportunity to interact with some truly inspirational people to whom I am eternally grateful, including Tom Tyning, Norton Nickerson, Peter Auger, and Mark Bertness. As soon as I could walk, my grandmother, Cleora Stimpson, started my lifelong compulsion to collect seashells and to learn the names of birds and plants. My parents, Carol and Richard Shumway, took me to many beaches along the East Coast and have always supported my interest in nature study and bird-watching. My father impressed on me from day one the value of a college education, never dreaming that I would someday be a college professor. My wife, Lisa, continues to support my interests and tolerate my occasional need to go bird-watching or for a long walk on a beach.

Without the support and influence of these people, my life would be very different, and this book would never have been possible. I thank them from the bottom of my heart. The spirits of Gram, Dr. Nick, and Ben will always be with me when I walk on the beach.

This book is dedicated to my son, Cooper Wesley Shumway, my favorite beachcombing buddy.

ABOUT THE AUTHOR

Scott Shumway is a professor of biology at Wheaton College in Massachusetts where he teaches courses in marine biology, botany, and environmental science. He is a devoted bird-watcher and beachcomber. Dr. Shumway began collecting shells on the sandy beaches of Ocean City, New Jersey, almost as soon as he could walk. He has undergraduate degrees in biology and environmental studies from Tufts University where he was introduced to the salt marshes of Cape Cod by Dr. Norton Nickerson. His study of salt marshes continued at Brown University where he received a doctorate under the guidance of Dr. Mark Bertness. He has also conducted research on sand-dune ecology on Cape Cod National Seashore and on Sandy Neck in Barnstable, Massachusetts.

CAROL SHUMWAY

PREFACE

My love of the ocean began when I was a child vacationing with my parents and grandmother in Ocean City, New Jersey. I had the misfortune of growing up in a city over 100 miles from the nearest beach. For the first eighteen years of life, I was exposed to this wonderful environment for only one week each year, but I relished every second of it and still do. I spent many hours walking the beach dividing my time between examining stranded sea creatures, shells, and seaweeds and watching pretty girls. Not much has changed over four decades, except that I now spend most of my time studying the marine organisms rather than the two-legged creatures.

An old photograph of a three-year-old boy with his red shovel and pail proves that I knew at an early age that there was much to see and do at the shore. I quickly learned that the burrowing activities of tiny Coquina Clams could provide hours of fun. I also discovered that these clams occur in a multitude of different color patterns. My habit of capturing them alive fifty at a time and bringing their stinking remains home in my pail earned me some outrage from my parents. My father taught me to dig for clams but failed to tell me there were other critters (mostly other critters) buried in the sand as well. I still remember the day when I ran down the beach screaming in pain with a recently exhumed Lady Crab attached to my thumb.

Thanks to my grandmother I evolved into a collector of shells, polished stones, and beach glass. My obsession with collecting shells and finding sea creatures washed up on shore was accompanied by a desire to identify them or to know their names. Field guides helped to some extent, but it was years before I knew what the fast-burrowing clams (Coquina) or egg-shaped crabs (Mole Crabs) really were. These guides were acceptable for identifying most beach creatures but revealed little or nothing about what the animals were actually doing. How they made their living, what they ate, how they captured their food, how they were adapted to living in such a dangerous environment, and how they impacted their neighbors remained a mystery. It was not until I was a graduate teaching assistant for an invertebrate zoology class that I discovered how clams burrowed in the sand or how they captured their food. I never knew why many of the surf clam shells that I collected contained round holes as if predrilled for stringing on a necklace. I never knew why some of the clam shells were riddled with tiny holes and catacombs as if attacked by termites. I never knew that the stranded Horseshoe Crabs that I would bravely return to the sea were important links in one of the largest shorebird migration stopover sites along the entire eastern flyway or that this site was only a few miles away from where I played on the shore. Nor did I know that these crabs were living fossils and that the same species has crawled about sandy beaches almost unchanged for millions of years. Nor could I have predicted that their blue blood would become an important lifesaving tool in biomedicine.

A few blocks away on the other side of the island, I was introduced to miles of salt marsh as far as the eye could see. My mother warned me not to walk in the marsh because I would surely sink out of sight. In 1991 I received a Ph.D. from Brown University based on five years of research, conducted while walking and crawling in salt marshes. I rarely sank in the marsh. My mother had lied, but she didn't know any better. Today we bird-watch together in the salt marsh.

These experiences have made me realize that it is important to know the names of the plants, animals, and algae with which we share planet earth. I have learned that while knowing their names is important, it is not enough. Rarely is it enough for us to learn just the name of the people we meet. We inevitably ask where they live, where they grew up, if they have any children, and what they do for a living. We might even discover their favorite foods and exercise activities. In the case of the ten million other species that share the planet with us, it is also essential to know what they are doing. How they interact with their surrounding environment and with one another is of great interest and importance. Knowing this information instills in us a greater appreciation for the interconnectedness of nature and the important roles that seemingly insignificant species can play in their world. Therefore, this book will aid with the identification of many species found in coastal environments, but its primary goal is to explain how coastal environments function and the roles that various species play in these environments.

Despite the crowds of people, I often feel alone when I go to the beach and immerse myself in the natural world that surrounds us. That people can go to the beach and NOT be intrigued by the critters crawling beneath their feet or swimming beside them is something that astounds me. I feel a deep sadness for them, that they are missing out on experiencing the wealth of interdependent life that surrounds them or the satisfying sense of wonder that comes with taking a closer look at this life. It is for them that I write this book, and it is the reader's job to share this knowledge with them.

QUEBEC

NEW
BRUNSWI

St. Lawrence River

MAINE

St. John ⊙

Bay of Fundy

Montpelier
⊛

Augusta
⊛

N
S
C

Lake Ontario

ADIRONDAK
MOUNTAINS

VT

⊙ Portland

Gulf of Maine

NEW YORK

Albany ⊛

Concord
⊛

N H

Boston ⊛

Hudson River

MA

Hartford
⊛

Providence ⊛

CAPE COD

R I

C T

Long Island Sound

PENNSYLVANIA

APPALACHIAN
MOUNTAINS

Harrisburg
⊛

⊙ New York

Philadelphia ⊙

⊛ Trenton

Delaware River

N J

Baltimore ⊙

⊛ Dover

M D

Delaware Bay

CAPE MAY

Washington, D.C. ⊛

Annapolis ⊙

D E

Potomac River

Chesapeake Bay

Atlantic

Ocean

VIRGINIA

Richmond
⊛

James River

CAPE CHARLES

Norfolk ⊙

Raleigh
⊛

Albemarle Sound

NORTH
CAROLINA

Neuse River

Pamlico Sound

CAPE HATTERAS

Outer Banks

N

S C

0 Kilometers 250

0 Miles

INTRODUCTION

The beach is home to a fascinating array of life-forms. Microscopic bacteria, large seaweeds, flowering plants, worms, clams, crabs, sea urchins, fish, birds, whales, and more all call the beach and surrounding ocean waters home. Representatives from nearly every major branch on the evolutionary tree of life can be found on the east coast of North America. A wonderful diversity of habitats makes this possible. Waves pound rocky and sandy shores. Calm water flows through estuaries, salt marshes, and seagrass beds. Hordes of migratory birds and fish come and go from these habitats as they seek out temporary places to feed or struggle to survive the early stages of their lives. Humans also flock to the beach as year-round residents or in large vacationing hordes. In addition to their aesthetic value, coastal habitats provide us with many economic benefits, including putting food on our plates. Whatever our reasons for visiting the beach, it is hard to miss the abundance of life that is present. Understanding how these living organisms interact with one another and with their environment is the goal of the study of natural history.

Understanding the world around us is a tremendous challenge. It is like attempting to assemble a large jigsaw puzzle, except there are no edge pieces, the exact number of pieces is unknown, and the "picture on the box" is incomplete at best. Because scientists are constantly reassessing the interactions among species, the shapes of the pieces are constantly changing. Some interlock tightly while others fit loosely. Despite these challenges understanding how pieces of the puzzle fit together is immensely rewarding and is what drives scientists, as well as the rest of us, to continue asking questions about the world around us.

Natural history tells a story that interweaves living organisms with one another and with their environment. Putting it all together is the challenge faced by us naturalists as we seek to understand the interconnectedness of all life. No matter how much we learn about our world, there is always more to learn. This is what keeps us fascinated with our world, causes us to value nature, and drives scientific inquiry. It is easy to be overwhelmed by the majesty of nature. A natural historian, however, is awed by the interplay of species and their environment that creates this natural world. The natural world is not static; it is constantly changing, and the components are interconnected in a highly complex manner. However, it is not so complex that we cannot at least begin to understand how it works.

For example the flounder that you ate for dinner last night was caught in the Atlantic Ocean a few miles offshore and then shipped several hundred miles to your local grocery store. That fish spent its first few months of life in the protected environment of an estuary where it fed upon small clams and worms that filtered zooplankton from the water. Zooplankton consume tiny algae that rely upon a steady stream of nutrients and sunlight. Those nutrients may originate from the effluent of a wastewater treatment plant located along the river feeding into the estuary. This may well be the same facility that your household plumbing system is connected to. You are a part of this complexity.

Biogeography, or Why Species Live Where They Do

This book focuses on the natural history of the western Atlantic coastline from the Bay of Fundy to Cape Hatteras. This geographic range is justified by the distribution patterns of the organisms that inhabit this large area. The Gulf of Maine is bounded by Nova Scotia, New Brunswick, Maine, and Cape Cod. Its designation as a separate region on a map seems arbitrary until you study the oceanic currents that bring cold water from the north and swirl around the bay in a giant counter-clockwise gyre. Temperature is probably the most important factor determining whether or not a species can live in a particular geographic area, whether it be at sea or on land. Only true cold-water species can inhabit the Gulf of Maine. Marine biologists refer to this area of the sea and associated coastal marine environments as the Boreal Biogeographic Province, or simply the **Boreal Region.** It is bordered to the north by the frigid waters of the Arctic Province. The Virginian Biogeographic Province, or **Virginian Region,** extends south of Cape Cod to Cape Hatteras.

Cape Cod serves as a barrier to the cold Labrador Current flowing from the north and the warm waters of the Gulf Stream flowing from the south. As a result it is also an effective distribution limit for many marine species sensitive to the different temperatures found on either side of the cape. While some boreal species are found south of Cape Cod, they are often restricted to deeper depths where water temperatures remain low.

Similarly Cape Hatteras demarcates an area where temperate waters meet up with warmer southern waters. The Carolinian Province south of Cape Hatteras is a transition area between temperate species to the north and subtropical species that become more common to the south. The boundaries of the provinces are set by the flow patterns of large-scale oceanic currents interacting with the geographic features of the land and continental shelf. This book covers the Boreal and Virginian Regions.

Marine Ecology and Levels of Inquiry

Study of the living world is driven by curiosity and the desire to gain a better understanding of the world around us, regardless of whether or not the study is being carried out by a child, an average beachcomber, or a research scientist. This study can take place at many different levels. As an example let us think about barnacles living on a rock. The first level of inquiry may be directed at the **individual.** What species is it? What should we call it? Does it have any special features that enable it to live in this particular environment? How does it feed and what does it

Population of barnacles living on an intertidal rock   SCOTT SHUMWAY

eat? What eats it? How does it protect itself? How long will it live? How does it reproduce? Does it have a larval stage?

A group of individuals of the same species living in the same area comprises a **population.** The next level of inquiry may be directed at the population of barnacles living on the rocks at this particular beach. How many individuals are there within this population? How does this number change over time? What factors influence the numbers of new individuals entering the population?

Groups of populations of different species occupying the same area make up a **community.** Many questions can be asked about how different species interact (or not) with one another within a community. In general these interactions can be characterized as being competitive, predatory, or symbiotic. Do barnacles and the mussels growing on the same rock compete with one another for a place to anchor on the rock? Do the snails crawling over the rock eat barnacles, mussels, both, or neither one? And how might predatory snails influence the relative abundance of these other two species? Do barnacles and mussels occupy distinct locations on a rock? And if so, what determines exactly where each species is found?

Our questions about communities were restricted primarily to how living organisms interact with one another. Yet they also interact with the nonliving part

Why do barnacles and mussels grow like this with one species above the other?
ANDREW K. HOWARD

of the environment (water, soil, air), which, together with the living communities, is known as an **ecosystem.** Because of their large size and the difficulty of studying each component, ecosystems are often studied from the point of view of movement of energy and nutrients throughout the living and nonliving components. **Energy** from the sun is captured by photosynthetic plants and algae. These organisms are then consumed by other species, and the energy is passed up a food chain. For example, the barnacles consume photosynthetic algae, gaining a share of energy and nutrients from their prey. They in turn become food for sea stars or snails, which are ultimately dependent upon the sun's energy originally captured by the photosynthesizers. Clearly the amount of energy available within an ecosystem and the pathway that it takes through living organisms have a strong influence on the species that live in the ecosystem.

Unlike energy, which moves in a one-way nonrenewable fashion through the food chain, **nutrients** are recycled. Therefore you might ask: What happens to an ecosystem when nutrients, like nitrogen, are in short supply? Or what happens when there is a surplus of nutrients? Do all species simply "do better" or are there negative consequences of too many nutrients? Where do nutrients come from? How do they cycle through living organisms and the environment?

Biodiversity and Evolution

Scientists have named and described about 1.5 million different species of living organisms. We know this list is inadequate, particularly for fungi and bacteria and all species living in rain forests and the deep sea. The actual number of species on our planet numbers between ten and thirty million. The collection of variation of life is commonly called **biodiversity.** The number of different species sharing the planet with us is just one component of biodiversity. We may also ask why some ecosystems have more species than others. Why are some species common and others rare?

How did all of this diversity or variation of life come about? The biodiversity that we see today and in the fossil record is the result of nearly four billion years of **evolution.** It is the variation in an individual's DNA that makes it slightly different from other members of the same species and greatly different from other species. Changes in DNA, called mutations, occur regularly and are the source of new variation.

Mutations can do one of three things. They can be neutral, meaning that no new gene products result from the change, especially if the mutation takes place in a region of the DNA molecule that does not code for anything (and there is a sur-

Rocky intertidal community.   SCOTT SHUMWAY

Alien Invaders

The aliens have invaded and are taking over! Ever since humans first migrated out of the plains of Africa, they have transported plants and animals to new locations. Species transported by humans to new geographic locations where they have never lived before are known as alien species, introduced species, or nonindigenous species.

Approximately 100 species of fish and 300 species of invertebrates and algae have successfully invaded the estuaries and coastal regions of North America over the past 200 years. Species such as the Common Periwinkle and Green Crab are so well established that it is hard to imagine that they have not always been here. Almost all of these introductions have been unintentional. So how do species manage to move from one part of a coastline to another, from one side of an ocean to another, or between oceans? Shipping and fisheries account for 89 percent of documented invasions.

Common Periwinkle (upper left), Green Fleece (upper right), European Green Crab (lower left), and Asian Shorecrab (lower right) are non-native species that now inhabit the shores of North America. SCOTT SHUMWAY AND ANDREW K. HOWARD

For most of human history, ships have been made of wood with hulls that would accumulate lush growths of marine organisms, known as a fouling community. Ships moved slowly and remained in port for extended periods of time. When the ship put to sea, the fouling community that had built up in port naturally followed. When cargo was unloaded at the next port, the seaweeds and animals of the fouling community had the opportunity to unload as well, either by dropping off the hull or by dispersing their larvae or spores. The commercial fleet has since changed to iron and steel ships with toxic antifouling paint on their hulls. These ships travel at high speed and spend little time in port before heading back out to sea. They accumulate very few fouling organisms. However, they are still extremely efficient transporters of aquatic life-forms.

Ships utilize ballast to avoid becoming top heavy while carrying a light load. Wooden ships employed dry ballast consisting of rocks and soil. When new cargo was loaded, the ballast rocks were ditched on the shoreline. The seeds of many plant species were spread this way. Modern ships have huge ballast tanks that are pumped full with water. At the next port the ballast water is pumped back out into the ocean along with an assortment of microbes, plankton, larvae, invertebrates, and fish. In recent decades the rate of species introductions by ballast water has increased exponentially with little sign of slowing down.

Why should we be concerned? One result of species introductions is the homogenization of the world's coastal biota. The uniqueness of coastal biodiversity is being eroded away as the same species are transported from coast to coast and subsequently spread at the expense of native species. An introduced species has left behind its natural competitors, predators, and the diseases that normally act to control its population growth. Providing it can find suitable shelter and food, the newcomer is in an ideal situation for growth free of its natural enemies. Under these conditions invasion may be rapid and the consequences for native species severe. The invader may impact native species by consuming them, consuming their food, altering the conditions of the environment, or occupying the best living space. While many of the effects on native species have gone undocumented, scientists now realize that these effects have been severe in the past and are growing in severity as the numbers of invasions increase. Examples covered in this book include the Common Periwinkle, Green Fleece, European Green Crab, Asian Shore Crab, Purple Loosestrife, and Common Reed Grass.

Rocky coast on Campobello Island in New Brunswick, Canada, at the mouth of the Bay of Fundy   SCOTT SHUMWAY

prising amount of this "junk" DNA). A mutation can be deleterious, resulting in an important enzyme or protein not being produced or being produced in lower quantities. It might also result in production of a different protein that is harmful. At the extreme a deleterious mutation may be lethal and kill a cell or entire organism. Once in a while a mutation will prove to be beneficial, increasing an individual's chances of survival or of reproducing. Perhaps the mutation results in production of an enzyme that works well under colder water temperatures or a protein that is toxic to predators. It is not too hard to realize that individuals with these beneficial mutations are more likely to survive than others that lack the mutation. They are also more likely to reproduce and to pass on their genes to offspring.

This process of differential survival and reproduction is known as **natural selection.** The small-scale process of evolution just described can, over time, lead to larger-scale evolutionary processes resulting in the formation of distinct species. According to the **biological species concept,** all members of a species are theoretically capable of reproducing with one another. **Speciation** typically involves **geographic isolation** followed by **reproductive isolation** of one population from another. In other words, some group of individuals is geographically separated from the rest of the species. Continental land masses, ocean basins, large-scale ocean currents, and sharp changes in water temperature are all highly effective at isolating groups of marine organisms from one another. Once isolated from the rest of the species, a new population will continue to evolve in response to the surrounding environment. Ultimately these changes may be so great that the population becomes significantly different from the rest of the original "species," such that it is functionally a new species. The ultimate test is that the two groups have diverged so much that they are no longer capable of reproducing with one another, even if they were growing in the same area.

Features of an organism, or *traits* as biologists like to call them, that make it better suited for survival in a particular set of environmental conditions are called **adaptations.** Much of the natural history of the Atlantic seashore is the story of how living organisms are adapted to their particular habitat.

Our Place in the Big Picture

Finally we must accept the stark realization that our species, *Homo sapiens,* is an integral part of marine ecosystems and that the influence of this species is disproportionately great and often negative. We eat fried clams, oysters on the half shell, crab imperial, stuffed flounder, shrimp cocktail, fish and chips, and sashimi tuna; therefore we are predators in marine food chains and sometimes reduce populations to dangerously low levels. We disrupt ecosystems by filling coastal wetlands, building vacation homes over sand dunes, and erecting seawalls. We pollute the oceans with sewage, agrochemicals, heavy metals, and excess heat. We are also changing every part of the planet through global warming, increased carbon dioxide gas, and ozone layer depletion. How our species ultimately chooses to accept (or not) responsibility for these impacts remains to be seen. It is only through an understanding of how the natural world around us functions, that we as individuals can make informed choices about how we wish to interact with this world.

How to Use This Book

This book provides an introduction to the natural history of coastal ecosystems with chapters for each of the major habitat types found along the east coast of North America. **Rocky shores** and **sandy beaches** are familiar to most beachgoers as the places of crashing waves. **Sand dunes** are terrestrial habitats that are strongly influenced by wind and salt spray coming off the ocean. They often form on barrier spits with a wave-swept sandy beach on one side and salt marsh on the other. **Estuaries** are protected from waves and occur in enclosed bays where fresh and salt water mix. Estuaries are fringed with **salt marshes** and **tidal flats** while **seagrass meadows** grow in their main channels. Thanks to the popularity of whale watches and deep-sea fishing excursions, the **open ocean** is habitat that only recently has been accessible to beachgoers. Chapters on each of these habitats begin with an overview of the environmental and biological features that make them unique. This is followed by a description of the food chain and the ecology of the algae, plants, and animals that reside in the habitat. Because winter is a time when only a

American Beachgrass, Seaside Goldenrod,
Beach Heather, and Northern Bayberry
growing on a sand dune on Cape Cod
SCOTT SHUMWAY

privileged few people visit the beach and because the habitats can be so different, the **beach in winter** is set aside as a separate chapter.

This introduction and the following two chapters provide an overview of the study of natural history, the shape of the coastline, and food chains. They should be read first. Each habitat chapter is designed to stand alone, enabling the reader to pick and choose at will. Sections on individual species may be targeted for reading independently of the rest of the chapter, although the rest of the chapter will provide the physical and biological context for the daily lives of the resident species.

The book is about the natural history of the species and natural processes that you can actually observe when you go to the beach. While it can be used to identify common species, it is not intended as an identification guide and does not attempt to describe every species on the beach. It is intended to help the reader understand our surrounding environment, much of which is covered in seawater. It is perhaps best read while reclining in a beach chair, feet buried in hot sand, with the sound of breaking waves and calling gulls in the background.

Salt marsh in Tuckerton, New Jersey   SCOTT SHUMWAY

The Coastline

Where the Ocean Meets the Land

A look at any map of the east coast of North America or "Our Backyard from Space" (borrowing from a recent publication on the Gulf of Maine) reveals many interesting features. The coastline is far from straight, nor is it smooth or oriented in a strict north-south line. It is an irregularly shaped intersection of land and sea that angles from northeast to southwest. The coastline is permeated by fingerlike indentations, dotted with islands, and even has a few awkward-looking projections hanging off that seem to be out of place. If you were to study the coastline from north to south, you would encounter distinctive features that are readily identifiable even from outer space.

A closer look at the Gulf of Maine reveals the Bay of Fundy, an area of water seemingly trapped by Nova Scotia, New Brunswick, and the northern reaches of Maine. The unique shape of this basin contributes to the most extreme tides in the world. The entire coast of Maine is interrupted by fingerlike projections where rivers meet up with ocean water. Areas where freshwater mixes with seawater are known as estuaries. The elongated basins of these estuaries reflect the scouring action of ancient glaciers. The rocky outcrops

"Our Backyard from Space"—Satellite image of the East Coast from the Gulf of Maine to the Outer Banks of North Carolina
NASA VISIBLE EARTH

"Our Backyard from Space"—Satellite image of Bay of Fundy, Gulf of Maine, and Long Island Sound   NASA VISIBLE EARTH

that characterize much of the coast of Maine and its coastal islands are a testament to the clearing capabilities of these ice masses.

Cape Cod juts into the ocean like a giant flexed arm made of sand. A closer look at the Massachusetts coast reveals several large sand spits and barrier beaches at Plymouth Harbor, Sandy Neck, Provincetown, Nauset, and Monomoy. These spits are constantly being reshuffled by waves, currents, and storms. History has shown that the sand spits off Chatham, at the elbow of Cape Cod, may be connected to the cape one day and islands the next, and vice versa. Beachgoers are well aware that rocky shores with cold water predominate north of Cape Cod and sandy beaches with progressively warmer waters are found as you travel south. Past glacial activity of 15,000 years ago is largely responsible for the locations of rocky and sandy beaches, whereas modern currents determine water temperature.

Immediately to the southeast of Cape Cod are two medium-sized estuaries. Buzzards Bay and Narragansett Bay harbor important habitat for shellfish and juvenile finfish. They are also lined with the important industrial cities of New Bedford and Providence. The many indentations of the coastline allow even the tiny state of Rhode Island to have extensive estuarine habitat.

Long Island hangs off southern New England like an afterthought deposited by the farthest advance of ancient glaciers. It shelters the waters of the sound and much of the Connecticut coastline from the crashing waves of the open Atlantic. The southern tip of Long Island and the small indentation known as New York

Harbor shelter one of the world's busiest commercial shipping ports, as well as the mouths of several rivers, and thousands of acres of wetlands.

The Jersey Shore is composed of numerous barrier islands with names like Long Beach Island, Atlantic City, and Wildwood. Broad sandy beaches with pounding surf attract millions of human visitors every summer while the estuaries and salt marshes separating these islands from the mainland attract millions of unseen fish visitors. The large Delaware Bay estuary separates southern New Jersey from the Delmarva Peninsula. The industrialized cities of Wilmington, Philadelphia, and Trenton line its shores. Millions of shorebirds descend upon these shores for a few days each spring in order to gorge

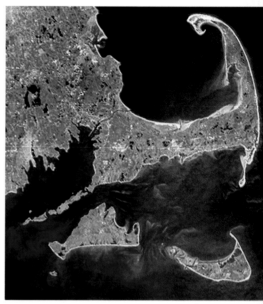

Cape Cod, Martha's Vineyard, Nantucket, and Buzzard's Bay   NASA VISIBLE EARTH

themselves on Horseshoe Crab eggs so that they have enough energy to fly back to their Arctic breeding grounds. It is in essence an unmarked rest area at the southern terminus of the Garden State Parkway.

The eastern side of the Delmarva Peninsula is lined with barrier islands, salt marshes, and sandy beaches much like the Jersey coast. The peninsula itself looks like a puzzle piece that doesn't quite fit into the rest of the continent. However, it shelters the largest and most important estuary in all of North America. Chesapeake Bay was formed when river valleys became flooded by rising sea levels at the end of the last glacial period. Its name is synonymous with the Blue Crabs and oysters that have historically seemed like inexhaustible resources.

The Carolina coast juts out into the ocean with a string of barrier islands that shelter the estuaries of Pamlico and Albemarle Sounds. Cape Hatteras forms the boundary between the Virginian and Carolinian provinces, as well as the southern limit for this book. The areas to the south are similarly lined with sandy beaches, barrier islands, salt marshes, and estuaries.

The Human Footprint

The Atlantic coastline is a heterogeneous mix of rocky shore, sandy beach, and estuaries lined with salt marshes and tidal flats. The heterogeneity leads to a large diversity of species found over a fairly short distance. Within this same landscape is another mosaic imposed by the human inhabitants. Pristine shores protected as national parks and wildlife refuges are surrounded by vacation resorts, large urban areas, and some of the world's busiest commercial ports. While we think of the seashore as a very narrow strip where the land meets the sea, the coast is part of and heavily influenced by larger watersheds that feed into estuaries and nearshore waters. Suburbia, agriculture, and industry occupy the land in the surrounding watersheds. Home and factory wastewater, as well as fertilizer and pesticide runoff, often make their way to estuaries and coastal beaches.

Ever since humans arrived on the east coast of North America, the seas and estuaries have offered up a huge bounty of fish and shellfish. Huge middens filled with the shells of oysters and clams represent the garbage dumps of coast-dwelling Native Americans. Early European colonists harvested shad and herring during their spring migration runs. In the Gulf of Maine, a fishery quickly developed for salt cod. Wellfleet became famous for oysters, and the Chesapeake, for Blue Crabs. As refrigeration methods and transportation technology advanced, fisheries were transformed to cater to a fresh seafood market. The offshore fishing grounds of George's Bank provide cod, flounder, and other groundfish. While most of these fisheries are still active today, some are in danger of becoming unviable due to many years of overharvest. New fisheries for sea urchins and deep-sea fish are emerging. Aquaculture of mussels and salmon is gaining in popularity. All of these culinary examples point to the fact that we have made ourselves an influential rung on many marine food chains.

The Ocean

The ocean provides a unique environment that is made possible by the unusual properties of water molecules and a variety of salts that are dissolved in it. The ocean is also a place of constant movement due to currents that span entire ocean basins, windblown waves, and rising and falling tides. The shape of a particular stretch of coastline and its bottom countours influence the way that this moving water impacts the shoreline and its inhabitants.

Properties of Seawater

Water, H_2O, is a very unusual molecule. Life cannot exist without it. Its special chemical properties are responsible for it being the molecule of life. Geometrically the water molecule forms a **106°-angled V-shape** with hydrogen atoms attached to opposite sides of an oxygen atom. The molecule is bound together by the oxygen and each of the hydrogens sharing a pair of electrons. The sharing, however, is asymmetric with the negatively charged electrons spending more time around the oxygen than the hydrogens. The *oxygen therefore has a slight negative charge* while the *hydrogen tips of the molecule have a slight positive charge.* Such details may seem insignificant at first glance, but this asymmetry in charge (polarity to a chemist) is the key to the unusual nature of the water molecule.

The positively charged hydrogens are attracted to the slightly negatively charged oxygens of adjacent water molecules. These weak attractions, known as **hydrogen bonds,** cause water molecules to stick together. They stick to other surfaces (adhesion) as well as to themselves (cohesion). You can easily test this by dipping a finger in and out of a glass of water. Adhesive forces cause the water to stick to your finger while cohesive forces keep the droplet together. The slight charges on water molecules also attract other charged molecules, or ions, such as the ones found in seawater. These attractive powers are what enable water to be the universal solvent that dissolves many different chemical substances.

Pure water has a low freezing point (32° F or 0° C) and a high boiling point (212° F or 100° C). As a result it is present as a liquid on the surface of the earth. A large amount of heat is needed to raise the temperature of a given volume of water. Therefore, *ocean waters warm up and cool down very slowly.* This protects marine organisms from sudden changes in temperature, something that they are ill equipped to deal with. This also helps moderate the air temperatures of coastal regions.

As water gets colder, it sinks; whereas warm water rises to the surface. As cold water sinks, it brings with it dissolved nutrients. During summer months warm surface waters may become effectively isolated from deeper cold water. Layering or **stratification** by temperature results in warm surface waters that are nutrient poor. The boundary between warm and cold waters is called a **thermocline.** Where stratification is an annual event, waters are eventually mixed when upper layers become cold and the thermocline breaks down. This mixing returns nutrients back to the surface and is usually followed by an increase in phytoplankton.

Stratification can also occur in response to differences in water **density.** Seawater is denser than freshwater because it contains a variety of dissolved ions. Where the two mix, such as in an estuary, the less dense fresh or brackish water floats on top of the salt water.

The various solutes dissolved in seawater lower its freezing point relative to pure water. Another unique property of water is that, upon freezing, it becomes less dense and floats. Ice sometimes forms in brackish (low-salinity) tide pools and salt marshes. In the process it solidifies around the resident seaweeds, barnacles, mussels, and marsh grasses. The floating ice moves upward with rising tides and downward as tides recede. The entrapped organisms are helpless against these up and down movements and may be crushed or ripped from their homes. It goes without saying that this is primarily a northern phenomenon that is more severe in Maine than on Long Island and is nonexistent in Virginia. In general, however, marine species are protected from freezing conditions by the low freezing point of seawater, as well as its almost constant movement.

The saltiness, or **salinity,** of seawater is due to a cocktail of various charged chemicals or *ions.* Certain positively charged ions are attracted to, and bond with, certain negatively charged ions to form what chemists refer to as salts. We usually equate sea salt with sodium chloride. Sodium and chloride are indeed the most abundant ions in seawater, but nearly a dozen different ions including sulfate and magnesium contribute to the overall salinity. The relative proportions of these ions usually remain constant, so that salinity is often determined by measuring just chloride or sodium content. It is reported in units of parts per thousand (ppt or

Better Understanding through Chemistry

Many scientists get very excited about chemical reactions and amounts of certain chemicals in the environment. Most folks, however, do not share this enthusiasm for chemistry and think of it as an esoteric subject reserved for Nobel laureates. Some people cringe at the name thanks to unpleasant memories of high school or college science classes. This is unfortunate and is simply the wrong attitude!

Nothing in this world exists that is not made up of chemical elements. Nutrition —whether it be ours, garden plants', or sea creatures'—is all about obtaining the chemicals necessary for life in the proper amounts. The science of chemistry is all about studying chemical reactions or how chemicals interact with one another to form new substances. All living organisms from microbes to Blue Whales are merely reaction vessels or chemistry sets in which chemical reactions are constantly occurring. Most of the activities of an organism are focused on obtaining the necessary ingredients to fuel these reactions and to prevent accumulation of toxic wastes. In order to get the big picture, you must be willing to think positively about chemistry!

o/oo) or practical salinity units (psu). Open ocean water measures in at about 35 ppt. Most marine organisms have an internal salt concentration equal to that of the surrounding seawater. Disruption of this internal balance caused by sudden fluctuations in salinity, such as occurs in estuaries, can prove fatal.

Currents and Ocean Circulation

Ocean waters are in constant motion. Large-scale **currents** driven by prevailing winds move throughout the ocean basins. Heat energy from the sun warms the surface of the earth. The equator is heated much more than the poles. Heated air masses rise up from the equatorial regions. As the warm air rises, it is replaced by air from midlatitudes that moves toward the equator. Eventually the air is recirculated as it falls back down at 30 degrees north and south latitude. The result is surface winds that flow toward the equator. In the Northern Hemisphere these winds, known as the northeast **trade winds,** blow from the northeast toward the equator. The Southern Hemisphere is a mirror image. Northeast trade winds and southeast trade winds blow in a westerly direction and merge at the intertropical convergence zone along the equator. Between 30 and 60 degrees latitude in both hemispheres, **westerlies** blow from west to east. (Wind currents are named after the direction from which they blow.)

These large-scale wind patterns blow across the surface of the ocean, and the

friction that is generated causes the surface waters of the ocean to move in a pattern that roughly reflects the wind patterns. Of course continents get in the way
and the ocean currents are deflected. Because we live on a round planet that is
spinning on its N-S axis, a phenomenon known as the **Coriolis effect** causes wind
and water currents to deflect to the right in the Northern Hemisphere and to the
left in the Southern Hemisphere. The Coriolis effect deflects the water currents
generated by the northeast trade winds to the right, forming a gigantic clockwise
gyre that spans most of the North Atlantic Ocean. The waters of the North
Atlantic subtropical gyre are carried from the equator up along the east coast of
North America by the **Gulf Stream.** The warm waters of the Gulf Stream have a
large influence on the water temperatures along the east coast of the United States.
The Gulf Stream hugs the continental shelf from Florida up to Cape Hatteras
where it veers off into the center of the Atlantic before either circulating back
toward the equator or continuing as the North Atlantic current responsible for
warming the shores of the British Isles.

The coastal waters north of Cape Hatteras are much colder, and this overall
current pattern and resulting temperatures are largely responsible for the differences in species on either side of this boundary. In comparison the waters off
northeast Canada and the northern portions of the Gulf of Maine are influenced
by the frigid waters of the **Labrador Current** that flows in a southeast direction out
of the Arctic and the Nova Scotian Current that it feeds. Once again, there are distinct differences in types of species found on either side of this boundary.

Evidence of the warming powers of the large currents can be seen, and felt, in
the presence of the tropical island of Bermuda due east of the Carolinas. Even after
it diverges out to sea, the effects of the Gulf Stream are felt along much of the
Atlantic coast up to southern New England. This explains why the waters of Nantucket are so much more pleasant than the rest of New England and why the south
shore of Cape Cod is warmer than the north.

These ocean currents are not devoid of life. Marine organisms take advantage of
the opportunity to be transported around the ocean with relatively little effort. Larvae of marine worms and snails can be dispersed from the coast of North America to
the shores of Europe. Freshwater eels swim down streams throughout North America
and into the ocean where they enter the North Atlantic gyre that transports them to
breeding areas in the middle of the ocean. Newly hatched sea turtles crawl away from
nests on sandy beaches and swim out to sea until they collide with the Gulf Stream,
where they will spend the first year or more of life floating in warm currents.

Waves

Wind also generates the waves that make boats bob up and down on the high seas as
well as the waves that crash onto beaches. All waves have distinct features, whether
they are the waves of the ocean or the wave generated by flicking a length of rope up
and down. A wave rises to a maximum peak and sinks to a minimum trough. The
vertical distance between the peak and trough is known as the *wave height.* The hori-

zontal distance between successive peaks is the *wavelength* while the time between peaks is the *period*. Surfers pay close attention to wave height and period. Scientists also study these features to predict the impacts of waves on coastlines.

It is important to note that waves move through water. The water itself rises up and down in a circular fashion but does not follow the shoreward movement of the wave. This situation changes dramatically when the wave moves across a shallow bottom. At this point the true bottom of the wave begins to experience drag as it impacts the substrate below. The bottom of the wave is forced to slow down while the velocity of the crest remains constant. Eventually the wave crests as the peak starts to overtake the trough. Gravity takes over and the wave breaks or tumbles over itself. At this point the considerable energy stored up in the moving wave is released upon the shore. Anyone caught off guard and struck by a breaking wave is well aware of the intensity of this energy. It is hard to believe that barnacles, mussels, and seaweeds can live on rocks hit repeatedly by this energy. Because waves are generated by winds, the higher the wind energy that created the wave, the higher the energy imparted on the shoreline when the wave breaks.

Longshore Currents

As waves strike sandy shores, sediment becomes suspended in the water. Under normal conditions there is a net transport of sand onto the beach. During the winter, however, winds are stronger, and waves strike with greater force. At this time sediment is eroded from the beach and transported offshore.

Winds cause these waves to strike the shore at an angle other than 90º, **generating longshore** currents that transport the suspended sediment parallel to the shore. As they move, longshore currents remove sediment from one location and redeposit it in a new location to form sand **spits**. These spits continue to grow as longshore currents deposit additional sand and may eventually form barrier beaches. **Barrier islands** may form when a storm surge washes over the spit, leaving behind a **tidal inlet** that divides the spit in two. Typically these barriers have wave-swept sandy beaches on one side, sand dunes in the middle, a lagoon fringed with salt marsh on the back side, and tidal inlets that connect the lagoon to the sea.

Tides

Tides are an important feature of the coastal environment. There are two high tides and two low tides each day on the east coast of North America. The cycle is repeated day after day on a twenty-four-hour-and-fifty-minute schedule, such that the tide cycle is fifty minutes later from one day to the next. The exact height of a tide varies and is influenced most strongly by the gravitational forces of the moon.

The vertical distance between a high tide and the next lowest tide is known as the **tidal range** or tidal amplitude. This distance is usually used to refer to the maximum distance measured from the highest monthly tide to the lowest monthly tide. It varies geographically with northern latitudes generally having greater tidal ranges than areas closer to the equator. For example, the tides along the coast of

Humans versus Nature: Always Bet on Nature

Humans are engaged in a futile battle against the sea for domination of the coast. We build houses where sand dunes should be, only to discover that the houses are no better suited than sand dunes to withstand storm surges. Our engineering prowess enables us to construct concrete or rock barriers with the

SCOTT SHUMWAY

Seawall, Truro, Massachusetts

intent of absorbing the impact of the sea and protecting beaches and cliffs from erosion. We construct seawalls parallel to shore and groins at right angles to the shore. Unfortunately these all prove to be temporarily effective, as they don't really absorb the energy of the waves, but divert it. Seawalls refocus the wave energy to the area immediately below the wall. Over time the sediment beneath and to the side of the wall erodes away and the seawall collapses. Seawalls also redirect the energy in such a way that one homeowner may effectively protect his cliff face while the deflected wave force erodes away the unprotected cliff face of the neighbor.

Groins are designed to intercept longshore currents and to prevent beach erosion. In reality the longshore current strikes the groin and deposits its load of sand. This is the intended outcome. However as the current passes on the opposite side of the barrier, it has no sand to deposit and instead erodes away the beach. On beaches with multiple groins, the naturally flat shoreline becomes scalloped with lopsided sand accumulation on the up-current side of a pair of groins and loss of sand on the down-current side. In cases where a large jetty has been constructed to keep inlets open for navigation, barrier spits located downshore may have their supply of sand cut off and cease to grow or begin to lose sand from the beachfront.

SCOTT SHUMWAY

The same seawall, five years later

Maine are significantly greater than those in Virginia. Tidal range is further influenced by the depths and shapes of various basins. The 52-foot (16-m) tidal range of the Bay of Fundy is the most extreme on earth. Most of the living creatures that we see at the beach live within the intertidal, the area that is alternately covered and uncovered by tides.

Tides are really bulges in the surface of the ocean. They are created by the interaction of several forces. We generally think of the moon rotating around the earth, but in reality they share a center of rotation that is not quite at the center of the earth, resulting in **centrifugal force** acting on the surface of the earth. The centrifugal force causes a bulge in the ocean surface on the side of the earth farthest away from the moon. The two most significant forces creating tides are the **gravitational pulls of the moon and sun.** Because the moon is closer to the earth, its effects are greater and a bulge forms in the ocean surface closest to the moon. The combined result of the centrifugal force and the gravitational pulls are two bulges in the ocean surface on opposite sides of the earth.

Observing the phases of the moon is the best way to predict the range of the tides. If you were to play connect the dots between earth, moon, and sun, the highest and lowest tides (greatest tidal range) would occur when a straight line was formed. These are known as **spring tides** and occur twice a month, whenever there is a full or new moon in the sky. These are the highest and lowest tides of a lunar month (twenty-eight days or the time it takes the moon to orbit the earth). The smallest tidal range would occur whenever a right angle was formed by the connect-the-dots exercise and the moon is in its first or third quarter. These are known as **neap tides.** Other days of the month are intermediate between these extremes.

Coastal Geology

Have you ever wondered how the coast that we see today came to be shaped the way that it is? The features of our coast have been shaped by geological processes of the past and continue to be shaped by the geological processes of the present. Nothing about our coast is static. Waves and currents will constantly reshape the coast as they always have. Catastrophic winter storms and hurricanes will cause sudden changes in the contours of the coast. Sea level will rise and fall as it always has. Glaciers will return. Of course these coast-altering processes differ in time scale and have been listed from those that take place on a minute-by-minute basis to those that take place over thousands of years. When we go to the beach, we see a snapshot in geologic time. The same snapshot taken a day later will almost certainly look the same, but change is taking place, albeit imperceptible at this time scale. A few years later the snapshot might look different. Wait a few decades and it will definitely look different. Given the forecasts for global warming and associated rise in sea level, much of our coastline is scheduled for rapid changes easily measured over a time frame of a few years or decades.

The Undeniable Power of Ice

Geologic time is interspersed with alternating periods of large-scale **glacial activity** and periods of little to no glacial activity (interglacial). Much of the previous 75,000 years were characterized by large-scale growth and movement of glaciers. This period in time is part of the Wisconsinan glacial stage. The 50,000 years before that is known as the Sangamonian interglacial stage and that was preceded by the Illinoian glacial stage. These three stages are all part of the Pleistocene time period. By geological standards this is all fairly recent history.

The New England landscape was shaped during the last glaciation when a massive sheet of ice, known as the Laurentide ice sheet, covered the upper third of North America. Inland areas of New England were covered by a mile-thick sheet of ice, while the ice sheet over the present coast of Massachusetts was only 1,500 feet thick. During the Wiconsinan glacial stage, this ice sheet repeatedly increased and decreased in size.

As a glacier increases in size, it moves forward or advances across the landscape. As it does so, it acts like a giant bulldozer scraping up soil and rock and even breaking pieces from the underlying bedrock. The exposed rocky shores of Maine, often called the Bold Coast, are a stark testament to the scraping power of an advancing glacier. Some of these rocks bear scars, called **striations**, from having rocky debris ground along their surfaces as the glacier moved above them. The parallel orientation of these scratches indicates the direction the glacier was traveling.

When temperatures begin to rise, a glacier will start to melt; and as it does so, it **recedes** or retreats across the landscape and deposits huge amounts of sediment. Some of this material is deposited directly at the edge of the ice and is known as **till**. When a glacier halts its advance, large amounts of till are deposited to form a ridge or end moraine. As a glacier melts, tremendous amounts of water are released, forming **meltwater streams**. Most of the accumulated sediment is carried off by these streams and is known as **outwash**.

Approximately 21,000 years ago, the Laurentide ice sheet reached its maximum extension, or **glacial maximum**, to the south and east. The glacier began to recede, then readvanced for a brief period of time, and finally continued to melt. In the process end moraines were formed. When it readvanced, the weight of the ice sheet, combined with a bulldozing effect, pushed up the recent deposits adding topography. We see the results today as Long Island, Block Island, Cape Cod, the Elizabeth Islands, Martha's Vineyard, and Nantucket. The meltwater streams deposited vast outwash plains of sand and gravel. Ten thousand years ago the ice sheets were greatly reduced and within another 5,000 years were all but gone.

Glacial activity greatly influences **sea level**. As glaciers grow, they remove water from the sea and sea level goes down. As glaciers melt, water is returned to the ocean and sea level rises. At the time of the glacial maximum 20,000 years ago, sea level was 300 feet (91 m) below its present position and the shore was 75 miles

Rocky Coast in Acadia National Park, Maine   SCOTT SHUMWAY

(121 km) south of Nantucket. As the ice sheets melted, sea level began to rise rapidly and continued to do so until 7,000 years ago. The flooded outwash plains created an extensive shallow continental shelf that would soon become a rich habitat for finfish and shellfish. The rising seas flooded river valleys and created many of our present-day estuaries. To the far west of the continent, the melting Cordilleran

Glacial end moraine on Martha's Vineyard, Massachusetts   SCOTT SHUMWAY

and Laurentide ice sheets parted from one another, allowing a passageway for humans migrating from Asia to North America. These new arrivals would make it to the East Coast in time to witness the rapid rise in sea level and to exploit the wealth of seafood starting to grow in the shallows.

Mid-Atlantic Coastal Plain

South of New England the earth's surface slopes gently from the Appalachian Mountains all the way to the edge of the continental shelf, forming a broad coastal plain composed of sandy soils. These are ancient soil deposits that predate the formation of the Atlantic Ocean, which began 180 million years ago as North America separated from the supercontinent of Pangea. Present-day rivers running through these coastal plains on their way to the sea continue to transport huge amounts of sediment to the coast. Waves and currents constantly rework this sediment and over the past 7,000 years have constructed a long series of barrier islands throughout the Mid-Atlantic.

Catastrophic Alteration of the Shoreline in the Present

Winter storms and hurricanes can drastically rearrange a shoreline within a few hours. Low barometric pressure and strong winds interact to produce elevations in water levels known as storm surges. These alone can cause devastation of natural and human features of the shore. However, if they coincide with normal high tides, then their magnitude and devastating impact are greatly increased. Storm surges can wash over barrier spits eroding away sand dunes in an instant and depositing beach sand over the marsh or bay on the inland side as washover fans. If the tide level is higher on one side of the weakened barrier than on the other, water can begin to rush through as though a dike were suddenly opened.

In 1987 a winter storm breached a barrier spit in Chatham, Massachusetts. Over time the breach widened, a tidal inlet formed, and the once protected bay was left exposed to waves. Within a few short years, the southern end of a barrier spit known locally as North Beach (or Nauset Beach) became severed from the rest of the spit forming an island. The breach continued to widen, and sand was deposited along one end of the breach until, in 1992, the island was joined to

An area on Cape Cod National Seashore where storm waves have eroded the foredune and an overwash event has breached the dunes SCOTT SHUMWAY

the mainland and is now called South Beach! Over time longshore transport of sediments will erode away more of North Beach and build up the southern end of South Beach possibly joining it with its neighbor North Monomoy Island. Of course a hurricane or winter storm could reshuffle all of this in an instant.

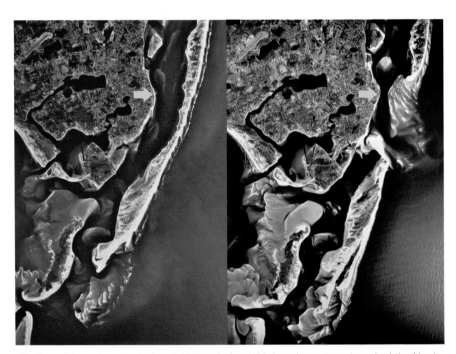

Chatham, Massachusetts, before (1985) and after (1991) a winter storm breached the North Beach spit in 1987. The 1991 photo shows a well-developed tidal inlet separating North Beach from the island of South Beach. In 1992 South Beach rejoined the mainland just below the lighthouse indicated by the yellow arrow. U.S. GEOLOGICAL SURVEY

Food Chains and the Forgotten Plankton

All living organisms need energy to survive. Energy wars have been fought on our planet for nearly four billion years and, even today, much of daily life is spent acquiring energy to grow and to achieve the ultimate goal of reproducing. The energy to sustain life on our planet comes from the **sun.** Through the process of **photosynthesis,** light energy is captured and converted into chemical energy that can be either stored or used to fuel life's everyday metabolic reactions. Only photosynthetic plants, algae, and certain bacteria are able to carry out this energy conversion. All other life-forms are directly or indirectly dependent upon these producers for their own energy needs.

A **food chain** traces the capture and movement of this energy from one individual to the next. At the base of all food chains are photosynthesizers. (There are very few exceptions to this rule. The most notable are deep-sea vents where the sun never shines and primary production is carried out by chemosynthetic bacteria.) The photosynthesizers are fed upon by consumers that we commonly call herbivores. They are in turn consumed by predators or carnivores. There might be one or two levels of higher consumers, but rarely ever more than that.

It is rare for a food chain to have more than four or five levels. There is simply not enough energy available. The transfer of energy from one rung of the food chain to the next is an inefficient one. Much of the energy is used up in basic metabolism and growth. In fact only 10 percent of the energy acquired by one level is available to be passed up to the next level. This "10 percent rule" places a strict limit on how many levels there can be in a food chain.

Food chains provide natural historians with a convenient and accessible way of organizing the species found in a given habitat into feeding groups or **trophic levels.** There are **primary producers** *(photosynthesizers),* **herbivores** *(primary consumers),* **carnivores** *(secondary consumers),* and higher-level carnivores *(tertiary consumers).* Some food chains are based upon **detritus** (dead and decaying material) and rely upon **decomposers** to free up the energy stored in the bodies of dead plants and animals. The decomposers, bacteria and fungi, keep the world from piling up with corpses and release a lot of food in the process.

In the real world the transfer of energy rarely progresses in a simple ladderlike food chain in which only a single species occupies each rung. Instead there are multiple species of producers, many different herbivores, a few species of carnivores, and an even smaller number of top carnivores within a single ecosystem. A diagram of these feeding interactions resembles a complicated **food web,** rather than a neat chain.

Because of the importance of the energy of the sun, the distribution of species is often related to the capture of sunlight. When sunlight hits water, the wavelengths are absorbed and reflected by the water and particles in the water. Light levels decrease with depth to a point where there is insufficient light for photosynthesis to take place. The water above is known as the **photic zone.** Below is the aphotic zone. Photosynthetic organisms must inhabit the photic zone in order to survive. Because the producers are directly or indirectly the food source for all other species, the greatest concentration of living organisms occurs in shallow water or close to the surface.

In the marine realm photosynthesis is carried out by flowering plants, algae, and some types of bacteria. Flowering plants include seagrasses and salt-marsh grasses. Algae are divided up into single-celled microalgae and multicellular **macroalgae** or *seaweeds.* The greatest contribution to carbon fixation, the technical term for what happens in photosynthesis, is made by single-celled algae (diatoms and dinoflagellates) and cyanobacteria (blue-greens). Diatoms, dinoflagellates, and copepods are often referred to as "net plankton" because they can be captured using a fine-mesh plankton net (20–150 microns). There are a large number of much smaller plankton about which we know very little because of the difficulty of studying them. These include smaller flagellates, bacteria, and viruses that constitute a separate microbial food web. They are out of sight and out of mind to the average beachgoer. However, without them there would be very little, if any, life to see at the beach.

Plantlike Plankton

Plankton are living organisms that are unable to swim on their own and are forced to move at the mercy of the water currents. Most are microscopic. Those that carry out photosynthesis are **phytoplankton** (literally plantlike plankton).

    Diatoms are among the most beautiful of all living organisms, but you can only experience this beauty with the aid of a powerful microscope. They literally live in glass houses. Diatoms are encased in two valves made of silica, the major ingredient in glass. The valves fit one inside the other very

View of a centric diatom taken with a scanning electron microscope, showing the round end or valve view and the side or girdle view. Diatoms are made of two glasslike valves that fit together like the two plates of a petri dish.   JOANN M. BURKHOLDER

much like the two plates of a petri dish with one slightly larger than the other. Diatom cells range in size from .0004–.008 inch (10–200 microns).

Diatoms come in two basic shapes. **Centric diatoms** are circular when viewed from above. Viewed from the side they resemble either a petri dish or a barrel. They can occur singly or in a series of cells loosely joined together into a chain. The genus *Chaetoceros* has barrel-shaped cells with four long spines coming off of the sides. These spines link together with the spines of

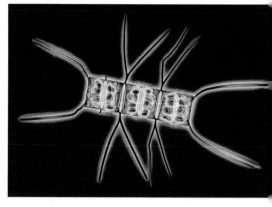

Chaetoceros is a centric diatom possessing elongated spines that link cells together to form chains SCOTT SHUMWAY

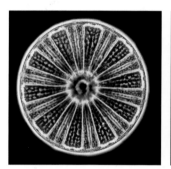

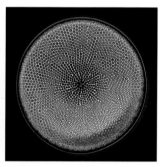

Three centric diatoms in "valve view" selected to show the intricate beauty of the patterns on their valves (Actinoptychus, Asterolampra, Coscinodiscus)
DR. PAUL E. HARGRAVES, HARBOR BRANCH OCEANOGRAPHIC INSTITUTION

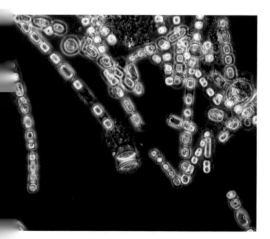
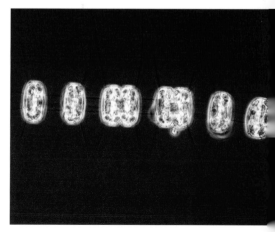

Two common chain-forming species of centric diatom (Skeletonema *and* Thallasiosira)
DR. PAUL E. HARGRAVES, HARBOR BRANCH OCEANOGRAPHIC INSTITUTION

An artistic arrangement of fifty different diatoms by microscopist Klaus Kemp KLAUS KEMP

Pennate diatoms are abundant in bottom habitats where they glide over the substrate DR. PAUL E. HARGRAVES, HARBOR BRANCH OCEANOGRAPHIC INSITUTION

other cells to form linear chains. **Pennate diatoms** are elongated in shape and look like submarines or coffins. Many pennate diatoms are *benthic* or bottom dwelling rather than planktonic. Bottom sediments and rocks are frequently covered by a film of diatoms.

The beauty of diatoms lies in their overall shapes combined with elaborate patterns that look as though they were etched into the silica valves. The series of holes and grooves within the valves are essential for properly identifying different species. Diatoms ooze slime from these grooves and, in the case of benthic pennate diatoms, use these secretions to glide over their substrate. So varied and beautiful are diatoms that in Victorian times they were adopted as an art medium. Microscopists would construct slides of "arranged diatoms" that spelled out written messages or formed a picture.

Dinoflagellates are single-celled algae that bear two uniquely positioned flagella, elongated, hairlike structures used for propulsion. One flagellum encircles the equator of the cell and lies within a grooved depression. The undulation of this **transverse flagellum** causes the cell to spin. Dinoflagellate comes from the Greek word *dineo* meaning "to whorl." The second or **longitudinal flagellum** is oriented perpendicular to the first and appears to trail from the cell. While their beating flagella enable them to swim up to 0.02 inch (500 microns) per second, this rate is still too poor to overcome most water currents.

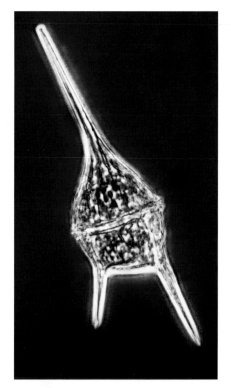

Dinoflagellates in the genus Ceratium *are characterized by a series of hornlike projections at either end of the cell* (Ceratium furca). DR. PAUL E. HARGRAVES, HARBOR BRANCH OCEANOGRAPHIC INSTITUTION

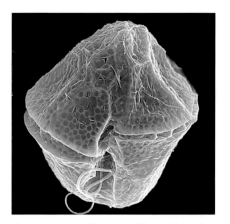

An armored dinoflagellate (Lingulodinium) *showing cellulose plates, horizontal groove (girdle), and vertical groove containing the trailing flagellum (photo taken with a scanning electron microscope) and an unarmored, or naked, dinoflagellate* (Cochlodinium) *showing horizontal groove and brownish pigmentation*
JOANN M. BURKHOLDER AND DR. PAUL E. HARGRAVES, HARBOR BRANCH OCEANOGRAPHIC INSTITUTION

The cells are 0.0007–0.078 inch (2–2,000 microns) in diameter. Their photosynthetic pigments give dinoflagellates a golden brown coloration. The biology of dinoflagellates is complex and poorly understood. Some species either do not carry out photosynthesis or obtain energy through a mix of photosynthesis and engulfing food particles. Sixty species are known to produce potent toxins, some of which are harmful to humans, fish, and shellfish. The cell wall of most species consists of a series of plates made of cellulose, giving them the appearance of being covered in armor. About 4,000 species have been identified, almost all of which are marine.

Cyanobacteria (blue-green bacteria) may occur in many forms inhabiting a diversity of habitats, such as tiny cells in the open ocean, as black paintlike bands on intertidal rocks, and as hairlike mats on the surfaces of salt marshes and tidal flats.

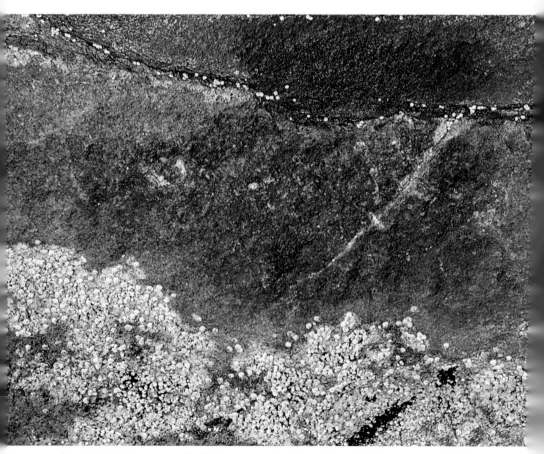

Intertidal rocks are covered with dense growths of cyanobacteria that are recognized by their dark blue-green coloration. SCOTT SHUMWAY

Animal Plankton

Planktonic organisms that must consume other plankton to survive and
are members of the animal kingdom
are known as **zooplankton.** They either
spend their entire lives or only a brief
part of their lives floating in the water
column.

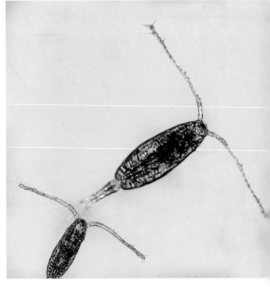

The best-known permanent residents are the **copepods.** These tiny
crustaceans, just visible to the naked
eye, are distinguished by having a reddish eyespot at the center of their
head. Planktonic copepods have long
antennae that are whipped about for
locomotion. The antennae also generate water currents that carry food particles to bristlelike appendages that
capture unicellular algae and pass
them to the mouth. They are known as

*Copepods spend their entire lives in the
water column where they graze on microscopic algae.*   SCOTT SHUMWAY

the "cows of the sea" for their lifestyle of grazing phytoplankton from the water
and are an important rung in many food chains, providing a link between primary
producers and secondary consumers. Many planktivorous fish and even some
whales depend upon copepods as their main source of food.

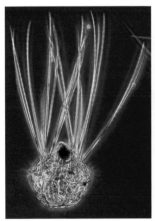

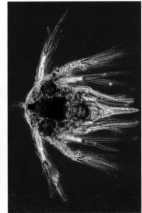

*Many invertebrates have a planktonic larval stage that spends a few weeks in the water col-
umn, such as this (l-to-r) polychaete worm larva, American Lobster larva, nauplius larva of a
barnacle*   DR. PAUL E. HARGRAVES, HARBOR BRANCH OCEANOGRAPHIC INSTITUTION; (C) 1999 FRAN HEYL ASSOCI-
ATES AND JASON GOLDSTEIN, NEW ENGLAND AQUARIUM, BOSTON, MASS.; SCOTT SHUMWAY

Part-time plankton are called **meroplankton.** Most of these are **larval stages** of invertebrates and fishes that are planktonic for only a few days or weeks. Most feed upon phytoplankton, whereas others never feed and hatch from eggs with a yolk sac that provides them with all the food they need to reach the next stage in life. These free-floating larvae are in turn an important food source for many fish and invertebrates, sometimes even adults of the same species.

Seasonal Changes

The total abundance of plankton, as well as the identity of the species that are present, changes throughout the year. These changes are mediated by light and nutrient availability, temperature, mixing of water from different depths, predation, and competition. During winter months uniformly cold water and surface turbulence created by high winds mix surface and deep waters together. Nutrients trapped in deep water or on the seafloor from the previous summer are brought to the surface. Despite this abundance of nutrients, phytoplankton abundance in the North Atlantic is limited by low light levels during the winter. Light levels are low due to short day lengths and the low angle of the sun. Furthermore, the mixing of water levels carries phytoplankton so deep that they are barely surviving and unable to build up enough energy to reproduce due to the lack of sunlight.

As winter ends, so do the intense winds that stir up the water. Phytoplankton are able to float closer to the surface. This is also the time when light levels increase in the temperate zone. As spring arrives and the earth continues its rotation around the sun, the Northern Hemisphere is no longer tilted away from the sun, and the sun's rays strike the ocean more directly and penetrate to greater depths.

The increased sunlight stimulates photosynthesis and reproduction in the phytoplankton, resulting in a population explosion called an **algal bloom.** Light, nutrients, and temperature are optimal for spring algal growth. Herbivorous zooplankton are still scarce, but this is about to change.

Warmer temperatures stimulate growth of copepods that are ravenous consumers of diatoms. Copepods are in turn fed upon by larger zooplankton and many species of planktivorous fish. For a period of time, there are sufficient nutrients to stimulate rapid reproduction of phytoplankton, and overall grazing effects are minimal.

As surface waters heat up, they become isolated from deeper, colder waters. This stratification results in a sharp boundary, or **thermocline,** between warm surface waters and much colder waters below. Over time the dead bodies of planktonic organisms sink below the thermocline where they are broken down by bacteria. However, the nutrients released by bacterial decay are temporarily trapped in the cold bottom layer. In the absence of mixing of water layers, nutrients become scarce and phytoplankton growth slows. Diatoms thrive in well-mixed, nutrient-rich water. As summer progresses, nutrient scarcity and copepod grazing drive down diatom numbers.

Harmful Algal Blooms

Some **algal blooms** are associated with shellfish poisoning in humans. Just how dangerous can microscopic algae be? Certain species produce potent neurotoxins that can have harmful, and sometimes lethal, effects on fish, birds, marine mammals, and humans. In low numbers they have no effect on consumers, but during population explosions when millions of algal cells are available for consumption, their toxins reach harmful levels. Because some blooms discolor the water, they are commonly called **red tides.** The toxic algae enter the food chain when they are consumed by planktivorous fish or filter-feeding bivalves, such as oysters, clams, and mussels. The toxins have little or no effect on the shellfish. However, the toxins are concentrated and passed up the food chain to subsequent consumers, including humans, with more severe consequences. Most reports of harmful blooms have occurred since 1972 with the duration of occurrence, frequency of occurrence, and severity all increasing during this time. In addition to the threats to human health, the effects on fisheries and tourism can be devastating.

Amnesic shellfish poisoning (ASP) is associated with a diatom, *Pseudonitzschia pungens,* that produces the toxin domoic acid. Symptoms include gastrointestinal and neurological disorders. In severe cases death may result. Consumption of mussels and scallops during recent blooms in the Gulf of Maine and off the Massachusetts coast has resulted in cases of ASP.

Paralytic shellfish poisoning (PSP) is caused by the dinoflagellate *Alexandrium.* Humans experience burning and numbness of the mouth and face within minutes of ingesting contaminated shellfish. In more severe cases paralysis of the limbs and respiratory system sets in, with death occurring if artificial respiration is not initiated. There is no antidote for either ASP or PSP; however, most victims recover fully from the symptoms within a few days. *Alexandrium* blooms are

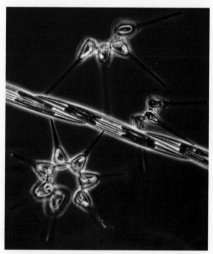

Pseudonitzschia pungens *is a pennate diatom with elongated cells that overlap to form colonies. It produces toxic domoic acid that is responsible for amnesic shellfish poisoning. The other colonies are* Asterionellopsis *diatoms.*   DR. PAUL E. HARGRAVES, HARBOR BRANCH OCEANOGRAPHIC INSTITUTION

continued

becoming increasingly common along the New England coast. They have even been implicated in the deaths of whales that fed on contaminated mackerel off Cape Cod. Spring blooms in the Gulf of Maine and in Cape Cod Bay appear to be stimulated by low salinity and warmer water associated with increased runoff from rivers.

In the summer of 2005, the Gulf of Maine experienced the largest red tide in its history. Record amounts of toxins and dinoflagellate cells were found in the water. The area covered and duration of the bloom were also record setting. An outbreak of *Alexandrium fundyense* forced public health officials to ban the harvest of clams, mussels, and oysters from Nantucket

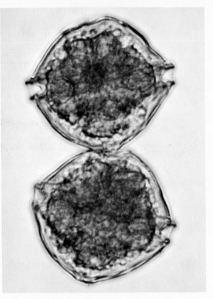

Two cells of Alexandrium, *the toxic dinoflagellate responsible for paralytic shellfish poisoning. A massive bloom of* Alexandrium *shut down New England shellfishing in the summer of 2005.*   DON ANDERSON

to the Bay of Fundy, putting many shellfishermen out of business for most of the summer. A much smaller bloom the previous fall left dormant cysts in the sediment. A May nor'easter corralled large numbers of algal cells from offshore and deposited them in the gulf. An unusually large amount of snow fell on New England earlier in the year. As it melted and ran off into the ocean, the diluted coastal waters became perfect for *Alexandrium* growth. By the end of May, a toxic bloom that would last for months was well under way.

The most insidious harmful alga is the fish killer, *Pfiesteria piscicida,* which actively seeks out live fish, kills them, and then eats them. Unknown to science prior to 1988, this dinoflagellate has been implicated in massive fish kills every year since its discovery. Based on a stage in its lifecycle featuring a pair of flagella, it is classified as a dinoflagellate; yet this is no ordinary dinoflagellate. *Pfiesteria* (pronounced fee-steer-ee-ah) lacks chlorophyll for photosynthesis and must obtain nutrients and energy by feeding on fish and other algae.

Pfiesteria has a remarkable twenty-four different stages in its life cycle. Stages come in three basic forms: amoebae, cysts, and zoospores. The amoebae slowly crawl along the bottom of shallow estuaries digesting algae and dead fish as they go. However, in response to fish excrement or fish secretions in the water column, the amoebae rapidly transform themselves into dinoflagellate-like zoospores that swim into the chemical cues produced by the swimming fish. When they contact a fish, the zoospores begin producing potent toxins (which have yet to be identified by scientists) that immobilize the fish and quickly destroy the skin. The zoospores then feed upon the ulcerated sores formed on the skin of the disabled fish. In the presence of a large food supply, the cells will begin to multiply rapidly. Soon after the fish dies, the zoospores may revert back to amoeboid stages, which will feed on the carcass. If conditions become unfavorable for survival or the food supply runs out, the *Pfiesteria* will transform into a cyst, which will sink to the bottom and lie dormant until stimulated to metamorphose into one of the other life stages.

The presence of large amounts of nutrients in a water body stimulates the growth of other algae that *Pfiesteria* can feed upon, leading to a *Pfiesteria* population explosion followed by massive attacks on fish. An outbreak in 1991 killed a billion fish in the Neuse River estuary in North Carolina. Unlike other dinoflagellate toxins, which can be concentrated in fish and then passed up the food chain to humans, *Pfiesteria* toxins do not appear to persist in fish. Instead humans can be affected by direct contact with dead and dying fish or contaminated water during a fish kill. Humans can also become ill from inhaling aerosolized toxins near a fish kill. Large outbreaks of *Pfiesteria* and resulting fish kills have been localized to the areas near the Albemarle-Pamlico Estuarine System (North Carolina) plus some smaller outbreaks in the Chesapeake. However, *Pfiesteria* is capable of experiencing blooms anywhere along the coast from North Carolina to Delaware.

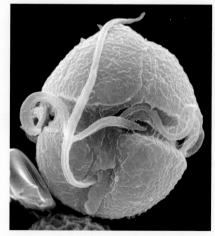

The fish-killing dinoflagellate Pfiesteria piscicida *viewed under a scanning electron microscope*   JOANN M. BURKHOLDER

Dinoflagellates often become more numerous at this point. Compared to diatoms, their smaller size endows dinoflagellates with a proportionately larger surface area relative to their volume. In terms of supplying a cell with nutrients, the higher this ratio is, the more efficiently the cell can pass nutrients across its outer surface. Therefore dinoflagellates survive better than diatoms under low-nutrient conditions because they are more efficient at taking up nutrients. Eventually copepods find it difficult to obtain food, and they too begin to decrease in abundance. Mid- to late summer is a time of low plankton abundance.

As surface waters cool in the fall and the thermocline breaks down, there will be a smaller phytoplankton bloom in response to increased availability of nutrients. This is short lived as shorter day lengths and less light once again limit phytoplankton production.

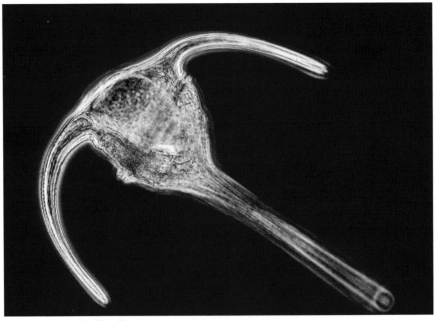

Ceratium tripos dinoflagellate   DR. PAUL E. HARGRAVES, HARBOR BRANCH OCEANOGRAPHIC INSTITUTION

Rocky Shores

Rocky shores line the Gulf of Maine, as well as portions of the Rhode Island and Connecticut coast. Enormous walls of granite rock meet the sea throughout much of this region. This rugged coastline was left behind by retreating glaciers 10,000 years ago. As the glaciers moved over the land, they scraped away topsoil and any loose rock. When the glaciers finally melted, the rocks and soil were deposited far from their original locations. The sheltered shores of New England and Long Island Sound are lined with rounded cobbles left behind by melting glaciers. Cape Cod and Long Island mark the southern most advances of the glaciers. Sandy beaches prevail south of here.

Exploring rocky shores requires careful attention to personal safety. A thin film of very slippery algae covers the rocks. Slipping on the rocks can be painful. Falling into the ocean can be fatal, especially if you are wearing hip boots or waders. Always keep track of whether the tide is rising or falling and the approach of the

Bold Coast at West Quoddy Head (Lubec, Maine) easternmost point in the United States
SCOTT SHUMWAY

next wave. Begin your explorations by getting a feel for the many different environmental conditions that make this a difficult place to inhabit. Then look around at the zonation patterns that appear on the rocks and make the seaweeds and animals look like they were applied to the rocks with a paint roller. Finally you are ready to examine the individual species and start asking how they are adapted for survival in this habitat and how they interact with their neighbors.

Rocky Intertidal: A Highly Stressful Place to Live

The **intertidal** spans the vertical shore-line submerged by the highest high tides down to the area exposed by the lowest of the low tides. It is one of the most stressful habitats on the planet. Crashing waves threaten to smash or dislodge organisms from the rocks

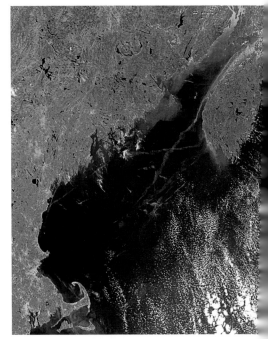

Gulf of Maine satellite view
NOAA PHOTO LIBRARY-NATIONAL MARINE FISHERIES HISTORIC IMAGE COLLECTION

while receding tides leave them vulnerable to drying out and exposed to potentially deadly heat or cold. Only certain species that are well adapted to coping with its various stresses are able to survive in the rocky intertidal.

The most obvious stress is the waves that constantly pound the shore. The species that live here must be able to resist being crushed or ripped off of the rocks by crashing waves. Barnacles and limpets have a conical shape that deflects the force of breaking waves and resists the shear forces acting to lift them off the rocks. Seaweeds have tough flexible bodies that allow them to be bent back and forth without harm. Mussels grow in dense clumps and have specialized anchoring threads that make it difficult for them to be dislodged. Snails use muscular feet and a coating of mucus to seal themselves to rock surfaces. Many species take refuge in crevices in the rocks in order to avoid the full force of the waves.

Waves can also dislodge rocks or toss floating debris onto the shore. Hurricanes and winter storms bring unusually strong waves that can rip organisms off rocks. The open rocky coast exposed to crashing waves is considered a high-energy environment. In contrast sheltered bays, inlets, coves, and the landward sides of islands that receive little or no wave action are low-energy environments. These differences in wave energy are accompanied by differences in the composition and abundance of species that live there. The total number of different species living in the rocky intertidal of New England is so low that even a casual observer can learn to identify most of the species found here, as well as to recognize patterns of species distributions and to discern the factors responsible for those patterns. Many of the same species of invertebrates and algae live on the rocks from the shores of the Canadian Maritimes to Long Island Sound. Although the tidal range changes along this gradient, and hence the width of the band of rock that these species call home, the patterns and processes are similar throughout.

Cobble beach at low tide (Bristol, Rhode Island)   SCOTT SHUMWAY

Within the vertical expanse of the rocky intertidal, the upper reaches are left high and dry for the longest duration and the highest frequency while the lower reaches may be exposed for only a few minutes each month. The time an organism spends out of the water is extremely stressful and has deleterious effects on its physiology, resulting in decreased metabolic rate, slower growth, less time to feed, lower reproductive output, or even death.

Desiccation or drying out is the greatest threat faced by intertidal species. They must avoid water loss during low tides when they are out of the water. Seaweeds possess gel-forming chemicals that absorb and retain water. Barnacles and mussels close their shells

Cobble beach at high tide   SCOTT SHUMWAY

tightly ("clam up") to trap moisture in their bodies. Snails seal off the opening to their shell with a trapdoorlike operculum. Mobile species like snails, starfish, and crabs seek out crevices, undersides of rocks, and tide pools (pockets of water left behind by receding tides) to wait out the exposure period.

Thermal stress is a problem because living organisms are controlled by a series of biochemical reactions mediated by enzymes, which function within a limited range of temperatures. When that range is exceeded, the chemical reactions essential to life cease to take place. Therefore extremes in hot and cold temperatures can set the northern and southern geographic limits of a species. Temperature can also influence the vertical distributions of species within the intertidal zone. Temperature stress increases with elevation as rocks farther upshore are out of the moderating effects of the ocean water for a longer time. Summer sunlight can heat rocks to lethal temperatures, whereas in winter intertidal species run the risk of freezing or being scoured by ice.

Zonation Patterns

Rocky intertidal species occupy well-defined zones that correspond to differences in elevation and are referred to as the high, mid, and lower intertidal. (The vast area below this is constantly submerged and is known as the subtidal.) Tides cover and uncover these elevation zones for differing amounts of time. The highest zone is covered by water for the shortest amount of time and exposed to the air for the longest. The low intertidal is submerged for the longest and exposed for the shortest. These differences have important consequences for the species that live here and are easily seen in the banding patterns that the species form across the rocks. The degree of wave exposure can also influence species distributions.

The **high intertidal** of **wave-exposed shores** is inhabited almost exclusively by Northern Rock Barnacles. This is the most stressful place to live as it is subject to both the extreme energy of breaking waves and the longest exposure times with the greatest risk of either drying out or overheating. Few other species can tolerate these conditions. The exceptions are lichens and cyanobacteria (blue-greens), which occupy a dark-colored band in the splash zone just above the barnacles.

A layer of blue-green bacteria (cyanobacteria) coats the surfaces of rocks in the splash zone of the uppermost reaches of the intertidal.   JOANN M. BURKHOLDER

Barnacles and mussels grow next to one another with barnacles occupying a band immediately above the mussels.
SCOTT SHUMWAY

The **mid intertidal** is inhabited by a dense growth of barnacles and mussels. Starting in January, barnacle larvae settle on the rocks and begin to grow. The bare space on the rocks made available by winter storms and cumulative mortality over the previous year will soon be filled by rapidly growing juvenile barnacles.

Many will perish due to intense competition with neighbors seeking growing space on the rocks. Starting in June, mussel larvae will begin to settle on the rocks. The mussels appear to prefer a rough surface for initial attachment and find the rough texture of barnacle shells to be ideal for settling upon. The newly settled mussels grow rapidly and smother the underlying barnacles. Over time the mussels outcompete and eliminate the barnacles from much of the mid intertidal, thereby restricting barnacles to higher elevations where the mussels are unable to survive the effects of desiccation. Snails and seaweeds are uncommon at these high-energy sites, most likely due to their inability to cling to the rocks under the force of the waves.

The **low intertidal** of exposed shores is dominated by Blue Mussels. Winter waves dislodge large clumps of mature mussels. Barnacle larvae colonize the bare space in early spring, but here too their occupation is short lived as mussels soon overrun them.

On **protected rocky shores,** where wave energy is much lower, the total number of species is greater. Barnacles still dominate the high intertidal, and barnacles and mussels inhabit the mid intertidal; but the amount of unoccupied rock surface is greater than on exposed shores. The difference is related to the abundance of Dogwinkle Snails, which prey upon barnacles and mussels. Snails can prevent complete occupation of the rock surface, as well as diminish the abundance of mussels to the point where their competitive effect on barnacles is negligible.

A dense canopy of brown seaweeds in the upper and mid intertidal further reduces barnacle abundance by providing a barrier to successful settlement by larvae seeking a suitable rock surface. More importantly the whiplash effect of the algae moving across the

Green Sea Urchins on low intertidal rocks just below Blue Mussels   SCOTT SHUMWAY

The upper intertidal of protected shores is covered with Knotted Wrack and other brown seaweeds.   SCOTT SHUMWAY

rock surface acts to wipe the rocks clean of invertebrate life.

The low intertidal of protected shores is dominated by the red seaweed Irish Moss rather than mussels. The transition from brown seaweeds in the mid zone to Irish Moss below is abrupt. Susceptibility to drying out prevents Irish Moss from living at higher elevations while greater longevity may contribute to its success down lower. The domination of Irish Moss on sheltered shores is made possible by its ability to regrow rapidly following disturbance in combination with the large numbers of predatory Dogwinkle Snails, which list mussels and barnacles as their favorite food.

Seaweed zonation in the upper and mid intertidal. From top to bottom: Knotted Wrack, rockweed, Irish Moss.
SCOTT SHUMWAY

Inhabitants of the Rocky Intertidal

Feeding style and position in the food chain (trophic level) are useful criteria for understanding the inhabitants of any marine community. At the base of the food chain are the photosynthesizing primary producers, which in the intertidal include microscopic algae and macroalgae or seaweeds. These organisms are consumed by mobile herbivores and sessile filter feeders. At the top of the food chain are predatory snails, crabs, and sea stars. The most common members of each group are considered below.

Algae are plantlike in that they photosynthesize and have similar physiological needs as true plants; yet because of their complex life cycles and photosynthetic pigments, they are considered members of the kingdom Protista. A film of microscopic bacteria and single-celled algae, primarily diatoms, covers the surfaces of intertidal rocks. Macroalgae or **seaweeds** occupy the greatest amount of space on rocky shores, and in so doing they provide food, shelter, shade, and hiding places for many different species. A holdfast shaped either like a mass of roots or a suction cup anchors seaweeds to rocks. While they may look like roots, holdfasts do not absorb nutrients. Instead, seaweeds use their entire bodies to absorb nutrients from seawater. A leaflike blade is used to capture sunlight to fuel photosynthesis. The blade is joined to the holdfast by a flexible stemlike stipe, which may be several feet long or nonexistent, depending on the species. A variety of specialized pigments are employed to harness the sun's energy for photosynthesis. Based on their photosynthetic pigmentation, seaweeds are subdivided into three phyla, green algae (Chlorophyta), red algae (Rhodophyta), and brown algae (Phaeophyta).

Seaweed body plans take on many forms. Some grow as sheets only a few cells thick. Upright forms branch and send out leafy blades, resembling miniature shrubs. Most are soft to the touch, yet tough, to resist being shredded by waves. Others encrust rocks, shells, and other algae never growing upright and looking more like a coating of paint than a living organism. Most grow attached to a hard surface like a rock, mollusc shell, or pier, while others are epiphytes (literally "plants that grow on other plants") specialized to attach to other algae. Many of these species lack universally agreed-upon common names and must be referred to using their scientific names.

The rootlike holdfast of this large kelp anchors the seaweed to rocks.   ANDREW K. HOWARD

Seaweeds

The green seaweed, **Sea Lettuce** *(Ulva lactuca),* resembles a leaf of lettuce minus the veins. The bright green blades are only two cells thick. These blades are a favorite food of herbivorous snails because they lack chemical defenses.

Sea Lettuce (Ulva lactuca)   SCOTT SHUMWAY

Enteromorpha intestinalis forms green tubes and, as its name implies, resembles a jumble of intestines. Oxygen gas produced by photosynthesis remains trapped in the tubes buoying the alga to the surface of tide pools. It too is a favorite snail food and obtains refuge in high elevation pools free of herbivores. The result is often a lush green growth in certain tide pools.

Brown seaweeds cover most of the intertidal and subtidal rocks. Most brown and red seaweeds are fortified with complex defense chemicals that render them unpalatable to herbivores.

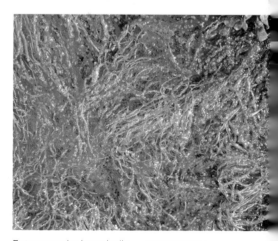

Enteromorpha intestinalis   SCOTT SHUMWAY

Fucus spiralis *often grows at higher eleva-tions than any other seaweed and is distin-guished from other rockweeds by the thin ridge along its swollen tips.*   SCOTT SHUMWAY

Tubed Weed (Polysiphonia lanosa) *growing on Knotted Wrack*   SCOTT SHUMWAY

Rockweeds in the genus *Fucus* are the most abundant intertidal seaweeds. Their brown bodies are loosely branched and adorned with bulblike swellings (called receptacles) at their tips. The swellings house reproductive structures, and tiny pockmarks on the surface provide points of release for the gametes. During certain low tides all of the rockweeds in an area will release millions of sperm and egg cells at the same time, allowing them to be swept up by the rising tide. This syn-chronous gamete release is highly advantageous in a species that depends on sperm and egg finding each other in the huge ocean.

Rockweeds are highly resistant to drying out. *Fucus spiralis* growing at high elevations is able to withstand losing up to 85 percent of its water. *F. vesiculosus* and *F. distichus* are found lower on the rocks. *F. vesiculosus* is the most common and may be distin-guished from the other species by pairs of air bladders scattered along the blades. The air bladders presumably make the plant buoyant at high tide, bringing the photosynthetic blades closer to the surface where sunlight is most intense.

Knotted Wrack *(Ascophyllum nodosum)* is the most common sea-weed of protected shores. To the unini-tiated it closely resembles the rockweeds. Closer inspection reveals that Knotted Wrack has many inflated air bladders along its length and the light brown blades grow into long, tough, narrow limbs that branch periodically. Unlike rockweeds these blades never have a midrib.

Another way to distinguish Knotted Wrack is by the presence of the epiphyte *Polysiphonia lanosa* (sometimes called Tubed Weed), which grows as a beardlike mass of dark red filaments joined at the base to its host. Wherever you find Knotted Wrack, it's a safe bet that *Polysiphonia* will be attached to some of it. *Fucus,* on the other hand, is never associated with *Polysiphonia.*

The prevalence of Knotted Wrack on protected shores is due to its inability to establish itself under wave-swept conditions, its longevity, and its defenses against herbivory. The young algae first beginning growth on a rocky surface are easily dislodged and can only establish successfully in protected areas with minimal wave action. So poor is their ability to establish that it is surprising they are able to become so abundant within the community. This abundance is maintained by being capable of surviving for up to thirty years and reproducing throughout this time. Because Knotted Wrack produces a single air bladder each year, it is possible to determine the age of an individual by counting the number of air bladders along its main axis.

Irish Moss *(Chondrus crispus),* a red seaweed, is the dominant species in the low intertidal of protected shores, occupying a band located immediately below the rockweeds. Irish Moss forms a dense canopy just above the rock surface and anchors to the rocks with a suction-cup holdfast that will remain in place even if the rest of the body breaks off. Should this happen, the alga can simply regrow from the holdfast.

Tufted Red Weed *(Mastocarpus stellatus)* often grows adjacent to Irish Moss and is very similar to it in appearance. Both are red algae, yet exhibit a deep brownish red coloration

The most common rockweed, Fucus vesiculosus, *bears numerous pairs of air bladders and a distinct midrib along the length of the blade*
SCOTT SHUMWAY

Irish Moss (Chondrus crispus) *with dichotomously branching blades is often the most common seaweed in the mid intertidal.*
SCOTT SHUMWAY

Tufted Red Weed (Mastocarpus stellatus) *often grows alongside Irish Moss, but can easily be distinguished by having bumpy reproductive structures along the blade.*
SCOTT SHUMWAY

that looks more brown than red. Their body plans consist of blades that repeatedly branch in two with only about a centimeter between branching points. Despite their similarities they are differentiated relatively easily. Tufted Red Weed blades have bumps associated with their reproductive structures while Irish Moss blades are always smooth. In addition Tufted Red Weed blades are cup shaped or rolled at the end while Irish Moss blades are not. Irish Moss will often appear bleached, yet healthy, while the other species never bleaches.

Coral Weed *(Corallina officinalis)* is the only branching red seaweed in New England that is impregnated with calcium carbonate (limestone). It has the texture of steel wool and looks like dense tufts of dark pink antlers. The calcium carbonate protects the algae from grazers but costs energy to make and blocks sunlight, so growth in this species is slow. Coral Weed provides an example of an evolutionary tradeoff. Is it better to grow quickly and reproduce as soon as possible without wasting energy on antiherbivore defense? Or is it better to grow slowly and not get eaten before the opportunity arises to reproduce? The seaweeds in this chapter illustrate some of the different ways that natural selection has answered this riddle.

Coral Weed (Corallina officinalis), *a red seaweed resembling miniature antlers with the texture of steel wool*   SCOTT SHUMWAY

Bare rock is unheard of in marine habitats. There always seem to be more algae and invertebrates attempting to live on a square inch of rock than can possibly be supported. Even rock that appears bare is actually covered by a film of microscopic algae and bacteria.

Usually "bare" rock will be covered with an **algal crust** resembling brown leather, red or brown paint, or pink bubblegum. A leathery brown crust that can be scraped off by fingernails or a knife is likely to be *Ralfsia,* while a blood-red paintlike covering that is not easily removed is *Hildenbrandia rubra.* Many red algae secrete calcium carbonate and grow over rocks as thin rocklike crusts that look just like flattened Bazooka bubblegum. Large areas

Crustose red algae impregnated with calcium carbonate and resembling a layer of bubblegum are common on intertidal and subtidal rocks.   SCOTT SHUMWAY

Seaweeds in Your Ice Cream!

What's in your ice cream? Read the ingredient labels on processed foods and you will find algin, agar, and carrageenan listed. Many seaweeds produce vegetable gums or *phycocolloids,* chemical substances found in cell walls that can form gels in low concentrations. Algin is harvested from Giant Kelp *(Macrocystis pyrifera)* off the coast of Southern California, where it forms massive kelp forests. Agar comes from certain species of red algae and is used extensively as a medium for culturing bacteria in microbiology labs. Irish Moss provides a local source for carrageenan.

Eminent algologists John Kingsbury and Philip Sze provide a recipe for a thickened milk beverage called Irish Moss blancmange.

"Rinse wet (fresh) Irish Moss, or soak dried moss in freshwater until soft. Discard any that is not reasonably clean and free of attached animals. Throw a small handful (a generous half cup) into a quart of milk in a double boiler and cook for twenty-five minutes. Strain the moss out with cheesecloth. Stir in some salt, sugar, and vanilla to taste. Pour into molds; chill until firm. Serve as is or with sugar and cream."

In the next paragraph they note, "Be sure you have Irish moss. Most others won't work."

Phycocolloids are used as thickening agents in pie fillings, salad dressings, chocolate milk, and other products. Because the human digestive system is unable to break down phycocolloids, they are used extensively as bulking agents in low-calorie desserts. Brewers will add algal extracts to ensure long-lasting tiny bubbles on a head of beer. Many ice creams contain phycocolloids, which retard ice-crystal formation providing a smooth creamy feeling in your mouth. Next time you see friends about to consume a pint of Ben and Jerry's finest, you may want to warn them about the seaweeds in their ice cream, and perhaps you'll get the pint all to yourself.

of these so-called encrusting corallines are known as algal pavements or urchin barrens and are often the result of sea urchins consuming everything else.

Mobile Herbivores: Algae-Eating Snails

The most common herbivores on rocky shores are snails (gastropods) that feed primarily on seaweeds. Like all gastropods, they possess a feeding apparatus called a radula. The radula is like a conveyor belt studded with hooked teeth of various sizes and shapes. It is extended through the mouth to rasp away at the food source, in this case seaweeds.

Hildenbrandia rubra *grows as a crust, only a few cells thick. Its red coloration is striking against a milky quartz background.*
SCOTT SHUMWAY

There are three species of **periwinkle** snail commonly encountered on rocky shores. Periwinkles are well adapted for living in the intertidal. At low tide they migrate to crevices in the rocks where shading and trapped water protect them from desiccation. They also hide beneath the protective canopies of seaweeds. Water loss is prevented by tightly sealing off the aperture using their *operculum,* a hardened proteinaceous trapdoor attached to the side of the foot. The seal is further weatherproofed by a secretion of mucus that helps hold the closed-up snail to the rock and prevents water loss. In some instances when the rocks become too hot, the snail hangs from

Common Periwinkle (Littorina littorea)
SCOTT SHUMWAY

the rock by a strand of gooey mucus until the tide returns.

The **Common Periwinkle** *(Littorina littorea)* is the largest and, as its name suggests, by far the most abundant. It has a dark gray to black and somewhat rounded 1.25-inch-long (3.1-cm) shell. It lives on most rocky shores and is particularly abundant on sheltered shores and in tide pools.

The **Rough Periwinkle** *(Littorina saxatilis)* is much smaller at less than 0.625 inch (1.6 cm). The whorls of its shell are grooved and resemble a miniature winding roadway ascending a mountain.

The round shells of the Smooth Periwinkles (Littorina obtusata) *blend in with the air bladders of Knotted Wrack.*   SANDRA E. SHUMWAY

The appropriately named **Smooth Periwinkle** *(Littorina obtusata)* has a very low, almost nonexistent, spire. The spherical shell is less than a 0.5 inch (1.2 cm) in length and is yellowish brown to brown in color. It is frequently found in association with Knotted Wrack, its preferred food, making it one of the few herbivores able to prey upon this well-defended seaweed. Its shape and coloration blend in well among the air bladders and reproductive structures of the brown seaweed. This is most likely an adaptation to avoid detection by birds.

In general the ranges of the periwinkle species overlap, and it is not uncommon to find all three in close proximity. The Common Periwinkle has expanded as far south as Maryland while the others range as far south as Cape May, New Jersey.

Easily recognized by their conical shells, **limpets** are primitive gastropods that cling to rocks with a large muscular foot. A limpet taken by surprise may be slid sideways off a rock, but once it tightens its hold on the rock, it is nearly impossible to dislodge without causing injury (to the limpet or your fingernails). The **Tortoise-Shell Limpet** *(Tectura testudinalis)* is the only limpet species common in the North Atlantic, where it grazes algae off rocks in the intertidal and subtidal. Its 1-inch (2.5 cm) diameter shell is shaped like a Chinese hat and sports a variable brown and cream tortoise-shell pattern for which it is named (*testudinalis* = turtle-like). This limpet is unusual in that it has a strong feeding preference for one species of crustose coralline red algae named *Clathromorphum circumscriptum*.

Tortoise-Shell Limpet (Tectura testudinalis)
SCOTT SHUMWAY

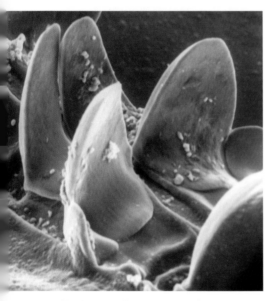

Teeth on the feeding radula of a limpet
BOB STENECK

The radula teeth of the limpet are hardened with deposits of iron and silica that keep them from being worn away by repeated rasping against the calcium carbonate impregnated alga. The extremely smooth surface of the alga enables limpets to maintain a strong grip in the face of waves and predators that threaten to dislodge them.

All limpets have homesites where they return when not actively feeding. Because the limpets feed primarily at night, any discovered during the day are most likely resting on their homesite, which is most likely a *Clathromorphum* colony. Fouling by epiphytes such as diatoms, filamentous algae, and sessile invertebrates is a constant threat to a slow-growing crustose alga with few ways of defending itself against colonization. Despite losing 800 cells to each limpet bite (and they never stop after just one bite), the alga grows best when grazed by limpets.

Sessile Filter Feeders

Sessile, or nonmotile, species like barnacles and mussels spend their entire adult lives attached to a rock. They are unable to move around in search of food. Instead they filter their food from the water column.

Barnacles look like inanimate lumps on a rock. In reality they are shrimplike crustaceans that live in the protected confines of a conical shell with their heads cemented to a rock and their feet waving in the water to collect food. They are filter or suspension feeders. They use feathery feet to filter suspended food particles, such as single-celled algae, from the water. Clearly they can only feed during the times when they are submerged. A set of movable plates (tergum and scutum) open to allow the feet to extend. At low tide the same plates clamp shut to prevent water loss. Tide pools are ideal locations to observe barnacles feeding.

How the Common Periwinkle Became the Most Common Snail

The Common Periwinkle is not native to North America. It first became established on the rocky shores of Nova Scotia around 1840 most likely after being introduced intentionally by European colonists as a food source. By 1870 it had reached the north side of Cape Cod, and twenty years later it was established in Cape May, New Jersey. It quickly became the most abundant snail and most important intertidal herbivore throughout most of this vast area. The snail is generally uncommon south of Long Island due to a lack of suitable rocky shores.

The Common Periwinkle is a generalist herbivore, readily consuming diatoms, seaweeds, and even the rhizomes of salt-marsh grasses. It is most abundant on protected rocky shores followed by the firm peaty edges of salt marshes. It is commonly found in densities of 650 individuals per square yard with a record of 14,630 per square yard. Given its wide diet and high density, the periwinkle has undoubtedly had a major impact on the distribution and abundance of its prey species, as well as native grazers with which it competes.

Perhaps the most stunning demonstration of the impact Common Periwinkles have had on natural communities comes from a study in which snails were removed from sections of a cobble beach in Narragansett Bay, Rhode Island. Within weeks of removal of the snails, the habitat began to change dramatically. The dark gray rocks were transformed into lush gardens of green algae that began to trap fine sediments. Worms and other burrowing invertebrates characteristic of soft-bottom habitat began to colonize the removal plots. This newly formed soft-bottom habitat might be an indication of what the shoreline would be like had the Common Periwinkle never appeared on the scene.

Clumps of salt-marsh grasses also grow on cobble beaches. Periwinkles consume the roots and rhizomes of Salt Marsh Cordgrass. When snails were removed experimentally, the marsh grasses experienced significant expansion. Periwinkles appear to have eliminated or halted the spread of salt-marsh habitat along these shores. Thanks to this snail, our natural coastal communities are not so natural after all.

Northern Rock Barnacle (Semibalanus balanoides)   SCOTT SHUMWAY

What appear to be lumps of shell on a rock are actually fierce competitors for living space, both between individuals of the same species and members of different species. As they expand in size, barnacles ruthlessly try to eliminate their neighbors, either by crushing them, prying them off a rock, or growing over them and excluding their access to food.

Two species of intertidal barnacle inhabit our region. The **Northern Rock Barnacle** *(Semibalanus balanoides)* is a cold-water species that lives as far south as Delaware. The **Little Gray Barnacle** *(Chthamalus fragilis)* is common from Delaware south to the Caribbean but may extend as far north as Cape Cod. The Northern Rock Barnacle covers most of the mid- to high-elevation rocky surfaces throughout its range. Where the two species overlap, the Little Gray Barnacle is restricted to a narrow band above the Northern Rock Barnacle. This distribution pattern is the result of differences in the two species' abilities to tolerate the more stressful physical conditions at higher elevations and differences in their ability to compete for space at lower elevations. The results hold true for zonation of many intertidal species.

The internal structure of the calcium carbonate plates that make up the shell of the Northern Rock Barnacle is a series of hollow tubes. This strong lightweight construction allows for fast growth and superior competitive ability. In comparison the shell of the Little Gray is solid in construction, grows slowly, and never gets to be half as big as that of its chief competitor.

The larger Northern Rock Barnacle is the superior competitor for living space on a rock and typically occupies the more desirable lower elevations. These areas are more desirable because they are covered by water for more time, allowing for more time spent feeding and less time drying in the hot sun. The Little Gray is perfectly capable of surviving the conditions of the lower intertidal, and even grows best there, but only when its rival is absent. However, where the two barnacle species overlap, Little Gray is only allowed to grow in the more stressful upper reaches of the intertidal where the less-tolerant Northern Rock Barnacle is unable to survive. North of Cape Cod, the uppermost reaches of the intertidal are not as hot, and therefore not as stressful to barnacles compared to southern shores. The Northern Rock Barnacle grows high on the rocks here. There is no refuge from the competitive superiority of the Northern Rock Barnacle, so there are no Little Grays.

Mussels and barnacles occur together on temperate rocky shores throughout the world. On the New England coast **Blue Mussels** *(Mytilus edulis)* form dense beds immediately below Northern Rock Barnacles. This species is also known as the Edible Mussel *(edulis* = edible) and for some reason enjoys a greater reputation as a culinary delight in Europe than it does in the United States. Nonetheless a growing aquaculture industry exists for this species in the Gulf of Maine.

Mussels are considered foundation species because of their bed-forming abilities and their tendency to bind together tangled masses of rocks, shells, and other live mussels. They anchor to rocks and other hard surfaces with strong threads of protein, known as byssal threads. This is the "beard" that Julia Child and friends instruct you to remove prior to cooking.

Adult mussels may reach 4 inches (10 cm) in length with a bluish black bivalve shell. At reproductive maturity individuals will release thousands of sperm or eggs into the water. Successfully fertilized eggs develop into larvae that pass through multiple stages. Upon encountering a suitable home, usually near a cluster of adult mussels, the larva will form byssal threads and attach to a rock, barnacle shell, or other mussel. It will spend the rest of its life within a few millimeters of this location.

Blue Mussels (Mytilus edulis) *in the mid intertidal*   SCOTT SHUMWAY

The Complex Life Cycles of Invertebrates

Many bottom-dwelling (benthic) invertebrates have a complex life cycle consisting of *planktonic* larval stages that float in the water followed by a benthic adult stage permanently cemented in place. A complete understanding of the biology of these species requires knowledge about what happens to them during their larval stages, as well as when they are adults. In the case of barnacles, bisexual adults reproduce annually by fertilizing neighbors using an elongated tubular penis to transfer sperm. Larvae form after fertilization and are brooded within the shell of the parent during early development. Larvae are released seasonally, in late winter for the Northern Rock Barnacle, into the surrounding water. The first larval stage or nauplius is shaped like a triangular shield with hairy legs, antennae, and a central reddish eyespot. After undergoing several metamorphoses to larger nauplius stages, they will change into a cyprid stage, which resembles a pinhead-sized football with legs. In response to chemical cues, the cyprid will permanently attach itself to a rock, shell, pier, or other hard surface and metamorphose into a juvenile barnacle resembling a miniature version of the adult. While viewing a nauplius requires the aid of a microscope, newly settled cyprids can easily be seen on rocks.

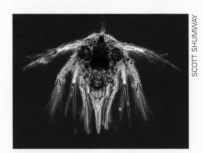

SCOTT SHUMWAY

Nauplius larva of a barnacle

Slight movement is possible by dissolving old threads and secreting new ones, allowing mussels to jostle for a slightly preferable location that may have better feeding or anchoring qualities or less crowding from other mussels. Mussels feed on planktonic algae by circulating water through their bodies using a pair of siphons. Their gills function in both respiration and feeding. Food particles are removed from the incurrent stream by the gills and then transported to the stomach while nonfood particles are shot out through the excurrent siphon.

Mussel beds may be found on rocks and even gravel on exposed and protected shores. They readily settle on top of barnacles and rapidly overgrow them, hence their ability to exclude barnacles from desirable locations.

Mussel populations in turn may be controlled by predatory Dogwinkle snails, which drill a tiny hole in the shell of their prey before digesting its tissue. Open mussel shells posing like small blue butterflies with a single pinhole in one of the valves reveal the work of a Dogwinkle. Green Crabs and Asian Shore Crabs also prey upon mussels but leave behind little more than shell fragments.

On protected shores in the Gulf of Maine, winter ice scour periodically denudes sections of rock of barnacles, mussels, and seaweeds. Rocks are repopulated when invertebrate larvae and algal spores settle on the cleared surfaces. If mussels become established first, they can successfully resist further colonization by seaweeds. Because recruitment by Knotted Wrack is rare overall, large clearings are likely to be invaded and held by mussels. These mussel patches persist over many years

Filter-feeding Blue Mussels (Mytilus edulis) *showing incurrent and excurrent siphons*
SANDRA E. SHUMWAY

surrounded by dense growth of Knotted Wrack. Some scientists point to the long-term presence in the same habitat of two different communities, one dominated by mussels and one by seaweed, as evidence for alternative stable states in the rocky intertidal. Each of these two community types is subject to rare events (ice scour) that alter the community composition in a way that could result in a switch to the other community state. The overall result is an environmental mosaic consisting of patches of mussel beds within a matrix of seaweed that is stable over time.

Predators of the Rocky Intertidal Zone

Snails, crabs, and sea stars are the major predators in the rocky intertidal. They drill, crush, pull apart, and/or dissolve their prey. The impacts on prey populations can be severe. Predation controls population sizes, particularly for juveniles. Just as with herbivory, predation can restrict certain species from living in certain locations. It can also benefit nonprey species by removing their competitors.

The 1.5-inch-long (3.8 cm) **Dogwinkle** *(Nucella lapillus)* is the most important predatory intertidal snail. Similar "Thaid" Snails (after the genus *Thais* to which early taxonomists assigned the Dogwinkle) are found in the temperate rocky inter-

Dogwinkles, also called Dogwhelks (Nucella lapillus), *prey upon mussels by drilling tiny holes in their shells.*   SCOTT SHUMWAY

tidal throughout the world. (The Dogwinkle provides a good argument to learn scientific names! The common name for this species suggests a cross between a dog and a snail.) Dogwinkles prowl the intertidal in search of barnacles and mussels. Their feeding radula can easily defeat the protective plates at the opening of a barnacle shell. The hardened teeth of their radula can also rasp away at mussel shells until a round hole penetrates the shell. The snail secretes digestive enzymes through the hole and after a period of time slurps up the dissolved mussel like a nutritious milkshake.

Depending on the availability of one species or the other, Dogwinkles choose to consume mostly mussels or mostly barnacles but will switch should the relative abundance of prey shift. Feeding by Dogwinkles greatly reduces the abundance of mussels and barnacles on protected shores to the point where bare space may be maintained on the rocks and normally intense competitive interactions between these species are prevented. Dogwinkle shells come in a striking array of colors including solid white, cream, pale yellow, bright orange, and striped combinations of these along with purple stripes. Exactly what causes these variations is uncertain, although it is rumored that snails feeding on barnacles tend to be white while those feeding on mussels are brown or purplish.

Dogwinkles are more abundant on protected shores than on exposed shores. There are noticeable differences between snails from exposed and protected shores. Snails from exposed shores have a more elongated spire and wider opening (aperture), while snails from protected shores have a shorter spire and thicker shell, particularly around the aperture. What is the adaptive significance of these differences? A larger, more muscular foot, and hence a wider shell aperture, is advantageous for staying anchored to the wave-swept rocks of exposed shores. Protected shores, on the other hand, have a greater incidence of crabs that feed by chipping away the shells of their prey before pulling them out through their apertures. The thicker the shell and narrower the aperture of the snail, the more difficult it is for a crab to crush and consume it.

The **Oyster Drill** (*Urosalpinx cinerea*) is an inch-long (2.5 cm) gastropod with a grayish shell characterized by an elongate, sharply pointed spire with rounded whorls. They range from Nova Scotia to northern Florida. In New England they inhabit rocky shores. Elsewhere they live on oyster beds, which are essentially oddly shaped clusters of limestone rock. As their name implies, their prey include

A Boring Story

The story of how Oyster Drills attack shelled prey is a boring one—quite literally. The snail drills tiny holes in the shells of its molluscan prey. This feat is accomplished by alternating between two feeding apparatuses, the radula and the accessory boring organ. They can be thought of as being housed in two independent tubelike structures that can be extended and contracted as needed.

First a firm seal is made between the foot of the Oyster Drill and the shell of the intended prey. As in other gastropods the radula consists of a series of hardened teeth located along a conveyor-belt-like structure. The teeth of the radula are used to rasp away at the shell of the prey; however, this alone is not sufficient to drill a hole in an oyster or mussel. Once the radula can no longer rasp away shell, it is retracted and the accessory boring organ is inserted into the hole in progress. The tip of the boring organ is shaped like a mushroom cap, providing a tight fit to the hole. The organ secretes strong acids (pH as low as 3.8) that dissolve and weaken the prey's shell.

After a period of time, the boring organ is withdrawn and replaced by the radula, which goes to work at excavating the weakened shell, ingesting bits of shell in the process. As soon as the boring organ is retracted, the acidity of the excavation site returns to the pH of 8 characteristic of seawater. This is probably a good thing; otherwise the acid might dissolve the Oyster Drill's own radula and shell! The alternation continues until the radula finally makes a small hole through the shell. The round hole is up to .07 inch (2 mm) in diameter and slightly beveled. Finally, digestive enzymes are secreted and the radula scoops up the liquefied flesh formerly protected by the shell.

The moon snails that crawl over tidal flats employ a similar shell-drilling methodology. Their handiwork can be distinguished by closely examining their victims' shells. Dogwinkles leave behind pinprick-sized holes, while moon snails produce a much larger hole with a well-beveled edge.

Oyster Drill (Urosalpinx cinerea)

oysters, which they feed upon by drilling a hole in the shell and then digesting the soft body inside.

The gray-to-tan-colored shells of Oyster Drills blend in well with rock or oyster-reef backgrounds. In addition to this camouflage, they have few natural predators. Each summer females lay leathery, tan-colored, vase-shaped egg capsules on hard surfaces. Egg capsules are usually clustered with different capsules often having different mothers due to the aggregating behavior of spawning females. Over the next forty days, the larvae complete their development within the capsules and hatch out as tiny versions of the adult ready for their first meal.

Oyster Drills are active predators known to migrate toward potential prey in response to waterborne chemicals. Many species use chemicals to detect the presence of possible mates, good places for larvae to settle, or potential competitors, yet for Oyster Drills these chemicals signal the presence of food! Oyster Drills consume a variety of prey with a preference for barnacles, followed by mussels, and then oysters. This preference most likely reflects the ease of handling prey. Barnacles can be attacked without the need to drill through shell, while mussels tend to have thinner shells than oysters.

Oyster Drills are notorious predators on oysters and, as a result, considered pests by the humans who earn their livelihoods competing with them for food. The annual economic cost to the oyster industry is in the millions of dollars. In some areas as much as 80 percent of first-year oysters may be consumed by Oyster Drills.

Crabs are primarily subtidal species that scurry up the shore at high tide in hopes of a quick meal. They can often be found hiding under rocks at low tide or foraging in tide pools. Crabs and lobsters are members of a group of crustaceans known as decapods after their ten legs. Four pairs are used for walking while the first pair sport claws or chelae. Most crabs have one large crusher claw and a smaller cutter claw. The European Green Crab and Asian Shore Crab are most common, followed by Rock Crab *(Cancer irroratus)*, Jonah Crab *(Cancer borealis)*, and various species of mud crabs.

The **European Green Crab** *(Carcinus maenus)* is an opportunist able to eat just about anything it can get its claws on. The scientific name, *Carcinus maenus*, literally translates into "excited crab". Its dietary breadth is only matched by its physiological capabilities, which enable it to withstand a wide range of environmental conditions. Green Crabs can survive in water with temperatures as low as 32° F (0° C) or with nearly depleted oxygen levels. They tolerate salinity levels as low as four parts per thousand (seawater is 35 ppt), withstand prolonged exposure to air, and put up with starvation for as long as three months.

The carapace, or main shell, is fan shaped with three scalloped lobes between the eyes and five sharp teeth to either side starting just behind the eyes. Coloration is highly variable consisting of various shades of olive green and browns on the upper surface along with a mix of green, yellow, orange, or red on the underside.

A single female may brood up to 185,000 fertilized eggs. Juveniles reside in organically rich mud, mussel beds, filamentous seaweeds, Eelgrass, or marsh grass.

European Green Crab (Carcinus maenus)   SANDRA E. SHUMWAY

Growth rate in crabs is strongly influenced by food availability and temperature. Green Crabs will stop feeding at temperatures less than 45° F (7° C) and be unable to molt below 50° F (10° C). As a result crabs in warmer water grow faster, molt more frequently, reach sexual maturity sooner, and even reproduce more often than crabs living at the northern limits of the range.

The Green Crab is native to Europe and Northern Africa and was first reported on our coast in 1817. It most likely traveled here from Europe attached to the hull of a wooden ship or in rock ballast stored within the damp leaky hull of the ship. It remained rare until about 1900 when the Atlantic Ocean experienced a warming trend, raising water temperatures to within the optimal range for Green Crab growth and reproduction. Today it may be found from the Virginia coast to Prince Edward Island, and over much of this area, it has been the most abundant crab for the past fifty years. It is found primarily on protected shores but is able to survive just about anywhere except areas of intense wave action.

As global climate change raises ocean temperatures in the near future, the Green Crab will continue to expand its range northward. As a generalist predator and as a competitor with other crabs, it exerts a major impact on native species and communities. Green Crabs can consume up to seven Blue Mussels per day. Predation by crabs represents a major obstacle to successful colonization of rocky shores by mussels, snails, and barnacles, providing an opportunity for Irish Moss to become firmly established in the low intertidal.

Green Crabs are in turn food for fish, birds, other crabs, and lobsters. In some cases crabs may become unwilling hosts to the parasitic barnacle *Sacculina carcini.* This parasite, which is only recognizable as a barnacle in its larval stages, takes over the body of the crab, neuters it, and turns it into an egg incubating machine. The North American reign of the European Green Crab, however, may currently be challenged by the latest crab to invade our coast, the Asian Shore Crab.

In 1988 a college student discovered a crab in southern New Jersey that had never been seen before in North America. The native distribution of the **Asian Shore Crab** *(Hemigrapsus sanguineus)* ranges from Sakhalin Island in Russia to Hong Kong. How it ended up on the Jersey Shore will forever remain a mystery, but transport and release of larvae from the ballast water of a ship is the most likely means. In Japan up to 70 percent of the adult crabs are infected by a parasitic barnacle *(Sacculina),* while adults in the United States are parasite free. This observation supports the claim that *Hemigrapsus* arrived here as larvae, which are not susceptible to infection by parasites. The Asian Shore Crab now ranges from southern Maine to North Carolina and is the most abundant intertidal crab throughout this vast region.

The crab itself is rather innocuous looking. Carapace width rarely exceeds 1.5 inches (4 cm) with males being slightly larger than females. The overall color of the crab is reddish brown. The legs are distinctly banded with alternating reddish and white stripes reminiscent of a barber pole. No other crab in our area shares this feature. These crabs are homochelous, meaning their two claws are equal in size. The claws are intermediate in design between crusher and cutter types, so they can crush mollusc shells or slice tissue from shells.

Finding an Asian Shore Crab in the intertidal is not difficult. Any site sheltered from intense wave action and having a supply of rocks is likely to support these crabs as they hide beneath rocks to avoid predators and to stay moist at low tide. The Asian Shore Crab has become the most abundant species of crab on the cobble beaches lining the shores of Long Island Sound and Narragansett Bay. Range

Asian Shore Crab (Hemigrapsus sanguineus), *a recent invader*   GARRY KESSLER

expansion to the south may be slowed by a lack of beach rocks, although rock jetties and oyster beds may provide suitable habitat.

Like many successful invaders the Asian Shore Crab is not picky about what it eats. While most members of the grapsid crab family are vegetarians and favor algae and seagrasses, this species also consumes mussels, barnacles, snails, worms, and crustaceans. In the laboratory a single crab can consume up to one hundred small-sized mussels in a day!

The Asian Shore Crab most likely competes for limited resources with other crabs. It feeds and takes shelter throughout the mid to low intertidal, as do several species of native mud crabs and the European Green Crab. Green Crabs can crush larger mussel shells and ingest more mussels per capita. However, because the density of Asian Shore Crabs exceeds that of Green Crabs, it has a much greater overall effect on mussel populations. Mud crabs feed more on algae, detritus, and worms and are not likely to compete with these crabs for food.

However, all of these crabs spend a large amount of time hiding under rocks to escape predators and the drying effects of low tide. North of Cape Cod, Green Crabs take refuge beneath rocks while south of the cape the prime hiding places are occupied by Asian Shore Crabs, and Green Crabs are relegated to sand and mud substrate. Where the distribution of Asian Shore Crabs overlaps with Green Crabs and mud crabs, the Shore Crab is often the most abundant or the only crab present.

Sea stars are remarkable five-armed predators that, while primarily subtidal dwellers, frequently feed in the lower intertidal. They are commonly referred to as starfish even though they are in no way (they don't swim), shape (just look at them), or form (they don't have scales, fins, or a backbone) fish!

Sea stars usually have five arms radiating from a disklike central area. They have the amazing ability to regenerate lost limbs or to grow an entire sea star from a severed arm containing sufficient portions of the central disk.

The surface of a sea star is covered with spiny bumps, hence their classification as echinoderms, which literally means "spiny skin". Closer inspection reveals that this bumpy surface consists not only of spines, but tiny pincers for removing fouling organisms and debris as well as fleshy fingerlike projections used as gills and chemical sensors.

The underside of a sea star is properly called the oral surface as the mouth opens downward from the center of the animal. A groove extends along the length of the oral surface of each arm. Hundreds of tiny tube feet extend from the groove in four rows. Each tube foot is an independently extensible suction cup controlled by changes in internal water pressure. The sea star is able to coordinate these tube feet to grasp onto any hard surface, to move in any direction it wishes, and to contort its body into any shape imaginable. So tenacious is the grip of the tube feet that if you rudely pull a sea star from a rock, dozens of tube feet are often left clinging to the rock!

Bivalves, particularly Blue Mussels, are a sea star's favorite food items. Sea stars use their tube feet to latch onto the mussel shells with a veritable death grip and

GARRY KESSLER

The Northern Sea Star (Asterias vulgaris) *has a pale yellow madreporite and pointed tips to its arms while the Common Sea Star* (Asterias forbesii) *has a bright orange madreporite and rounded tips.*   R. WAHLE AND GARRY KESSLER

then begin to pull the valves apart. While the force of their pull may be great, the real secret to their success is that the sea stars can lock their tube feet in place without expending additional energy. They simply wait until the exhausted prey is unable to hold its shell closed any longer.

Surprisingly the sea star does not need to completely open the bivalve in order to feed upon it. All that is needed is a tiny gap between the shells. Then it can employ another secret weapon possessed only by sea stars—a stomach that can be slipped outside of its body and into narrow cracks. Sea stars actually have two stomachs, sort of like connecting sacs. One of these is extruded from the oral opening directly onto the tissues of the prey item. Whereas we chew our food and swallow to bring it to our stomach for digestion by chemicals, sea stars bring their stomachs to the food and digest their prey before ingesting it. Once the soft tissues of the bivalve prey have been digested into a slurry, they are slurped up along with the stomach. Quickly pick up a feeding starfish and you might observe the soft yellow-orange stomach sliding back into its body.

Sea stars have a small brightly colored spot on the upper surface called the madreporite, often mistaken for the less obvious nearby anal opening. The madreporite functions as an intake valve and pressure sensor for the water vascular system. A unique feature of echinoderms, the water vascular system is in essence a plumbing system responsible for circulation within the body and maintaining the water pressure that controls the tube feet.

Two medium-sized (4–8 inches [10–20 cm]) sea stars are commonly encountered in our range, either washed up onshore or foraging over rocks. They are very similar in appearance and in their ecology. They can vary greatly in color, but are most often dull orange to slightly purple in color. The **Northern Sea Star** *(Asterias vulgaris)* has a pale yellow madreporite, grows to be slightly larger (to 8 inches [20 cm]), has pointed tips to its arms, and becomes limp when lifted out of the water. The **Common Sea Star** *(A. forbesii)* has a bright orange madreporite, is less than 5 inches [13 cm] in diameter, and has rounded arm tips and a more rigid body.

Search for sea stars at low tide wedged beneath large rocks, at the waterline, and in tide pools. The two species overlap widely in distribution, particularly between Cape Cod and Cape Hatteras. Close to shore however, it is safe to assume that a sea star found north of Cape Cod with a yellow madreporite is a Northern Sea Star whereas a one found south of Cape Cod with an orange madreporite is a Common Sea Star. Because the Northern Sea Star prefers colder water, it inhabits deeper regions of the continental shelf along the Mid-Atlantic, a phenomenon known as boreal submergence in which cold-water species live farther offshore and in deeper water the farther south they go.

Because they prey upon bivalves, sea stars have long been in competition with commercial shellfishermen for mussels, oysters, clams, and scallops. In Long Island Sound the Common Sea Star has been implicated as a major oyster pest. A 1961 U.S. Fish and Wildlife Service publication documents the various and futile means that can be employed to control sea stars, including dragging large spaghetti mops or oyster dredges across the bottom and then dumping the catch in boiling water or dumping toxic chemicals on them to erode away the skin. A 1966 publication from the same agency entitled *Ornamental Uses of Starfishes* provides instructions on how to make an attractive *Asterias* Christmas-tree decoration.

The Rocky Subtidal and Its Inhabitants

The area beyond that which is exposed by the lowest tides is known as the subtidal. It is constantly submerged and inaccessible to most beachgoers. This unseen realm starts off shallow before dropping off to hundreds of feet in depth. The bottom features of the shallow subtidal are often similar to those found onshore, consisting of rock, gravel, sand, or even mud. Life abounds here. Rocks are covered by leafy seaweeds and sessile invertebrates such as bryozoans, sponges, hydroids, anemones, mussels, and tunicates. Herbivorous sea urchins, chitons, and limpets crawl over the bottom in search of seaweeds. Invertebrate predators include Jonah and Rock Crabs, lobsters, and several species of sea star. The most common predatory fish include Cunner and Tautog. A full appreciation of the subtidal can only be gained by strapping on scuba gear and going for a closer look. Even with scuba gear the undersea world gets cold and dark by about 30 feet (9 m) in depth. For the average beachcomber the mysteries of the subtidal are revealed by clues that have been seemingly spit up from the deep by strong waves that have ripped subtidal species from their homes and deposited their remains on the shore. A few species deserve attention because of their ecological importance or because you are likely to encounter them on the beach or on a dinner plate.

Tide Pools

As the tides recede each day, pockets of water are trapped in depressions in the rock surface. These **tide pools** range in size from the area of a kitchen sink to an entire kitchen and beyond. They serve as valuable refuges from exposure at low tide and are exploited by large numbers of organisms. Tide pools often mimic conditions found at lower elevations and provide visitors with a window into the subtidal. Encrusting red algae, kelps, sponges, sea anemones, nudibranchs, crabs, shrimp, amphipods, sea stars, sea urchins, tunicates, and an occasional small fish are all possible. When you explore the intertidal and associated tide pools, it always pays to lift up rocks. Undersides of rocks provide organisms with an escape from large predators and a cool moist place to ride out low tide. Lacy colonies of encrusting bryozoans will spend their entire lives here while mobile crabs, starfish, and snails seek refuge during low tide. The undersides of rocks are good places to find egg cases of snails. Challenge yourself to see how many different species you can find living on or under a single rock.

Although tide pools are a refuge from the drying effects of low tide, they may create other severe physiological stresses that may prove lethal to their inhabitants. During summer months they may heat up considerably, while the exact opposite may happen in winter. Ice may scour these areas in winter. Not only is receding salt water trapped in tide pools, but freshwater runoff from the land can render a pool brackish or even fresh. During summertime the heat of the sun evaporates water, but not salt, from these same pools, making them extra salty. Warm water contains less dissolved oxygen than cold water, creating the danger of oxygen depletion during the summer.

Some pools are bright green in color as a result of luxuriant growth of green seaweeds, primarily Sea Lettuce and *Enteromorpha intestinalis* followed by a high diversity of other less common species. These are known as ephemeral species because they are only present for a short period of time. A close look at these green pools will reveal a lack of Common Periwinkles.

In contrast pools without abundant green algae typically have several hundred snails grazing over a square yard of rock surface. The ephemeral algae grow rapidly each spring but are soon grazed by the herbivorous periwinkles, which prefer to eat these highly nutritious yet poorly defended algae. The algae that remain behind are species such as Irish Moss and rockweeds that contain chemical toxins that make them unpalatable, as well as red crusts and Coral Weed that are impregnated with calcium carbonate and understandably not good eating.

The better-defended seaweeds benefit from the feeding activities of the snails in two ways. Some of the ephemeral algae are fast growing epiphytes that attach to larger species such as Irish Moss. The ephemeral algae are actually superior competitors and could easily block out sunlight from the slower growing species that expend energy on defense compounds rather than increased growth. In pools with Common Periwinkles, these competitive effects are ameliorated because the snails preferentially consume the best competitors. In pools where periwinkles are not present, the ephemeral species dominate, and because of their competitive superiority, algal species diversity is low. In pools where periwinkles are present in large numbers, algal diversity is also low as only the least palatable species remain.

The greatest algal diversity occurs in pools where snail numbers are moderate and their grazing activity prevents the ephemerals from overgrowing other species but is not so severe as to eliminate ephemerals from the pool. In this case the fast-growing ephemerals and less palatable slow-growing species are able to coexist.

Some pools are bright green in color due to a high abundance of green seaweeds and low abundance of herbivorous periwinkles. SCOTT SHUMWAY

Kelp Beds

In the subtidal region algal size is no longer restricted to short-growing rock-huggers. Here large brown seaweeds, commonly called kelp, have graceful bodies that wave gently in the current. They form extensive **kelp beds** that, like terrestrial forests, have different layers to them. The canopy is dominated by species of *Laminaria* that may exceed 10 feet (3 m) in length; the understory, by fleshy red seaweeds; and the ground level, by encrusting coralline reds. Kelps are most common in shallow water 13–26 feet (4–8 m) in depth where they frequently attach to the shells of Horse Mus-

Kelp beds are formed by large brown sea-weeds. The seaweed with the holes in the blade is called Sea Colander (Agarum cribrosum).   BOB STENECK

sels *(Modiolus modiolus)*. This is not advantageous to the mussels on exposed coasts as the large seaweeds are constantly being tugged on by waves. Winter storms regularly rip the kelps and associated mussels from the bottom and toss them up onto beaches, providing beach-combers the opportunity to sample the subtidal. Horse Mussels thrive from 30–60 feet (9–18 m) in depth where they seem to be free of attached kelps. At this depth grazing Green Sea Urchins devour any and all kelp. In exchange the clusters of mussels provide a refuge from predation for small urchins that use their tube feet and spines to wedge themselves into the mussel bed. The spaces between mussels also provide a safe habitat for many species of invertebrate including urchins, brittle stars, and other bivalves. Outside of mussel beds each of these species is readily preyed upon by crabs, lobster, whelks, Cunner, Winter Flounder, and Pollock.

Horsetail Kelp *(Laminaria digitata)* occurs at the border of the subtidal and intertidal and is the easiest to observe. A short stipe gives way to a blade that divides close to the base. The resulting handlike morphology with floppy "fingers" is unmistakable and explains the choice of the Latin name *digitata*. **Sugar Kelp** *(L. saccha-*

Horsetail Kelp (Laminaria digitata) *against a background of Irish Moss* (Chondrus crispus)
SCOTT SHUMWAY

Scuba diver with Sugar Kelp (Laminaria saccharina)   BOB STENECK

rina) features a short stipe and a long blade that reaches 10 feet (3 m) in length and 6–10 inches (15–25 cm) in width. The frilly margins of the blade resemble curly lasagna noodles, but unlike noodles, the blades are extremely tough and resistant to tearing. A kelp with a very long stipe is likely to be **Hollow-Stemmed Kelp** *(Laminaria longicrurius).*

The aptly named **Sea Colander** *(Agarum cribrosum)* has holes scattered over the surface of the blade. The holes, large enough to insert a pinky finger through are not the result of herbivory, as Sea Colander is chemically defended against herbivores. The holes form during development, starting off small and getting larger as the blade ages. The reason for the holes is not known for sure, but they may increase water flow across the blade, and hence nutrient uptake.

The author holding Sugar Kelp (Laminaria saccharina) *that have washed up onshore*
ANDREW K. HOWARD

Hollow-Stemmed Kelp (Laminaria longi-crurius) *can grow to 15 feet (4.5 m) in length.*   BOB STENECK

Green Sea Urchins (Strongylocentrotus droebachiensis) *showing tube feet*
R. WAHLE

Sea Urchins

Sea urchins are the dominant subtidal herbivores. **Green Sea Urchins** *(Strongylocentrotus droebachiensis)* are common north of Cape Cod, whereas **Purple Sea Urchins** *(Arbacia punctulata)* are common south of the cape. Dense aggregations of urchins can sometimes be seen clinging to rocks during extremely low tides. Their well-protected bodies are like pincushions consisting of a globe-shaped shell surrounded by numerous spines. The spines are interspersed with highly maneuverable tube feet, each of which terminates in a suction cup. The mouth is found on the underside and is surrounded by five hardened teeth. Urchins graze on algae by extending and contracting these teeth, which are capable of rasping away almost any seaweeds or soft invertebrates that happen to get in their way.

Where large numbers of urchins occur, extensive areas of rocky substrate will be cleared of nearly all other living organisms. The result is an **urchin barren.** Only encrusting coralline red algae can resist urchin grazing, and barrens often look like they were painted over with a thin coating of pink bubblegum.

Historically sea urchin populations were controlled by predatory lobsters and occasional outbreaks of disease. Within the past few decades, a new fishery arose, and large numbers of Green Sea Urchins are now harvested for export to Japan, where raw urchin eggs are a culinary delicacy. The ecological impact of this fishery is predicted to be great. Urchin barrens are shrinking and kelp beds are increasing. On vertical rock surfaces, periodic urchin grazing cleared rock surfaces of algae, enabling the establishment of a diverse community of hydroids, bryozoans, soft coral, and tunicates. In the absence of urchins, leafy seaweeds cover these surfaces.

Urchins reproduce by releasing sperm and eggs into the water where, with luck, the two will meet. The odds of success are increased when urchins form dense mating aggregations prior to shedding gametes. There is great concern that the reduction in urchin numbers has lowered densities to the point where successful fertilization is unlikely.

American Lobsters

With two formidable claws and an elongated tail (abdomen), the **American Lobster** *(Homarus americanus)* cannot be confused with any other sea creature on our coast. The large crusher claw is used for crushing or chipping away at the shells of molluscs and sea urchins. The cutter claw is capable of more delicate maneuvering required to remove meat from the bodies of subdued prey and transfer it to the mouth. When confronted with danger, a lobster will raise up its claws in a defensive posture. If this fails to work, a powerful flick of the tail under its body rapidly propels the lobster backwards through the water.

These defenses combined with their ability to consume a variety of food enable some lobsters to reach at least thirty and possibly one hundred years of age. Because lobsters shed their shells (molt) repeatedly as they grow and because size

American Lobster (Homarus americanus)   BOB STENECK

Lobster Trivia

Here are some random tidbits for lobster eaters. There are three body segments. The head and thorax are fused on top into a cephalothorax. The mouthparts, two pair of sensory antennae, and eyes are part of the head. The molting hormone is produced in the eye stalk. Legs are attached to the thorax. The tough feathery white material in the thorax cavity are the gills. The elongated abdomen, or tail, bears a series of appendages called swimmerets as well as a tail fan. In males the first pair of swimmerets is enlarged and hardened with a groove for the transfer of sperm to a mate. Some people prefer to know the difference when purchasing lobsters. The green stuff found after the tail that is separated from the rest of the body is the liver while the pinkish red stuff is unfertilized eggs. Both are edible. The "sand vein" running the length of the tail is actually the lower end of the digestive tract and leads to the anus. Removal prior to consumption is optional. Reminding people around the dinner table of these bits of lobster trivia can sometimes earn you a share of their lobster as appetites begin to wane.

varies with growing conditions, it is difficult to estimate lobster age with great confidence. In fact, for such a well-known species, surprisingly little is known about some parts of the lobster life cycle.

Adult lobsters mate soon after the female has molted while her new shell is still soft. She will spend the next few months brooding up to 100,000 eggs attached to the underside of her abdomen. Constant beating of feathery appendages called swimmerets bring the eggs into contact with clean aerated water. Fishing regulations prevent the harvest of so-called berried lobsters. Lobster fishers who have captured a berried lobster are required to cut a V-shaped notch in the tip of the tail to signal that this individual is a breeding female who should be released to produce more lobsters.

Eggs hatch into a planktonic stage that floats near the surface and feeds on phytoplankton. Eventually they metamorphose into a bottom-dwelling form that resembles a miniature version of an adult. They are basically defenseless and must immediately seek shelter beneath rocks before they become food for predatory fish like Cunners. The shelter provided by the spaces between and beneath cobbles is essential to the early survival of lobsters. Only when they get larger and become able to defend themselves against predators will they begin to leave the shelters to forage.

As they mature, lobsters reach a size at which they are safe from all but the largest fish and are free to roam the ocean bottom at will. Lobsters forage mostly at night in search of clams, scallops, mussels, sea urchins, and even dead fish.

Lobsters are surprisingly mobile and capable of traveling the entire length of the Gulf of Maine. Some undergo winter migrations to deeper offshore waters, possibly to escape frigid waters or avoid being tossed onshore by winter storms.

Lobster coloration varies greatly, with mottled brown and olive being most common. A rare genetic trait causes some lobsters to be endowed with a beautiful blue coloration. Lobsters turn red only after high heat destroys the proteins that give them their natural coloration.

Commercial harvest of lobsters is one of the most important single species fisheries along the eastern seaboard. Although they range from Newfoundland to Virginia, the vast majority of the lobster harvest occurs in nearshore waters of Maine and southern Canada. They have been harvested commercially for more than a century, but only recently have lobsters become a luxury food available in most grocery stores and restaurants.

Lobsters are caught using baited traps left on the bottom and marked by a float featuring markings that are unique to a particular fisher. The overall design is simple with a funnel-shaped mesh opening that allows for easy entry, but not easy exit. Modern traps include a smaller exit vent that allows individuals too small for legal harvest to escape.

Historically the lobster harvest has fluctuated greatly. During the twenty-year period between 1920 and 1940, the lobster fishery experienced a severe drop in landings known as "the bust" by Maine lobstermen. Since 1990 the current generation of Maine lobster fishers has been enjoying record harvests. In 2004 the harvest reached seventy million pounds. The reasons for this boom-and-bust cycle are unknown. Overharvesting of Atlantic Cod may have eliminated a major predator from nearshore waters. Recent harvest of sea urchins has allowed kelp beds to proliferate, providing additional shelter for young lobsters.

For most of the past fifteen years, fisheries scientists have been issuing warnings that lobsters are severely overfished and that the current harvest is in excess of two to three times what should be allowed. It takes seven years for a lobster to reach legal size (3.54 inches [9 cm] carapace length). Ninety-four percent are harvested within a year of reaching legal size. Most lobsters caught in the Gulf of Maine are considered adolescents, physiologically capable of reproducing but yet to do so. In the absence of fisheries, pressure, lobsters typically live for twenty to thirty years and reach record sizes of forty-two pounds (19 kg), far larger than the pound and a quarter lobsters found in the grocery store. In spite of these concerns, the Gulf of Maine lobster stock is currently quite healthy and biologists have been forced to search for new explanations for how the fishery manages to be so successful. The fishers happily point to the size and V-notch regulations that they helped develop and to which they adhere strictly as the reason that they continue to enjoy bountiful harvests.

Sandy beach at Ocean City, New Jersey   SCOTT SHUMWAY

Sandy Beaches

Crashing waves, gulls laughing from above, children screaming with delight at the water's edge, the smell of suntan lotion, hot sand burning the soles of your feet—this is the coastal environment with which people are most familiar. Yet, aside from the gulls and a few jellyfish washed ashore, most people would be hard pressed to come up with a long list of living organisms that they encountered at the beach. So where are all the animals? Biologist John McDermott addressed this puzzle in a 1983 treatise on sandy beaches, saying, "To the casual observer it appears that the exposed sandy beach of temperate latitudes is, except for the conspicuous migrating shorebirds, a rather desolate and abiotic region of the sea."

Even though, compared to rocky shores and tidal flats, sandy beaches do appear to be lacking in living things, lacking they are not.

Sandy beaches are **high-energy environments.** Moving waves carry large amounts of energy that must be absorbed by the sand when they break upon the shore. This immense energy has the potential to either erode sand away from or deposit sand onto the shore. It can topple living organisms, carrying them out to sea or dumping them high on the beach. The sandy bottom is unstable and subject to redistribution by each successive wave. It is nearly impossible for a bottom-dwelling *(benthic)* organism to remain securely attached to the sand. This is why you don't see many organisms at the beach, unless, of course, you look closely. Millions of microscopic animals *(meiofauna)* live in the tiny spaces between sand grains. Most medium-sized residents *(infauna)* of sandy beaches burrow beneath the sand where they are sheltered from breaking waves. Rather than living in or on the sand, the largest species use the beach as a swim-up or fly-in snack bar.

The Swash Zone

The area along the shore where waves race up and down the beach is known as the **swash zone.** The top few centimeters of sand are full of living creatures that have the ability to burrow rapidly to keep from being carried off by the crashing waves and undertow. Mud worms, digging amphipods, Coquina Clams, and Mole Crabs are abundant members of the sandy beach infauna. Their small size (less than 1–2 inches [2.5–5 cm]) and digging speed contribute to the difficulty of seeing them. While the overall species diversity is low, the abundance of certain species is staggering.

Swash zone in Ocean City, New Jersey   SCOTT SHUMWAY

Invisible Animals between Grains of Sand

An invisible community of animals inhabits the wet spaces between sand grains. They are known as **meiofauna,** typically range in size from 0.001–.004 inch (30–100 microns), and occur in densities of up to ten million individuals per square yard (.8 sq m) of sand. Nematodes (roundworms) and harpacticoid copepods (characterized by short antennae) are the most abundant, followed by various invertebrate

Harpacticoid copepods are members of the meiofauna, a group of tiny animals that live between sand grains.   SCOTT SHUMWAY

larvae, worms, tardigrades (water bears), ostracods (seed shrimp), and mites. Many of these strangely named microscopic animals have only recently been identified by scientists, and little is known about them other than that they are probably valuable food sources for larger invertebrates.

Tiny but Numerous Animals

A single species of **mud worm** *(Scololepis squamata)* has been found to average 4,000 worms per 1 square foot (0.1 sq m) on a New Jersey beach. These barely visible mud worms are distinguished by a pair of slender tentacle-like palps that are extended over the surface to pick up sediment for deposit feeding. They construct loose tubular burrows that are frequently dislodged by wave action, making them easy targets for predators.

Digging amphipods (haustorids) are shrimplike crustaceans with laterally flattened bodies that rarely exceed 0.325 inch (.83 cm) in length.

Swashbuckling Clams and Crabs

The two most visible species of the swash zone are a small colorful clam and an egg-shaped crustacean that ride the swash much like children with their skim boards. Tiny **Coquina** or **Wedge Clams** *(Donax variabilis)* are common from New Jersey to the Gulf of Mexico. Less than 0.75 inch (2 cm) in length and brightly colored (pink, purple, orange, creamy white, banded, and/or rayed), they can occur in densities of thousands of individuals per square yard (.8 sq m). Coquina are suspension feeders and extract single-celled diatoms from the water as it rushes past. They extend their delicate siphons to feed either while they are lying horizontal at the surface or burrowed vertically just below the surface. If displaced by a wave, they can extrude their foot, right themselves, and with a few jerking motions be burrowed below the surface before the same wave washes back down the shore.

These ingenious little bivalves actively migrate up and down the beach with the changing tides, enabling them to always be in the best location for simultaneously capturing food, obtaining oxygen, staying moist, and avoiding predators. The method by which they migrate has been dubbed "swash riding." Coquina always

Coquina or Wedge Clams (Donax variabilis) *are rapidly burrowing bivalves that feed in the swash zone.* SCOTT SHUMWAY

seem to be burrowed into the sand just seaward of the rising or falling tide. As the tide rises, they will literally jump out of the sand by repeatedly extending their muscular foot. This jump is timed to match the arrival of a wave that will carry them up the beach. When the swash reaches its maximum excursion up the beach, the tiny clams will rapidly burrow into the sand before they can be swept back out to sea. Not only do Coquina ride waves like miniature body surfers, but they carefully select waves that are most likely to carry them a great distance. The mystery of how Coquina are able to do this was solved by lab experiments in which they were exposed to sounds similar to those made by a breaking wave. Only the sounds of large waves stimulated the Coquina to jump out of the sand! Exactly how they sense wave sounds is still unknown. As the tide recedes, the Coquina simply reverse the process and ride the swash to a lower elevation.

Some Coquina have bushy brown **hydroid colonies** *(Lovenella gracilis)* fouling their shells. The colony is shaped like a spreading bush with each branch tipped with stinging tentacles used for defense and food capture. When fouled Coquina are burrowed in the sand, the brown colonies reveal their location, not just to us, but to foraging crabs. Clams bearing hydroids are more likely to be excavated and consumed by hungry Ghost Crabs and Speckled Crabs. However, the stinging capabilities of the hydroids seem to offer some protection to the Coquina from certain predatory fish. So, depending on the types of predators present, hydroids may be a blessing or a curse to Coquina.

Mole Crabs, *Emerita talpoida,* burrow and feed in the surf zone from Cape Cod to the Gulf of Mexico. The shells of these peanut-sized crustaceans are the color of pink flesh with the texture of a small bird's egg. Because they lack pinching claws, Mole Crabs are perfectly safe to handle. During the summer females carry masses of bright orange-yellow eggs beneath their legs and abdomen. Young males become sexually mature at a mere 0.125 inch (3.2 mm) in length and begin mating with mature two-year-old females. The following spring males will resume

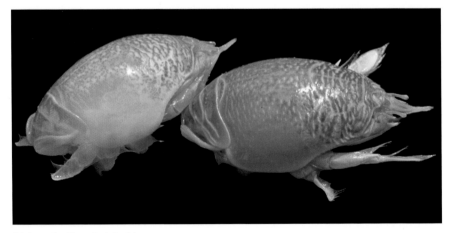

Mole crabs, Emerita talpoida   SCOTT SHUMWAY

Do You Believe in Ghosts?

Small holes, about 1 inch (2.5 m) in diameter, are scattered between the high-tide line and the base of the foredunes. Small scratch marks radiating from the opening of each hole are visible first thing in the morning. They mark the entrances to **Ghost Crab** *(Ocypode quadrata)* burrows. Ghost Crabs are appropriately named and can be found on most beaches south of Cape Henlopen, Delaware. Their 2-inch-wide (5-cm) bodies are the color of light sand and difficult to spot unless they are in motion. Tracking them may make you a believer in ghosts! A predawn bicycle ride down the beach with a flashlight is the best way to sneak up on these phantoms. The genus name, *Ocypode,* means "swift footed." They seem to realize that they have been spotted and quickly dart down the nearest burrow hole. Ghost Crabs often leave you wondering, "Did I see one or not?"

At night the crabs scurry down to the water's edge to prey upon Coquina and Mole Crabs. At dawn the crabs return to their underground burrows where they are safe from hungry birds and the heat of the day. They do not return to the same burrow as their foraging brings them several hundred meters from where they began the night before.

Ghost Crab (Ocypode quadrata)   SCOTT SHUMWAY

mating, this time with females of their own age. Then, males disappear, either dying off or possibly undergoing a sex change into female crabs.

Mole Crabs scurry about on five pairs of hairy walking legs and can be found rolling in the surf as waves wash up the beach slope. As they tumble back out to sea, they suddenly latch onto the bottom and disappear into the sand. They burrow backwards orienting the body downslope and leaving just their eyestalks and two pairs of antennae sticking out of the sand. Feathery second antennae filter diatoms and other algae out of the water as the waves recede. The antennae then transfer the trapped food to the mouthparts. Mole Crabs feed in an ever-changing environment; and as the tides move, so does the preferred Mole Crab habitat. Crabs track this movement by crawling out of the sand and allowing the water to tumble them either up- or downslope before burrowing in again.

High-Tide Predators

Numerous swimming species forage in the surf zone at high tide. The vast majority of these are **juvenile fish** that make good use of their ability to swim in very shallow waters that are inaccessible to larger predators. Juvenile **Atlantic Silverside** *(Menidia menidia),* **Spot** *(Leiostomus),* **White Mullet** *(Mugil),* **Northern Kingfish** *(Menticirrhus saxatilis),* and **Bluefish** *(Pomatomus)* frequent this area where they readily prey upon worms, amphipods, small clams, and Mole Crabs. Other species that feed here include **Sand Shrimp** *(Crangon septemspinosa)* and **Lady Crabs** *(Ovalipes occellatus).*

The Wrack Line: Playing Beachcomber Detective

The highest reach of the tide is delineated by a ribbon of debris, or **wrack,** made up of stranded seaweeds, Eelgrass blades, and other flotsam. This trash heap of the beach constitutes a miniature ecosystem that should be explored carefully. The presence of Eelgrass signifies that seagrass beds are not far from shore. Eelgrass blades dry quickly, but seaweeds remain damp for longer periods of time thanks to water-retaining gels designed to help them withstand drying out at low tide (see "Seaweeds in Your Ice Cream" in the "Rocky Shores" chapter). The wrack provides a moist habitat for species that have the misfortune of being trapped here as well as a home for species that exploit it as a smorgasbord of decaying delights. As the wrack decays, it provides food for bacteria, fungi, and amphipods, as well as fertilizer for plants growing on the foredune.

As you begin picking through a pile of wrack, small shrimplike crustaceans called **amphipods** literally jump out. They have an elongated abdominal, or tail, section that can be folded under the legs and then rapidly extended, flicking the amphipods into the air. Their resemblance to jumping fleas gives them the common names **Beach Flea** and **Beach Hopper.** They range in size from just barely visible to 1 inch (2.5 cm) in length. Their activity levels increase at night when they can move around without risk of drying out or being consumed by shorebirds.

Wrack line on a Virginia beach   SCOTT SHUMWAY

The flotsam provides clues to the hidden realm that lies beyond the breakers. The shells, skeletons, and dead bodies that litter the beach are tantalizing evidence that there is indeed a world to which we are not privy. Piecing together these bits and pieces to reconstruct the animals, plants, and communities "out there" is part of the fun of beachcombing. Most of the shells and stuff that wash up on the beach is from animals and plants that reside subtidally just offshore. Some of the "clues" likely to be discovered on the beach include shells of snails and bivalves, molted carapaces of crabs,

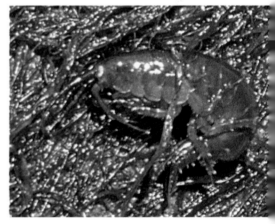

Search beneath stranded seaweeds and damp wrack for amphipods, also known as beach fleas.   SCOTT SHUMWAY

eggs, egg cases, bones, and driftwood. Bivalve shells commonly found washed up on sandy beaches include clams, jingles, oysters, mussels, ribbed mussels, angel wings, scallops, arks, and cockles. The shells often offer up clues to the forensic beachcomber as to how their inhabitant lived and died.

Common beach shells: surf clam with moon snail hole, shell eroded by boring sponges, Razor Clam, cockle, inner and outer surface of American Oyster, Blue Mussel, jingle shell, and Coquina   SCOTT SHUMWAY

Clams

The largest shells on the beach from the Gulf of St. Lawrence to Cape Hatteras usually belong to the **Atlantic Surf Clam** *(Spisula solidissima)*. These clams reside burrowed into the sand from the low-tide line down to nearly 200 feet (60 m). They can live for thirty-one years and reach a maximum size of 9 inches (23 cm). Growth lines encircle the shell but only give an approximation of age as they are not necessarily deposited annually. They spawn by releasing gametes into the water. Perhaps the key to their success is that an individual can release up to thirteen million eggs at a time.

Clams have a pair of siphons used for feeding. One sucks water into the body where it crosses gills that take up oxygen and filter out food particles. The other siphon spews out excess water and waste. Planktonic diatoms and ciliates make up most of their diet. Surf clams are in turn preyed upon by moon snails, crabs, Horseshoe Crabs, sea stars, Haddock, Atlantic Cod, and humans.

Sex-Changing Snails

The **Common Atlantic Slippersnail** *(Crepidula fornicata)*, also known as Slipper Limpet, doesn't look much like a snail as its shell is not coiled. Instead, the shell is roughly oval in outline, up to 2 inches (5 cm) in length, and strongly convex with a large opening where a muscular foot holds the animal firmly to a rock or shell. A shelf that runs halfway along the undersurface gives the upside-down shell the appearance of a slipper (*Crepidula* means "little sandal"). Slip-persnails live in stacks with larger individuals on the bottom and successively smaller snails above. Up to a dozen snails can inhabit a single stack. The bottom snails are always female while the uppermost snails are male. The advantage of this system for locating mates is obvious. Upon learning the scientific name for this species, one may jump to the conclusion that it refers to this relationship. Latin scholars would tell you, however, that *fornicata* means

Common Atlantic Slipper Snails (Crepidula fornicata) *are often found in stacks with females on the bottom and males on top.* SCOTT SHUMWAY

"arched," as in the shape of the shell. When Linnaeus, the father of taxonomy, named the species in 1758, he only had a single shell and never saw them in a stack. The scenario gets even more interesting when the middle members of the stack are considered. They are often intermediate between male and female conditions. This is a sex-changing snail and, once they get large enough, the males closest to the bottom will undergo profound changes in their anatomy and become female.

Commercial Clam Facts

Surf clams are harvested commercially using hydraulic dredges. Water from high-pressure nozzles dislodges clams from the sand ahead of a chain-link bag that is dragged across the ocean floor behind a boat. Most harvested clams are fifteen to twenty years of age. About 30,000 metric tons of clam meat are harvested annually from U.S. waters with the final product sold as chopped sea clams, chowder, strips, cakes, and juice. The largest harvesting areas are located off New Jersey and the Delmarva Peninsula. Most chowders and fried clam dishes are made using Atlantic Surf Clams. Other species harvested include Ocean Clams or Ocean Quahogs from deeper waters and Quahogs (Hard-Shell Clams) and Steamers (Soft-Shell Clams) from estuarine tidal flats.

Slippersnails don't move around much, and the curve of their shell closely matches the rock or shell that they are living on top of. They are filter feeders, which is unusual for snails. They feed by generating a current that circulates water under their shells where food particles, mostly phytoplankton, are bound up with mucus before consumption.

Slippersnails are abundant on protected shores where small cobbles are abundant, or scattered across a muddy bottom. Stacks are found at the low-tide line and throughout the shallow subtidal. Single shells, however, are commonly scattered along sandy beaches.

Holey Shells

You have probably collected a clam shell with a nearly perfectly round hole drilled through the shell close to the umbo (oldest part of the shell) and wondered how the hole got there. Such drilled shells look like they are predestined to be strung on

Lobed Moon Snail (Neverita duplicata) depositing "sand collar" egg case
SANDRA E. SHUMWAY

a necklace. The hole was made by a **moon snail,** either the Northern Moon Snail, *Lunatia heros* (to 4 inches [10 cm], more common north of Long Island), or the Lobed Moon Snail *Neverita duplicata* (to 3 inches [7.6 cm], Massachusetts Bay to Gulf of Mexico). Their globe-shaped shells are often found washed up onshore. Moon snails crawl about subtidal sandy and muddy bottoms using a large muscular foot that, when extended, covers up part of the shell. Moon snails make their living bulldozing through the top centimeters of sediment in search of burrowing bivalve molluscs.

Once it contacts a clam, the moon snail uses its radula to scrape away at the shell. A snail's radula is like a conveyer belt of hardened teeth fixed to a ribbon that moves back and forth across the prey. Acid secreted by the snail helps dissolve the calcium carbonate shell while the radula drills a hole into the softened shell. Once through, the snail is able to secrete digestive enzymes that break down the body of the clam, which is then slurped up like a nutritious mollusc milkshake.

Shells will also wash up riddled with multiple holes and catacombs. In some cases they are more hole than whole. They have been attacked by **boring sponges** (*Cliona*) (see photo page 117), which occupy a network of spaces within the shell.

Boring sponges secrete acid, which dissolves the calcium carbonate shell. In the process tiny chunks of shell are excavated and ejected by the sponge, which then grows into the newly mined space. This is an important bioerosion process and helps explain why the seafloor is not completely covered with seashells. In a living specimen the sponge will appear as yellow bumps projecting from small holes in the shell surface. Shells of bivalves, especially oysters, are frequently attacked.

Body Parts

On some days the beach seems to be littered with dead crabs. Hold off on the funeral as these are most likely **molted shells** rather than dead bodies. Crabs and other crustaceans must periodically shed their rigid external skeleton and form a new one in order to grow larger. This process of molting is described in detail for Blue Crabs in the "Estuaries" chapter. The molted shell looks like a dead crab, but is usually hollow inside. Actual crab death usually involves the entire crab being swallowed whole or crushed beyond recognition. Dead crabs washing up on shore are quickly dismembered by scavenging gulls. Live Horseshoe Crabs are an exception; they are occasionally left stranded and must crawl back to the sea before they are overcome by heat and desiccation.

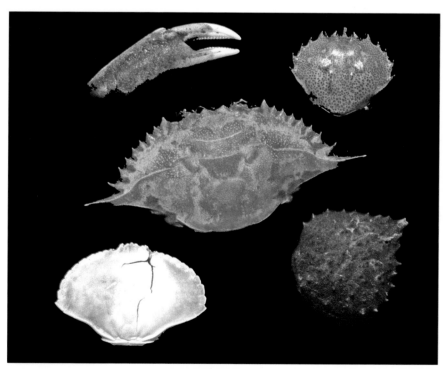

Body parts—molted shells rather than dead bodies. Claw of a spider crab and molted cara-paces (clockwise) of Lady Crab, spider crab, Rock Crab, and Blue Crab (center).
SCOTT SHUMWAY

Hermit Crabs

Sometimes a stranded snail shell will have a new owner living inside. Whereas most crabs protect themselves with pinching claws, hardened shells, and swift movement on four pairs of legs, **hermit crabs** have evolved to dwell within discarded snail shells. Their abdomen lacks a hard covering and is curled to fit within the whorls of a gastropod shell. Most have dimorphic claws (one larger than the other) and all scurry upon only two pairs of legs. When threatened, they withdraw into the protective safety of their snail shell. Hermit crabs can readily exit and enter snail shells, but are able to hold on tightly enough to avoid forcible removal by other creatures.

Two species are common in our range. The **Long-Clawed Hermit Crab** *(Pagurus longicarpus)* occupies small shells, such as those of periwinkles and Oyster Drills. If the crab is large and living in either the shell of a moon snail or whelk, it is likely to be the **Flat-Clawed Hermit Crab** *(Pagurus pollicaris)*. While hermit crabs range widely throughout the subtidal, they are easily viewed on quiet sandy bottoms at low tide, sometimes trapped in tide pools of sandy beaches or sand flats where they feed on detritus and diatoms.

Hermit crab (Pagurus)   GARRY KESSLER

If a shell is no longer large enough to accommodate a growing hermit, the crab will either find a new discarded shell or engage in a ritualized battle with another hermit for rights to its shell. A series of claw taps to the shell determine the winner in a contest where no one gets injured.

The shells occupied by hermit crabs are often covered with pink fuzz commonly called **Snail Fur.** The fuzz belongs to a colonial hydroid in the genus *Hydractinia* that lives only on snail shells occupied by hermit crabs. The exact nature of the interactions between hydroids and hermit crabs continues to be debated. The hydroid cannot move on its own but, thanks to the hermit crab, enjoys the food- and mate-finding benefits of mobility.

The hydroid captures food and defends itself with stinging tentacles. Potential predators on the hermit crab are deterred by these stinging capabilities. Larvae of Slippersnails that might foul the hermit's home are readily consumed by the hydroid. What is less certain are potential negative impacts of the hydroid on its host. Hermit crabs with hydroids produce fewer eggs than those without hydroids. In addition hydroids appear to interfere with reproduction, as male hermit crabs attempting to mate with a female are met with a series of stings from the hydroid!

While this may seem to be a case of jealousy, the stinging cells of hydroids generally fire upon contact.

Sand Dollars

Sand Dollars *(Echinarachnius parma)* live subtidally on sandy and muddy bottoms where they are deposit feeders with a taste for diatoms. Sand Dollars are common from Labrador to New Jersey and are best found stranded on the beach after a storm. The **Keyhole Urchin** *(Mellita quinquiesperforata)* is a southern dollar with five mysterious slits in its shell and can sometimes be found on Virginia and North Carolina beaches. Both species are covered with small spines that aid in locomotion and, along with smaller hairlike cilia, help move food toward the mouth centrally located on the undersurface. Gills protrude from the shell in a pattern resembling a five-petaled flower.

Sand Dollar (Echinarachnius parma) *showing numerous short spines and petalloid gills.*
GARRY KESSLER

Live Sand Dollars are tan or purplish brown in color. An indelible purple pigment easily leaches out of live and dying Sand Dollars. Bright white shells are visible only after bleaching in the sun.

Few predators favor Sand Dollars, perhaps because they are mostly shell with little nutritional value. The exception is Winter Flounder, which preys heavily upon small Sand Dollars.

Egg Cases of Giant Snails and Skates

The giant snails commonly called **whelks** or conchs are predators that spend their time plowing through the surface sediments of the subtidal in search of mollusc prey. **Knobbed Whelk** *(Busycon carica)* and **Channeled Whelk** *(Busycotypus canaliculatus)* are harvested commercially to be sold in ethnic markets as scungili or exported to Europe and Asia. Their shells rarely wash up onshore and are prized by beachcombers.

Knobbed Whelk (Busycon carica)
SCOTT SHUMWAY

Their unusual **egg cases** are often found in the wrack line. They are dull mustard colored and look like inflated coins linked together by a string. When shaken, the cases sound like a child's rattle. Inside of each sac is a collection of miniature whelks. Unlike most snails that have a free-floating larval stage, whelks are direct developers. They bypass the larval stage going straight from the egg to tiny versions of the adults all within the protective egg case that normally remains on the bottom. Once you find an egg case on the beach, the young whelks have died. If you crack open one of the sacs, you can shake out the exquisite miniatures.

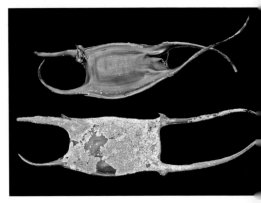

The cartilaginous fish known as **skates** *(Raja)* attach their egg cases, called **mermaids purses,** to seaweeds. When the baby skate reaches a certain size, it wiggles its way out of the egg case as a small version of the adult. The cases found beached and dried are either ones from which babies have hatched or were prematurely detached and tossed ashore.

Mermaids purse, the egg case of a skate
SCOTT SHUMWAY

Jellies

The jellylike animals that you encounter while walking the beach or swimming among the waves are not all jellyfish! These jellies come from several different groups within the animal kingdom. **True jellyfish** are members of the class Scyphozoa (meaning "cup animal"). Like other members of the Cnidaria phylum (hydroids and sea anemones), they have stinging cells (nematocysts) used for prey capture and defense. Jellyfish and other cnidarians can sting with the severity ranging from a sensation undetectable by humans to instant severe pain leading to death within minutes. Luckily for us, the latter is rare in the Western Atlantic.

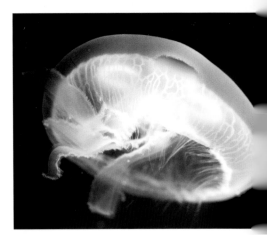

True jellyfish—Moon Jelly, Aurelia aurita
© 2000 DENISE CONE AND JASON GOLDSTEIN, NEW ENGLAND AQUARIUM, BOSTON, MASSACHUSETTS

The jellyfish body consists of a clearish jellylike disk or bell, a downward-facing mouth surrounded by four arms and associated stinging tentacles, and visible four-leaf-clover pattern (the gastric pouches and gonads). If one or more of these features are lacking, the animal is probably not a true jellyfish.

The **Moon Jelly** *(Aurelia aurita)* is the most common jellyfish along the East Coast. Currents sometimes carry these beautiful jellyfish close to shore by the thousands, especially in late spring. Their sting is mild, short-lasting, and not much to worry about.

The **Lion's Mane Jellyfish** *(Cyanea capillata)* is commonly 8–18 inches (20–45 cm) in diameter but can reach much larger sizes and is reported to be the largest jellyfish in the world. The sting of the Lion's Mane is toxic and potentially fatal to humans. They are most common in summer and early fall.

Lion's Mane Jellyfish (Cyanea capillata)
© 2000 DENISE CONE AND JASON GOLDSTEIN, NEW ENGLAND AQUARIUM, BOSTON, MASSACHUSETTS

The appropriately named **Mushroom Cap Jellyfish** *(Rhopilema verrilli)* is a southern species that occasionally washes up on beaches as far north as Long Island Sound. A few unusual species, known as **stalked jellyfish** *(Haliclystus)*, live anchored to rocks and seagrasses north of Cape Cod.

Water jellies or *Hydromedusae* (*Aequorea* in the class Hydrozoa) are easily confused with true jellyfish, but can be distinguished by numerous lines radiating from the center to the margins of a thickened jellylike disk.

The most notorious Atlantic jelly, the **Portuguese Man-of-War** (*Physalia physalia*—order Siphonophora in class Hydrozoa), is easily distinguished by a gas-filled float that keeps it suspended at the surface of the water and acts like

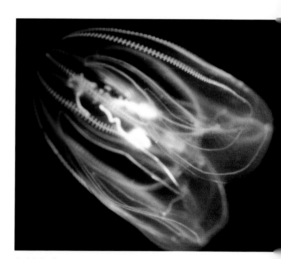

Leidy's Comb Jelly (Mnemiopsis leidyi).
© 2000 DENISE CONE AND JASON GOLDSTEIN, NEW ENGLAND AQUARIUM, BOSTON, MASSACHUSETTS

a sail, catching the wind and propelling the animal through the water. A mass of stinging tentacles up to 50 feet (15 m) long lie below the float. Man-of-War stings are severe. If you see one in the water or washed up onshore, *don't go anywhere near it.* Portuguese Man-of-War is a tropical species rarely found in our area, but the Gulf Stream can transport it as far north as Cape Cod.

Invasions of 1–6-inch-long (2.5–15-cm) "baby jellyfish" are more often than not swarms of **comb jellies** or *Ctenophores.* (True baby jellyfish are microscopic when born and already have adult features.) Comb jellies are shaped like elongated spheres and are contenders for the most beautiful creatures of the sea. Their clear delicate bodies are nearly invisible, except for the constantly beating combs that often luminesce in waves of green or purple flashes. *Ctenophore* means "comb bearer" and refers to the eight rows of tiny combs that run the length of the body. The beating combs draw water through the body and help in locomotion. Food is captured by discharging sticky cells (colloblast) that adhere to prey.

The **Sea Gooseberry** *(Pleurobrachia pileus)* appears in dense swarms in summer and is a voracious predator of fish eggs and larvae. It is distinguished by being the size and shape of a grape and having a pair of elongated tentacles. **Leidy's Comb Jelly** *(Mnemiopsis leidyi)* and **Common Northern Comb Jelly** *(Bolinopsis infundibulum)* are distinguished by two elongated lobes coming off their spherical bodies and reach 4 and 6 inches (10 and 15 cm) in length, respectively.

Beach Birds

The most conspicuous animals on any sandy beach are, with the exception of humans, the shorebirds. Some species build their nests on or near the beach. Of these some are year-round residents while others migrate south for the inhospitable winter months. An even greater diversity of species consists of mere visitors that stop to feed during their spring migrations to breeding grounds far to the north or during fall migrations to wintering grounds far to the south. A few species that nest in the Arctic consider New England and Mid-Atlantic beaches to be fine places to spend the winter. The gulls, terns, plovers, and peeps that spend their summers on our sandy beaches are covered in this chapter. Winter visitors are covered in the "The Beach in Winter" chapter.

Gulls

An army of **Herring, Laughing,** and **Great Black-Backed Gulls** forages along sandy beaches in search of a meal, mostly in the form of crustaceans, worms, insects, and fish. Gulls are generalist feeders that capture their prey by dipping into the water while swimming or by walking along the shore at low tide. They can often be seen dropping sea urchins, crabs, and molluscs onto rocks and parking lots in an effort to crack their shells. Some have also learned to feed at trash bins and landfills, resulting in a population surge.

Great Black-Backed Gull (Larus marinus) *with chick*   SCOTT SHUMWAY

The **Great Black-Backed Gull** is distinguished by a dark gray-black back (mantle), white head, and yellow legs. It is one of the largest and most aggressive gulls in the world and will eat eggs or young from the nests of other gulls, as well as terns and plovers.

Herring Gulls are slightly smaller with a light gray back, white head with some tan streaking, red spot at the tip of the bill, pink legs, and wings with black tips and white spots. The Herring Gull is our most common gull, breeding from Cape Hatteras north to the Canadian Arctic. Massachusetts and New York have the greatest number of nesting Herring Gulls with 35,000 and 25,000, respectively. Range expansions into Maryland, Virginia, and North Carolina are recent events that coincide with displacement from New England breeding areas by Great Black-Backed Gulls. Future growth is limited by the availability of suitable nest sites and food.

Herring Gulls (Larus argentatus), *first year bird and adult*   SCOTT SHUMWAY

Ring-Billed Gulls are similar to Herring Gulls but have a broad black ring near the tip of the bill and yellow legs. They pass through eastern U.S. seashores during migration and over the winter but breed much farther north along the Bay of Fundy.

Laughing Gulls are easy to identify by their black heads and loud "laughing" cries, which announce that you have arrived at the beach. Other black-headed (hooded) gulls are less common in our area and do not have the "ha-ha-ha-ha-ha-haah-haah-haah" call which you will either love or find terribly annoying. New Jersey supports the

Pair of Laughing Gulls (Larus atricilla) *courting*   SCOTT SHUMWAY

greatest number of Laughing Gulls with over 58,000 breeding pairs.

The descriptions given thus far of the four gulls are for mature individuals in breeding plumage. During their first three years, most gulls go through a progression of plumages starting with mottled brown and white leading into their adult plumage.

Gull Populations and Conservation

During the 1800s and early 1900s, hunting of birds for food, hat decorations, and eggs nearly annihilated most species of gull, tern, and plover. That there are any left today is a credit to the resiliency and adaptability of these species. Some gulls are currently benefiting from human activities and increasing their numbers and ranges at the expense of other birds. Herring and Great Black-Backed Gulls have adopted human refuse as a major part of their diets. They are no longer simply "sea gulls," but landfill and dumpster-diving gulls. While food gleaned from garbage dumps is less nutritious than fresh seafood, it is abundant and easy to come by. As a result up to half of the food items taken by these gulls may be human-generated refuse. This menu addition has helped gulls increase in numbers, as well as provided a reliable food source for over-wintering juvenile birds. However, chicks fed garbage by their parents tend to do less well than those raised on a more natural diet. Gulls are also adept at following fishing boats and feeding on the offal tossed overboard. Fish guts, on the other hand, are a highly nutritious food source. Increases in gulls over the past hundred years were likely aided by overfishing of large predators like Atlantic Cod and whales, resulting in increases in the numbers of smaller fish. Whatever the reason, the population sizes of our three most common gulls have increased tremendously since protection laws were established.

They have also expanded their breeding areas beyond historical ranges. They nest in colonies with a preference for islands that are inaccessible to terrestrial predators. Because islands free from human development are rare and in high demand for nesting, several different species will often nest within the same colony. The larger more aggressive gulls are currently displacing the smaller species in competition for nest sites. Laughing Gulls may be suffering the most as they are the smallest, least numerous, and most restricted to coastal sites. Great Black-Backed Gulls are continuing to expand their range to the south and are having a negative impact on Herring Gulls as well as endangered Piping Plovers and Least Terns. In at least one wildlife reserve, Great Black-Backs have been poisoned in an effort to protect the rare species that nest there. The impacts of widespread closure of landfills and overfishing of medium-sized fish may soon reverse some of the progress these gulls have made.

Gulls may also be a hazard to aircraft and are shot as part of a control program aimed at reducing collisions with airplanes at New York's JFK Airport. This program has reduced collisions significantly but also eliminated about 2–3 percent of the U.S. nesting population of Laughing Gulls.

Gulls rely upon a variety of calls, postures, and attack behaviors to convey their feelings toward potential mates, competitors, and predators. Nests are low-tech scrapes on the ground and are lined with plants and feathers. If you stray too close to a nesting colony of gulls or terns, be prepared to be screamed at, be dive-bombed, have your head grazed, be showered with vomit, be defecated upon, or all of the above—just another reason to always wear a hat at the beach.

For the most part our gulls are only partially migratory; they tend to either stay put for the winter or travel moderate distances to more southern coastlines. Most Laughing Gulls migrate to Central and South America. Several other species of gulls are sometimes observed as winter migrants and are mentioned in the "Beach in Winter" chapter.

Terns

Terns are aerial acrobats possessing narrow pointy wings designed for fast flight and forked tails that act as rudders allowing for sudden changes in direction. Sharp bills aid in capturing fish and invertebrate prey. Terns are plunge divers that are able to sense fish below the water while flying 10–20 feet (3–6 m) in the air. Terns prepare themselves for a dive by fluttering in place for several seconds before plunging headfirst into the water. Their quarry is primarily small fish, but crustaceans and squid may be taken as well. If a dive is successful, the bird will fly up from the water, shake itself free of excess water, and then swallow its prey headfirst. Terns often forage, nest, and migrate in groups. An individual bird foraging by plunge diving will often attract others to the same area. Presumably the other birds are capitalizing on the original bird's discovery of a school of fish.

Terns prefer to nest on sand and gravel beaches above the high-tide line but below vegetated dunes. They readily take advantage of overwash areas where sand has been deposited on former tidal flats as well as blowouts in foredunes. This places them in close proximity to avian and mammalian predators, as well as in conflict with humans. In some cases they may misjudge the location of the high-tide line and lose nests to flood tides. The nest, called a scrape, is no more than a depression in the sand formed by the bird kicking its legs and moving its body side to side. A few shells placed at the perimeter may complete the low-investment but well-camouflaged nest. The eggs of terns and other shorebirds have evolved to resemble speckled beach stones.

The Common Tern (Sterna hirundo) *with a freshly caught Sand Lance*   GARRY KESSLER

The Least Tern (Sterna antillarum) *nests on sandy beaches, has a yellow bill, and is an endangered species.*   DENNIS DONOHUE – WWW.THROUGH-MY-LENS.COM

Distinguishing one tern species from the next can be a frustrating exercise. Most terns have a bright white body with shades of gray on the back, a head capped in black, black wing tips, and a bill that is red, orange, and/or black. Outside of the breeding season, the bill colors often shift to black while the head cap becomes white. Common, Least, Roseate, and Forster's Terns nest along the east coast of the United States. The **Common Tern** has an orange bill with a dark tip and is, indeed, the most common nesting species. The **Least Tern** is the smallest tern, the only one with a yellow bill, and one of the least common. **Roseate Terns** have a black bill, lighter wings, and a rosy wash to the breast but are rare. **Forster's Tern** has an orange bill with a black tip, orange legs, light-colored wing tips, and a tail that sticks out beyond the primary feathers while the bird is at rest. Forster's differs from the other species by nesting and foraging almost exclusively in fresh- and salt-water marshes. **Arctic Terns** pass through briefly in spring and late summer on the longest of all bird migrations. They nest in the Arctic and migrate to the Antarctic. This 22,000-mile (35,400 km) round-trip journey means that they spend much of the year migrating, live in almost constant daylight, and never experience winter.

Plovers

The **Piping Plover** (*Charadrius melodus*) is a federally endangered shorebird that nests on beaches from New Brunswick to North Carolina, as well as regions of the Great Plains. It is a small (6.5–7-inch-long [17–18 cm]) shorebird that is miraculously well camouflaged to blend in with beach sand. It has a sand-colored back and wings (lighter in females), light breast, black necklace, black and orange bill, and orange feet. You are not likely to spot this bird unless it is in motion. When it does move, it glides over the sand as though it were on wheels. When disturbed, it will take to the air giving a "pipe-pipe-pipe" or "woo-up" warning call. A similar bird with a dark brown back and wider breast band is likely to be the more common **Semipalmated Plover** *(Charadrius semipalmatus).*

Strict nest-site requirements and the feeding behavior of its precocious young have contributed to the Piping Plover's status as an endangered species. Piping Plovers arrive on nesting beaches in March and April and soon initiate nest construction above the high-tide line. The nest itself is nothing more than a shallow depression or scrape in the sand, usually excavated by the male who wiggles his chest back and forth over the sand and kicks stones away with his feet. The dark-speckled, buff-colored eggs look just like an average beach pebble and never exceed four in number. It is quite easy to walk past a nest or on one without ever knowing it was there. Both parents take turns incubating the eggs over the next twenty-eight days. Plover eggs and chicks are vulnerable to a wide range of mammalian and avian predators including skunks, raccoons, dogs, cats, rats, and gulls.

As soon as they hatch, the chicks are responsible for getting their own food. Here lies a major stumbling block in their survival. The flightless precocious young must walk over the beach to the water's edge to feed on crustaceans, worms, and other small invertebrates. They must do this without becoming a predator's next meal, without getting flattened by a four-wheel-drive vehicle, and without overheating on the hot sand. For the next twenty-one to thirty-five days, the parents are constantly on the lookout for danger and sound warning calls signaling the

The Piping Plover (Charadrius melodus)   DENNIS DONOHUE—WWW.THROUGH-MY-LENS.COM

Shorebird Protection

Piping Plovers and Least and Roseate Terns are all on the U.S. Endangered Species List and often nest on the same beaches. Their nesting beaches are often targeted for special protection. Basic tactics involve keeping pedestrians, dogs, and vehicles away from known nest sites during breeding season. In some cases wire-mesh enclosures are set around nests to protect the birds and eggs from predators such as foxes, skunks, raptors, and owls. These simple measures, while often controversial because of the ways that they restrict use of beaches by humans, are usually effective. The total Piping Plover population is estimated to be about 5,900 birds; half of which nest along Atlantic beaches. Inland populations are declining while coastal populations are slowly increasing in numbers due to basic protection measures.

young to freeze when danger is near. Virtually any moving object is considered a threat including vehicles, people walking on the beach, dogs (even those on a leash!), hawks, and even kites, which are mistaken for hawks. It is possible for a young plover to spend so much time avoiding danger that it is either unable to get enough food or overheats on the beach. Although the parent birds don't feed their young, they will go to great measures to distract potential predators from the chicks or nest. In the face of danger, a parent bird may begin flapping its wings on the ground and slowly move away from the nest or chick while dragging a wing behind it as though it were injured. This "broken wing" display draws the attention of the predator to the parent and away from the vulnerable young. The parent will eventually burst into flight leaving the bewildered predator to wonder what happened.

Vehicles traveling on the upper beach present an obvious danger to nesting birds. Wheel ruts are an obstacle to the chicks, who must cross them in order to feed at the water's edge. Flightless chicks, who choose the path of least resistance and travel along wheel ruts, may not escape in time when the next vehicle approaches. Beachgoers frequently leave behind garbage that attracts skunks and raccoons to the beach. These animals will just as easily feed on fresh plover eggs as they would leftovers.

Many other shorebirds are commonly observed migrating along our coast, staying for a few weeks in late summer or spring or for the entire winter. These species include Black-Bellied Plover, Semipalmated Plover, Greater and Lesser Yellowlegs, Hudsonian and Marbled Godwit, Ruddy Turnstone, Red Knot, Sanderlings, various sandpipers including Purple and Semipalmated, Dunlin, and Short- and Long-Billed Dowitchers. Some are covered in the "Estuaries" and "Beach in Winter" chapters.

Sea Turtles: Tracks in the Sand

There are eight species of sea turtle in the world. All are in a state of decline, and most are in danger of extinction. They spend almost all of their time at sea and only come ashore for the purpose of laying eggs. Stranded turtles are usually disoriented, sick, or cold-stunned (hypothermic). Leatherback, Loggerhead, Kemp's Ridley, Atlantic Hawksbill, and Green Turtles inhabit our coast, although they are more likely to be found in warmer tropical waters. The Leatherback is the largest sea turtle, reaching one ton (.9 metric ton) in weight and more than 8 feet (2.4 m) in length. At one hundred pounds (45 kg), the Kemp's Ridley is the smallest, as well as the rarest, with a global population of only 1,500 individuals.

Loggerhead Turtles (*Caretta caretta*) are the only ones to nest on our beaches from North Carolina to Florida. They are medium sized for sea turtles, achieving 38 inches (97 cm) in length and 200-400 pounds (90-180 kg) in weight. Mating takes place just offshore in an event that has rarely been observed. Females migrate onto sandy beaches under the cover of darkness. They use their flippers to excavate nest holes just above the high-tide line. Approximately 110 soft leathery eggs are deposited into the hole and then covered with sand. Before returning to the sea, the mother will use the underside of her body, the plastron, to tamp down the sand above the nest. The tamping marks and tracks in the sand are often the only evidence that a turtle has ever visited the beach. After incubating for about two months, the baby turtles hatch from their eggs and immediately face the most hazardous moment in the life of a sea turtle. The 1–2-inch-long (2.5–5 cm) babies must crawl to the water before being eaten by birds, mammals, and crabs that are waiting along the way.

The emergence of the newly hatched turtles takes place at night. Apparently the horizon over the ocean is lighter than other directions and the turtles use this as a navigation tool to find their way to the sea. (Recent construction of well-lit tourist resorts now provides a deadly distraction for baby turtles searching for the open ocean.)

If they survive the march to the sea, the baby turtles must now orient into the breaking waves and out to sea. They

Tracks left behind by a nesting Loggerhead Turtle (Caretta caretta)   SCOTT SHUMWAY will not set foot on solid ground again until they return to nest years later. This in-between time has stymied biologists trying to study sea turtles. So great was the mystery that biologists referred to "the lost year" to describe the void in knowledge of basic sea turtle biology. By swimming away from shore, the baby Loggerheads encounter large-scale ocean currents and are swept up in the North Atlantic Gyre. The turtles spend the lost year, really closer to eight years, floating and feeding in these currents. Young Loggerheads spend an extended period of time residing in the Sargasso Sea, a subset of the Atlantic Gyre named after the large amounts of seaweed that float here. (This is also the famed breeding area for the eels that live in the streams of North America and Europe.) Large rafts of **Sargassum**, a floating brown seaweed for which the area is named, provide places to hide from sharks and other large predatory fish.

Loggerhead turtles have a compass sense and are able to use the earth's magnetic field to fine-tune their navigation throughout the ocean. Adult turtles forage close to shore and inside estuaries, including Chesapeake Bay, where they feed upon crabs, molluscs, and shrimp. Their massive heads and jaws enable Logger-heads to crush their otherwise well-protected prey. The name Loggerhead refers to a heavy iron ball mounted on the end of a pole and once used to melt and spread pitch to seal the seams on a wooden ship.

Sea Turtle Bycatch

The future survival of sea turtles is dependent upon strong international environmental legislation and enforcement that protects turtles at all stages of their life cycle. Sea turtles are frequent victims of *"bycatch,"* a sterile term that refers the senseless deaths of nontarget species captured in the nets of fishermen. Turtles must return to the surface to breathe approximately every five minutes. If tangled in a net, they can easily drown. Shrimp trawling kills more sea turtles than any other human activity. As many as 10,000 sea turtles die in the nets of shrimp trawlers each year in the Gulf of Mexico. Specialized turtle exclusion devices have been successful in decreasing turtle mortality in shrimp nets. The longline fisheries for swordfish and tuna kill many Logger-heads, as they will readily attack a baited hook. Each year the Spanish long-line swordfish fleet operating in the Mediterranean captures 20,000 juvenile Loggerheads, half of which hatched from U.S. beaches. Closer to home Log-gerheads and Kemp's Ridleys fall victim to gill-net fisheries targeting Summer Flounder from New Jersey to North Carolina.

Sand Dunes

Rolling hills of sand naturally cover the area between the beachfront and salt marsh on barrier spits and barrier islands. Determined hikers can find themselves completely surrounded by sand dunes. There are hollows between dunes where the wind seems not to blow and sound seems not to travel, but the sun burns with a fiery intensity. In contrast the tops of dune ridges provide spectacular views of a rolling landscape of sand interspersed with patches of green vegetation bordered on one side by the crashing surf of the Atlantic Ocean and the flat lush green salt marsh on the other side. On one day the air may be dead calm, the sun's rays mercilessly hot, and each step will seem heavier than the previous one. The next day a stiff breeze will make walking difficult and raise up such a storm of stinging sand that you will be forced to run for cover. The following day the breeze may be mild, the colors of the sand, grass, and sky will be the purest shades of white, green, and blue imaginable, and you will never want to leave this paradise.

These are areas of constantly shifting sand inhabited by a few species of hardy flowering plants. The species that live here are terrestrial, yet they must be able to withstand constant exposure to salt spray and to recover from occasional intrusion by high tides and storm surges. Sand dunes form on the back sides of barrier beaches. Some of the sand deposited on beaches by waves and longshore currents is further transported by onshore winds. Over time this sand piles up to form a **dune ridge** or foredune parallel to the shore.

Wind will forever reshape these sand dunes. By having sand removed from the windward face, blown over the crest, and deposited on the leeward face, sand dunes migrate away from the beach. Eventually a new foredune ridge will be formed. Over a long period of time, rows of parallel dunes will run the length of the beach with the oldest dune located farthest from the beach. The oldest dunes may support the growth of scrubby pine and oak trees to form maritime forests.

In some cases the sand will be molded into a series of U-shaped mounds of sand known as **parabolic dunes.** Prevailing winds hollow out the base of a parabolic dune and deposit sand on the far side. The inside of the U-shape will usually be devoid of vegetation due to the instability of the sand. The depressions hollowed out between dunes are called interdunal **swales.**

Evidence that dunes actually migrate can be seen in live trees, and sometimes roads and houses, being covered by sand. Dark lines, resembling a bathtub ring on the face of a dune, are revealed by migrating dunes. These are remnants of the soil

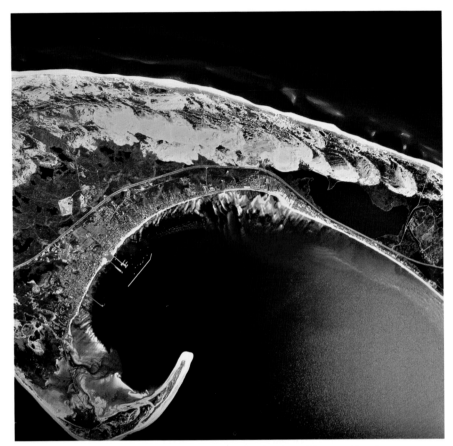

Aerial view of parabolic dunes on Cape Cod National Seashore (Truro and Provincetown, Massachusetts)   U.S. GEOLOGICAL SURVEY

from ancient maritime forests. In some cases standing dead trees are uncovered many years after being buried.

Catastrophic events can cause major rearrangements of dunes. Storm winds hollow out holes known as **blowouts** and assault plants with salt spray. Storm surges blast openings through fore-dunes in what are known as **overwash events.** When this happens, sand is deposited behind the dune as an over-wash fan. In some cases the water that overran the dune drains back into the sea, enlarging the opening as it does so.

The same dunes as seen from the ground
GARRY KESSLER

Blowout showing the power of wind to constantly reshape the dunes   SCOTT SHUMWAY

A Lousy Place for Plants to Grow: Foredunes and Backdunes

Sand dunes are anchored in place by the roots of plants growing there. However, the dry, nutrient-deficient, unstable sand makes for very difficult growing conditions. Water percolates quickly through the porous sand, leaching away what few nutrients are present and depositing them well below the reach of plant roots. The poor water-retention abilities of sand cause dune soil to be very dry, even in areas where there is plenty of rain.

Take a walk through a dune on a windy day and you will find yourself sand-blasted. While you can run for shelter, the plants rooted on the dunes must stick it out or die. In addition to abrasion, delicate plants, particularly seedlings, must deal with being partially or completely buried by sand. Mature plants respond to periodic burial by proliferating roots into the newly deposited layer of sand. The real trouble comes when sand erodes away and roots are exposed or are no longer anchored in the ground. The only salvation in this case is for the plant to be prepared in advance by having deep roots with many branches to anchor the plant and to access scarce water and nutrients.

The area where the upper beach meets the first row of dunes is known as the **foredune.** It is an inherently unstable environment loosely held together by a tangle of plant roots. Decaying seagrass and seaweeds stranded by tides (wrack) provide a source of nutrients for foredune plants. Small amounts of nutrients

Foredune   SCOTT SHUMWAY

Backdunes and swales of the Sandy Neck Barrier Beach (Barnstable, Massachusetts) looking toward Cape Cod Bay
SCOTT SHUMWAY

contained in salt spray are taken up directly through the leaves of some plants. At the same time plants living in this area must be able to withstand the potentially toxic effects of constant exposure to salt spray.

The rows of dunes beyond the foredune, if they are present, are referred to as **secondary** or **backdunes.** During the summer these are areas of intense heat and mysterious life-forms. Camouflaged grasshoppers have bodies that look like collections of tan, brown, and gray sand grains; these give the impression that clumps of sand are able to suddenly jump from the ground and fly away. Quarter-inch-diameter (6-mm) holes in the sand are the secret burrows of spiders. Probing the holes with lengths of beachgrass shows that these burrows can be a foot (30 cm) or more deep. A web lining prevents the burrows from collapsing. Earthstar fungi *(Geoaster)* are like armed puffballs that expand and contract their rays in response to changing moisture conditions. In the process they release spores to be dispersed by the wind. Occasionally a low-flying Northern Harrier will rise up over a dune crest only to disappear below the next. These raptors are visual foragers flying low in search of rodents such as White-Footed Mice and Meadow Voles. Deer, coyotes, rodents, Diamondback Terrapins, snakes, toads, and even caterpillars leave tracks in the sand that are often the only clues to their presence in the dunes.

Common Sand-Dune Plants

The most common sand-dune plant throughout most of the east coast of North America is **American Beachgrass** *(Ammophila breviligulata).* As winds blow the beachgrass blades, they trace circular patterns in the sand, leading to the common name "Compass Plant." These grasses are stabilizers of sand dunes and may be found growing from the base of the foredune to the edge of maritime forest or to the salt marsh on the back side of a barrier spit. Beachgrass grows as clusters of vertical shoots (ramets) that emerge from a spreading horizontal rhizome that may be several yards in length. Beachgrass shoots and their straplike blades reach 3 feet (.9 m) in height and send up a robust flower spike in midsummer. The shoots slow down wind movement over the dune while the roots tightly anchor the sand in place. South of Virginia beachgrass is replaced by **Sea Oats** *(Uniola paniculata)*.

Seaside Goldenrod *(Solidago sempervirens)* forms leafy rosettes that produce stunning inflorescences of bright yellow flowers. The name *sempervirens* suggests that the leaves are evergreen, but in the northern part of its range, leaves turn brown during the winter. A perennial storage rhizome, the size of a large human finger, allows the plant to persist from year to year and to slowly increase the numbers of rosettes and flower stalks. The leaves are often under attack by two species of chrysomelid beetle. The yellow-and-black-striped adults, as well as the all-black larvae, of *Trirhabda canadensis* can consume almost the entire leaf leaving behind a midrib and a pile of frass. *Microrhopala vittata* is a leaf miner whose larvae live within the leaves and devour them from the inside. During the fall and winter White-Tailed Deer browse on the leaves.

Northern Bayberry *(Myrica pensylvanica)* is a shrub with the remarkable ability to grow on dune crests and backdunes, at the perimeters of swales, and in the understory of maritime forests. How it is able to grow in habi-

American Beachgrass (Ammophila breviligulata)   SCOTT SHUMWAY

Seaside Goldenrod (Solidago sempervirens)
SCOTT SHUMWAY

tats with such a wide range of soil moisture and sunlight is unknown. The woody shrubs grow to 6 feet (1.8 m) in height and produce a dense canopy of dark green leaves. The leaves are highly aromatic and rarely consumed by insects, suggesting chemical protection. The fragrance is also found in the gray waxy coating on the outside of the fruits. Bayberry candles are produced by boiling off this wax. Bayberry shrubs are dioecious, meaning that the flowers are either male or female and are produced on separate plants. Translated from Greek, *dioecious* literally means

Northern Bayberry (Myrica pensylvanica)
SCOTT SHUMWAY

"two houses," one for the males and one for the females. As a result of this system, only the female Bayberry shrubs produce fruit.

Seed dispersal is carried out by flocks of migrating birds, such as Yellow-Rumped Warblers and Tree Swallows. Yellow-Rumps were once called Myrtle Warblers because of their association with this plant, which is sometimes called Myrtle. The birds consume the entire fruit but only digest the energy-rich waxy layer. Because the waxy layer is so thin, the birds must eat large numbers of fruits. The seeds within are extremely hard and simply pass through the digestive tract unharmed, landing in a new location away from the parent plant.

Bayberry shrubs have clusters of small fingerlike swellings, or **nodules,** on their roots that house symbiotic bacteria *(Frankia)* that carry out nitrogen fixation. These bacteria absorb nitrogen gas from the soil and transform it into a form that plants can use. The bacteria share their excess nitrogen with the Bayberry. Nitrogen fixation is inhibited by oxygen, and the root nodules provide a low-oxygen environment conducive to this reaction. Therefore both partners benefit, and the relationship is a mutualism. Careful searching around Bayberry shrubs adjacent to blowouts may reveal root nodules uncovered by the moving sand. Plants growing beneath Bayberry shrubs also benefit as fallen Bayberry leaves decay and release their nutrients into the soil. Beachgrass and Seaside Goldenrod growing beneath Bayberry grow larger and produce more flowers than those growing in the surrounding dunes.

Wax-Myrtle *(Myrica cerifera)* is common from New Jersey south and closely resembles Bayberry, except that it grows taller and has narrower leaves that are evergreen. In some locations these two species form dense impenetrable thickets. Salt spray driven by onshore winds sculpt thickets into lopsided hedgerows.

The dull gray-green mats of **Beach Heather** *(Hudsonia tomentosa)* and their deep roots are important stabilizers of dunes as far south as North Carolina. At first glance the plants may not even appear to be alive, but a closer look will reveal tiny hairy leaves clustered along thin woody stems. For one to two weeks in early June, this homely plant transforms itself into a stunning mass of bright yellow flowers. Another common name assigned to this species is "Poverty Grass" because of its ability to grow in such poor soil. Clearly this plant is not a grass and presents

Beach Heather (Hudsonia tomentosa) *in bloom*   SCOTT SHUMWAY

yet another reason why common names should be abandoned in favor of scientific names.

The number of other dune plants is not large, and none of them occurs in the abundance of the species mentioned so far. **Sea Rocket** *(Cakile edentulata)*, **Common Saltwort** *(Salsola kali)*, **Common Cocklebur** *(Xanthium strumarium)*, and **Beach Pea** *(Lathyrus japonicus)* are foredune specialists. **Seaside Spurge** *(Euphorbia polygonifolia)*, **Sand Jointweed** *(Polygonella articulata)*, **Sickle-Leaved Golden Aster** *(Chrysopsis falcata)*, **Dusty Miller** *(Artemisia stelleriana)*, and **Wormwood** *(Artemisia caudata)* are common herbaceous species. **Beach Plum** *(Prunus maritima)*, **Poison Ivy** *(Toxicodendron radicans)*, **Red Cedar** *(Juniperus virginiana)*, **Bearberry** *(Arctostaphylos uva-ursi)*, and **Rugosa Rose** *(Rosa rugosa)* grow as woody shrubs or vines in secondary dunes and thickets. **Marsh Hay** *(Spartina patens)*, **Seaside Panicum** *(Panicum amarum)*, and **Hair Grass** *(Deschampsia flexuosa)* are grasses of backdunes and swales.

Interdunal Swales—Wetland Oases

Low-elevation areas between dune ridges are known as **interdunal swales** or **dune slacks** and are wetland oases in the dry dunes. Swale soils are almost always damp to the touch, even in midsummer, and digging reveals that the water table is not far below the surface. Coyote, fox, and deer dig holes or use holes of others to access the fresh drinking water. When the groundwater table rises in the spring, swales are inundated by several inches of water, transforming them into freshwater

Beachgoers Beware: Lyme Disease and Deer Ticks

Dune shrub thickets, maritime forests, and other uplands near the coast are hot spots for contracting a debilitating illness transmitted to humans by ticks. Ticks are arachnids that feed on mammalian blood. The tick life cycle consists of larval, nymph, and adult stages, each of which requires a blood meal. The latter two stages may pass on disease-causing bacteria acquired while feeding on previous hosts. Dune thickets and coastal uplands are often crawling with ticks in search of a blood meal.

The **Deer Tick** *(Ixodes scapularis)* is the vector by which Lyme disease is transmitted from one mammalian host to another. The Deer Tick is usually smaller and darker than the common Dog Tick that transmits Rocky Mountain spotted fever, but not Lyme disease. **Lyme disease** is a debilitating, sometimes fatal, illness that is caused by the bacterium *Borrelia burgdorferi.* The Lyme disease bacteria carry out their life cycle in two separate hosts, a Deer Tick and a mammal—usually Meadow Voles, White-Footed Mice, squirrels, fox, and White-Tailed Deer.

Lyme disease was first discovered in Old Lyme, Connecticut, in 1975 after several children began to exhibit arthritis-like symptoms. In reality the disease has been around for hundreds of years; however, the transmission to humans has become more common as ideal deer habitat is forced to overlap with vacationland and suburbia. Lyme disease symptoms mimic influenza, Bell's palsy, and arthritis, making it difficult to diagnose.

The best strategy is to know what Deer Ticks look like and avoid them by wearing permethrin-based tick repellent, avoiding dense vegetation in tick hot spots, and checking yourself frequently for crawling or biting ticks. It takes several hours for a feeding tick to transmit the bacteria to a human host, so spotting a tick crawling on your leg is not a cause for panic! Unfortunately the minute, nearly impossible to see, nymph stages also transmit the disease.

Deer Tick bites often leave behind a growing *bull's-eye rash*. If you should experience such a rash, go to your doctor immediately. The rash is frequently followed by a flulike infection and then debilitating joint pain. The key to preventing more serious symptoms is early treatment with antibiotics.

Interdunal swale inundated with water
SCOTT SHUMWAY

The same swale during the summer
SCOTT SHUMWAY

pools. Amphibians, including American, Fowlers and Eastern Spadefoot Toads, migrate to these vernal pools to call, mate, and lay eggs.

Wetland Plants of the Interdunal Swales

Swales are populated by wetland plants able to tolerate waterlogged soils. The most numerous plants are often rushes and sedges that spread via horizontal rhizomes. **Mud** and **Canada Rushes** (*Juncus pelocarpus* and *J. canadensis*) are common in the centers of swales while **Greene's Rush** *(J. greenei)* grows at the drier edges between

Swale showing summertime growth of Mud and Canada Rushes (Juncus pelocarpus and J. canadensis)   SCOTT SHUMWAY

Sand-Dune Conservation

Humans are slow learners and have repeatedly destroyed the protective vegetative cover on dunes only to watch the sand blow away. The first European colonists cut down the forests growing on the dunes of Cape Cod. In 1662 laws were passed to prevent further destruction of the sand-dune vegetation, and in the 1700s attempts were made to plant beachgrass in hopes of stabilizing the migrating dunes, which had begun to engulf the village of Provincetown. Three centuries later the National Park Service is still planting beachgrass on Cape Cod National Seashore.

Single passes by an off-road vehicle or a hiking boot can kill beachgrass vegetation. For barefooted pedestrians beachgrass has a special defense. The growing tip of a beachgrass rhizome is extremely sharp where it emerges from the sand. After a single mistake a barefoot beachgoer will hobble home having learned to walk between, not on top of, beachgrass shoots.

swale and dune. **Nutsedge** (*Cyperus dentatus*) is highly unusual in that its seeds are capable of germinating while still attached to the parent plant. Eventually the seedlings will detach from the parent and put down roots. This phenomenon is known as vivipary, or live birth, and is uncommon in plants. However, it is easy to see how a relatively large and well-fortified seedling with established roots may have an advantage over newly germinated seedlings the following spring.

American Cranberry (*Vaccinium macrocarpon*) carpets the surface of many swales, particularly on Cape Cod. Cranberry vines are actually creeping woody shrubs, which never grow more than a few inches off the ground. Vines spread across the surface of the ground sending up numerous vertical stems covered by whorls of tiny half-inch-long (1.3-cm) leaves. The similarity between the flower shape and the beak of a bird gave the plant its true name of "Crane Berry." The pinkish flowers begin to appear in June and attract buzzing bumblebees that vibrate the flower at just the right frequency to release pollen. Fruits develop in the ensuing weeks, maturing deep red berries in early autumn.

Hidden among the Cranberry are small plants with reddish leaves that appear to be covered in dewdrops. These are **Spatulate-Leaved Sundews** (*Drosera intermedia*), and the sticky dewdrops are suspended on hairs covering the leaves. These beautiful gems are death traps for inquisitive insects that become captured and slowly digested by plant enzymes, which then transfer nutrients to the leaves. Insectivorous plants rely upon insect meals as valuable nutrient supplements, even though they take up nutrients with their roots as do most other plants.

American Cranberry (Vaccinium macro-carpon)   SCOTT SHUMWAY

Spatulate-Leaved Sundew (Drosera inter-media)   SCOTT SHUMWAY

Several species of orchids reside in swales. In early summer the pink blooms of **Grass Pink** *(Calopogon pulchellus)* and **Rose Pogonia** *(Pogonia ophioglossoides)* orchids contrast sharply with the underlying deep green Cranberry leaves. In later summer, **Nodding Ladies' Tresses** *(Spiranthes cernua)* may appear by the hundreds with inflorescences of delicate white, downward-facing flowers.

Chesapeake Bay is a drowned river-valley estuary that is economically important for the harvest of fish, oysters, clams, and crabs. SCOTT SHUMWAY

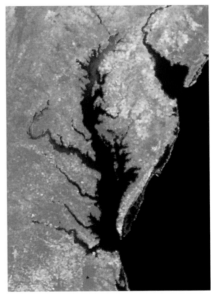

Satellite image of Chesapeake Bay
NOAA PHOTO LIBRARY–NATIONAL MARINE FISHERIES HISTORIC IMAGE COLLECTION

Estuaries

An **estuary** is a semienclosed body of water subject to freshwater runoff from the land and salt water from the sea. Estuaries are found wherever freshwater from a river meets the ocean. Boston and New York Harbors, Penobscot, Buzzards, Narragansett, Delaware and Chesapeake Bays, and Pamlico Sound are some of the major East Coast estuaries. They are of great ecological importance for many species and contain enormous quantities of commercially valuable fish and shellfish, including Blue Crabs, oysters, and clams. Many fish use the food-rich and predator-poor estuarine waters as nursery grounds for their young. The mouths of estuaries provide sheltered locations for all kinds of shipping and are ideal places to construct industrial complexes that take in raw materials and ship out finished goods. They are highly desirable places for humans to live, work, and play.

Scientists identify estuaries and the surrounding salt marshes as **critical transition zones**—middle grounds between terrestrial, freshwater, and marine habitats. The water, mineral nutrients, organic material, and living organisms flowing off of the land or down rivers must pass through these transition zones on the way to the sea. The same is true of pesticides, fertilizers, sewage effluent, and industrial waste. As these components pass through marshes and estuaries, they become incorporated into biological processes and are often transformed along the way. This transformation may result in chemical changes and/or may incorporate them into the local food chain. These pollutants may also drastically impact the well-being of the organisms and ecosystem processes that take place within the transition zones. Here lies the danger, as these transition zones act as biological buffers to the surrounding marine ecosystem. They are also areas characterized by relatively low species richness, yet the key species that do live there perform extremely important roles in the functioning of the ecosystem.

Extensive oyster beds line the shallow waters of many estuaries where they filter huge quantities of water every day. They are in essence the estuarine equivalent of a HEPA filter, removing algae, microbes, and nutrients from the water and building more oyster biomass. Over-harvesting of oysters in the Chesapeake Bay has been implicated in the buildup of nutrients, deterioration of water clarity, and outbreaks of toxic algae and disease-causing microbes. Because oyster larvae prefer to settle upon the shells of old oysters, once oyster beds have been depleted it is not a simple matter to restore the system.

The establishment of nonnative species can have devastating effects on critical transition zones by replacing important species but not their important functions in the ecosystem. In other words it is not possible to simply replace one species with another and get the same result. Interactions between species and interactions between species and their environment have been fine-tuned over thousands, if not millions, of years, and sudden changes through the addition or subtraction of species, nutrients, or habitat can throw the entire system out of whack. Humans have been doing just that for decades and are only just beginning to recognize the need to understand how their activities will impact natural environments. In some cases we are realizing the need to repair or restore damaged environments, but this activity is still in its infancy and is proving more difficult than we ever imagined.

This chapter highlights the important physical attributes of estuaries and the ecology of some of their most notable inhabitants. Although salt marshes, tidal flats, and seagrass meadows are all components of estuarine systems, they are separated into different chapters in this book for organization and presentation purposes. In nature they are all tightly linked and incapable of functioning independently.

Drowned River Valleys and Barrier Beaches

Atlantic-coast estuaries may be divided into two types based on their geologic history. Ten thousand years ago North America was in the midst of a glaciation. Sea level was 330 feet (100 m) lower than present due to the vast amounts of water stored in frozen glaciers. The mouths of rivers flowing from the land to the sea were located miles away from present locations. As the glaciers melted, rivers raged toward the sea, gouging the earth as they went. Over time the oceans were refueled and sea levels rose, flooding the river valleys in the process. These **drowned river-valley estuaries**, also known as coastal-plain estuaries, include Narragansett, Delaware, and Chesapeake Bays.

Over the past 5,000–10,000 years, shoreline sediments have been in a constant state of flux and have formed numerous sandbars, some of which developed into **barrier beaches** and **barrier islands.** A protected embayment, or **bar-built estuary,** is formed between the barrier and the mainland. Freshwater enters this lagoon as runoff from the mainland while a tidal inlet connects it to the ocean. The Mid-Atlantic coast is dotted by barrier islands with wave-exposed sandy beaches on their eastern side and bays lined with salt marsh on the western side. Plum Island and the Parker River Estuary, Long Beach Island and Barnegat Bay, Assateague Island and Chincoteague Bay, and the Outer Banks and Albemarle and Pamlico Sounds are some of the better-known pairs of barrier islands and estuaries along our coast.

The Stress of Constant Change

Estuaries are areas of **constantly changing environmental conditions.** Daily as well as seasonal variations in **salinity, tides, temperature, nutrients,** and **dissolved oxygen** interact to determine what species live in estuaries. The severity of these

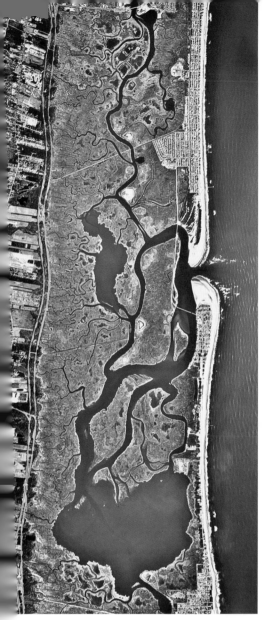

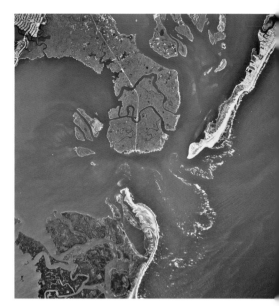

Southern tip of the barrier beach of Long Beach Island, New Jersey, and the mouths of the Great Bay and Mullica River Estuaries. A tidal inlet known as Little Egg Inlet separates Long Beach Island from a smaller barrier spit. The large penninsula to the upper left is salt marsh permeated with meandering creeks. The long line is a road leading to the Rutgers University Marine Field Station from where the photograph below was taken.
U.S. GEOLOGICAL SURVEY

Aerial view of the southern terminus of the Ocean City, New Jersey, barrier island Corson's Inlet, and the northern end of Strathmere, New Jersey. The mainland shows up as purple and is primarily agricultural. The Garden State Parkway shows up as two white lines running north-south at the edge of the mainland. Salt marsh permeated by meandering creeks is located between the mainland and barrier spits. In contrast the straight lines of mosquito ditches are evident closest to the mainland and islands.
U.S. GEOLOGICAL SURVEY

Salt marsh in Tuckerton, New Jersey, mouth of the Great Bay Estuary, and the southern tip of Long Beach Island   SCOTT SHUMWAY

fluctuating stresses keeps the overall species diversity in estuaries low. The majority of estuarine species are bottom-dwelling invertebrates that are well adapted to fluctuating salinities and live only in estuaries. Many species of fish live here as juveniles, yet few spend their entire lives in estuaries. The total species diversity is boosted significantly by these visiting species. Even among the species that do inhabit estuaries, only a small subset occurs in large numbers. Yet these species are often present in staggering abundance.

Salinity presents the greatest stress to species living in estuaries. The physiologies of freshwater species are unable to deal with increased salinities while those of most marine species are unable to cope with decreases in salinity. Only species capable of overcoming the challenge of fluctuating salinities are able to inhabit estuaries.

The salinity within an estuary ranges from being fresh in the uppermost reaches fed by rivers to full-strength seawater at the mouth. This salinity gradient fluctuates as rising and falling tides transport salt water into and out of estuaries in a cycle that repeats itself approximately every twelve and a half hours. Many estuaries also exhibit vertical salinity gradients with fresh or brackish water floating over more dense seawater.

This **salinity stratification,** or layering, can change seasonally and is often accompanied by **temperature stratification** of warm water over cold. The sharp separation of warm and cold waters is called a **thermocline.** Over time gravity causes nutrients to sink, leaving surface waters deficient in nutrients. Once a thermocline forms, nutrients become trapped in the deep cold layer.

The relative contribution of freshwater from rivers varies seasonally with maximum inputs in springtime. Therefore estuarine gradients in salinity can be steep and change, either gradually or abruptly, over the course of months or hours. Shallow estuaries are well mixed with little change in salinity from the surface to the bottom. In contrast the salinities of larger and deeper drowned river estuaries are weakly to strongly stratified with depth. Mixing of water of different depths is driven by tides, river flow, and wind.

Estuaries, like the open coast, are strongly influenced by **tides.** Within an estuary the rising tide is like a large moving wave. In some estuaries the water rises at the same time throughout and tides are described as a **standing wave.** In other cases, particularly in large estuaries, the tide moves like a **progressive wave,** with some locations experiencing high tide before other locations farther up the estuary. The Delaware Bay estuary has a six- to seven-hour tide difference from Cape Henlopen, Delaware, to Trenton, New Jersey. When the tide has receded to its lowest point at Cape Henlopen, high tide is just peaking 137 miles (220 km) away in Trenton, where the system is a tidal river.

The volume of freshwater entering estuaries from rivers increases in response to rainstorms and melting snow. At these times the salinity of an estuary plummets. Runoff water carries with it sediment, nutrients, and pollutants. The amount of sediment entering an estuary after a spring rainstorm can severely cut off light penetration and may clog the mouthparts of benthic filter feeders. Runoff from nearby agricultural fields contains a cocktail of fertilizers, pesticides, and animal waste that also changes the character of the water. The resulting **nutrient pollution,** or **eutrophication,** stimulates population explosions of phytoplankton. In some cases these algal blooms contain species that produce potent toxins that can injure fish and humans. After blooms peak and millions of algal cells die, the resulting decomposition by aerobic bacteria depletes the supply of **dissolved oxygen** in the water. With insufficient oxygen fish and shellfish begin to die. Their subsequent decay makes matters worse. Surprisingly this entire process can occur within a few days or a few hours!

Storm drains that collect road runoff are sometimes piped into the same treatment facility as household wastewater. The effluent from sewage treatment plants often drains into an estuary or river. During large storms the volume of material entering a treatment plant may exceed its capacity, and the only solution is to release the untreated water directly into the estuary. As this nutrient- and pathogen-rich material decomposes, it fuels the same eutrophication process stimulated by agricultural fertilizers.

Patterns in the Plankton

Most estuaries experience seasonal fluctuations in **phytoplankton** (plantlike plankton composed of single-celled algae) abundance with peaks in spring and fall that are driven by light and nutrient availability, as well as herbivore abundance. In shallow estuaries, such as Narragansett Bay in Rhode Island, the entire water column is capable of supporting photosynthesis leading to high levels of primary productivity. Nutrient supplies are enriched primarily by runoff from the surrounding land and river transport. When nutrient levels are high, such as after spring rains, phytoplankton densities also become high. These nutrients are also recycled quickly in estuaries as grazing zooplankton consume phytoplankton and then enrich the water with their waste products.

In the 178-square-mile (460-sq-km) Narragansett Bay estuary, a peak in phytoplankton abundance, or algal bloom, occurs in late winter/early spring. A single species of diatom, *Skeletonema costatum,* makes up 80 percent of all phytoplankton at this time. The bloom collapses in May/June as nutrients are depleted and grazing by copepod crustaceans increases. The algae are also consumed by a large community of benthic filter-feeding bivalves, particularly Quahog clams. A large population of benthic invertebrates can be supported in Narragansett Bay because the primary production by phytoplankton exceeds what can be consumed by the grazing zooplankton. A smaller algal bloom takes place in July/August as nutrients are recycled from the bottom. Because Narragansett Bay is so shallow and lacks a strong thermocline, mixing of water layers and nutrients continues even into the warm summer months. Algal blooms are also stimulated by periodic outbreaks of

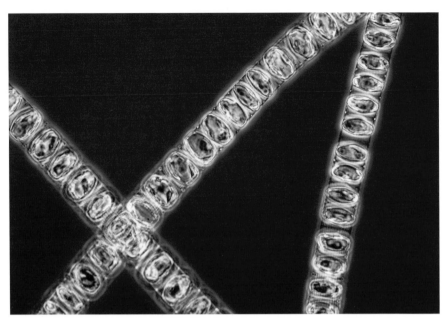

The chain-forming diatom Skeletonema costatum *is one of the most abundant species of estuarine phytoplankton.*   DR. PAUL E. HARGRAVES, HARBOR BRANCH OCEANOGRAPHIC INSTITUTION

zooplankton-eating comb jellies *(Mnemiopsis)* and Menhaden fish that greatly reduce the abundance of grazing copepods.

Animal Life in Estuaries

The animals that inhabit estuaries often occur in staggering abundance, a testament to their tolerance of the widely fluctuating physical conditions of their environment. Bivalve molluscs, crabs, shorebirds, and fish are among the most common inhabitants of estuaries.

Oysters: Structural and Sanitation Engineers of the Estuarine Ecosystem

The Eastern or **American Oyster** *(Crassostrea virginica)* is an estuarine species tolerant of a wide range of salinities from 5 to 40 ppt. Oysters are filter-feeding bivalves that grow attached to hard substrates. The tendency of larvae to settle upon the shells of live or dead oysters results in tight clusters ranging from a few individuals to expansive oyster beds.

Oyster shells often seem distorted, a reflection of their cramped living arrangements and the type of substrate they inhabit. Oysters on hard substrates tend to grow wider and have a greater curve to the lower valve compared to those on soft substrates where the lower valve is narrower and flatter. In all oysters the lower valve is curved while the upper valve (really left and right) is flatter. Their range of shell shapes and sizes exceeds any of our other native molluscs. In addition any single shell probably has one or two others permanently cemented to it.

Much of the study of oysters has been focused on their commercial value, rather than on their ecological importance within the context of oyster bed communities or estuarine ecosystems. These omissions have proven to be unfortunate and scientists have only recently acknowledged the important role of oysters as structural architects of estuarine communities and as living water purification filters of estuaries.

American Oyster, Crassostrea virginica, *shells are highly variable in shape and color.*
SCOTT SHUMWAY

Oyster beds form over time by successive generations of oysters settling, growing, and dying upon one another. What started as a few individuals may eventually become a sizable physical structure that provides habitat for many other species. Subtidally these structures are called oyster beds while those that are intertidal are called oyster reefs. Intertidal reefs are restricted to southern regions where winter exposure to cold temperatures is not a problem.

Oyster beds are three-dimensional islands of hard substrate projecting upward from expanses of mud and sand. They are a refuge for sessile species that require a hard attachment point as well as for mobile species in need of a firm substrate to

Oyster bed in Wellfleet, Massachusetts   SCOTT SHUMWAY

Oyster Life Cycle

American Oysters reproduce in late spring by releasing large quantities of gametes into the water. Synchronous gamete release combined with gregarious living greatly increases the probability of successful fertilization. After three weeks in the water column, the planktonic larvae, presumably responding to chemical scents released from adult oysters, settle on the shells of a member of the same species. For a brief period of time, the newly settled larva crawls over the bottom searching for an appropriate location for permanent attachment. Upon attaching to a hard substrate, referred to as "culch" by oystermen, the larvae metamorphose into spat and then grow into juveniles.

The life cycle deviates from the norm in that oysters change sex. Smaller individuals are typically male and will ultimately become female as they get larger. Natural sex change is not unique to oysters and often follows the general rule that larger individuals are female due to the extra energy needed to make eggs. In the case of oysters, food availability and other environmental conditions influence the timing of this gender change. Sometimes they will even revert back to males in response to these external conditions.

The production of large numbers of planktonic larvae may be one of the features of oysters that enable their populations to remain resilient in the face of periodic devastation from overharvesting, predator outbreaks, and natural disasters. Within an estuary larvae can travel with currents to locations where local conditions have wiped out an oyster population. Present environmental stresses, such as disease and pollution, are severely challenging this natural resilience of oyster populations.

forage over and a network of crevices in which to hide from predators. For crabs and fish that travel from adjacent seagrass beds and mud bottoms, oyster beds are like well-stocked lunch counters.

It is often tricky to view the diversity of life that inhabits oyster beds. An abundance of mobile polychaete worms crawl through the jumble of shells in search of prey. Small fish, such as blennies and gobies, barely 2 inches (5 cm) in length, inhabit the gaping shells left behind by deceased oysters. Even commercially harvested oysters that have been cleaned up for market may still be covered with bryozoans, hydroids, worm tubes, barnacles, and sea anemones.

Oyster Predators and Unwelcome Partners

Oysters are preyed upon by shell-drilling snails, shell-crushing crabs, flatworms, sea stars, and fish. Oyster fishermen have gone to great lengths to control these invertebrate pests that compete with them for access to oyster meat. In nearly all cases these attempts have either met with failure or presented an unacceptable risk to the natural environment.

Oyster Drills (*Urosalpinx cinerea* [see photo page 57] and *Eupleura caudata*) are the most common predatory snails, occurring in densities of up to 127 snails per square yard (106 per sq m) of oyster bed. The combination of shell-dissolving acid secretions and a rasping radula bearing hardened teeth enables the snails to drill small holes in the shells of oysters and other molluscs. The radula and digestive enzymes then consume the animal within. Juveniles and thin-shelled individuals are most susceptible to drilling by snails and crushing by crabs. An oyster may eventually reach a sufficient size at which it is impervious to drilling or crushing.

Mud crabs, like *Panopeus herbstii,* easily crush and consume up to twenty-one spat per day. This particular species also has a toothlike projection on its claw that enables it to crush larger shells. The most important crab predator is the **Blue Crab,** which scurries over oyster beds as they become covered by high tides. Spat (less than .6 inch [15 mm] in length) are easily crushed while larger shells are gradually chipped at the edges until the crab can insert its cutter claw to extract the oyster meat.

Shells washed up on a beach will often yield clues about the manner of death suffered by the inhabitant. The **flatworm,** *Stylochus ellipticus,* however, leaves no such traces. It slips through the cracks of gaping oysters and slowly devours the unsuspecting prey. The **Common Sea Star** (*Asterias forbesii*) is an important predator on oysters in Long Island Sound. Periodic good larval years are soon followed by plagues of sea stars that take a heavy toll on local oyster populations. Many fish, including **Toadfish, Cownose Rays, Summer Flounder,** and **Drumfish,** prey upon oysters.

Boring sponges (*Cliona*) excavate a network of galleries within the shells of oysters and other molluscs. The sponge body is almost completely enclosed within the excavated catacombs. Only small bumps of yellow sponge extend from the surface of the shell. These bumps barely project from the shell as they are readily eaten by predators. The sponge tunnels rarely extend all the way through to the live oyster. In cases where this does happen, the oysters

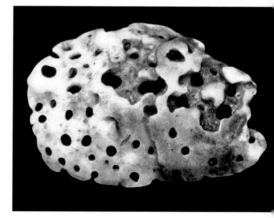

Boring sponge (Cliona) *damage to an oyster shell*   SCOTT SHUMWAY

The Seeds of Invasion

In the early 1800s we began transferring tiny "seed oysters" or "spat" along the East Coast in an attempt to restock depleted populations. Spat, attached to oyster shells, known to oystermen as culch, were shipped from larger populations in Delaware and Chesapeake Bays to beds from Maine to Long Island. This practice has been responsible for spreading diseases as well as many species other than oysters. American Oysters have also been introduced to Europe, the west coast of the United States, and Hawaii. As a consequence hitchhiking Oyster Drills, Slippershells, periwinkles, and numerous other species native to the western Atlantic have become established on the shores of Europe and the eastern Pacific.

In fewer than fifty years, a habitual hitchhiker, the green seaweed *Codium fragile,* has become established over much of the east coast of the United States. *Codium* has a dark green spongy tubular body that branches repeatedly to form a bushy plant up to 2.3 feet (70 cm) tall. Its feltlike appearance and feel gave rise to the common name **Green Fleece** long before Polartec was patented. Its eerie appearance washed up onshore or floating in the water has resulted in the equally descriptive common name of **Dead Man's Fingers.** The hulls of European ships docked in New York during World War II were covered with dense growths of this seaweed, some of which apparently jumped ship. Surprisingly, *Codium* is not native to Europe. It invaded European shores in 1900 on the bottom of ships traveling from Japan.

It now grows from Boothbay Harbor, Maine, to North Carolina. *Codium* attaches to rocks, oysters, mussels, clams, and scallops. The increased difficulty of harvesting scallops and oysters covered in a tangled mass of green algae has made *Codium* a sworn enemy of shellfishermen. However, the shellfish industry helped create the problem. Seed

Codium fragile   SCOTT SHUMWAY

oysters shipped from Long Island to Chatham spread *Codium* to Cape Cod in 1961. The small green bumps on the baby oyster shells turned out to be baby algae, in this case a noxious weed that would continue to spread on its own.

rapidly secrete new shell material to patch the damage. While the sponge does not directly kill or harm the living oyster, it does leave the shell severely weakened and susceptible to crushing by crabs and fish.

Still other species reside within the mantle cavity of live oysters. **Pea Crabs** (*Pinnotheris ostreum*) live symbiotically inside oysters, mussels, worm tubes, and echinoderms. For us they are a note-worthy, and sometimes crunchy, find within an oyster or mussel. Pea Crabs steal food from the oysters as it passes over gills that carry out both respiration and food sorting.

Mud worms (*Polydora* spp.) settle on top of oyster shells where they construct small tubes of mud. Some mud worm species, however, bore into the inner surfaces of the shells where the oyster attempts to cover them over by secreting new shell. The resulting "shell blisters" are easily observed either on the beach or on the half shell.

Symbiotic Pea Crab (Pinnotheris ostreum) *inside of a scallop. The white frills are the gills of the bivalve and provide a ready meal for the crab.* SANDRA E. SHUMWAY

There are three major oyster diseases, commonly known as **Dermo, MSX,** and **SSO.** The diseases weaken and often kill oysters. They don't seem to harm humans directly, but can wipe out most or all of a commercial oyster bed before the oysters reach harvestable size. The causative agents are protozoans. These single-celled life-forms have complex life cycles, the stages of which scientists are still trying to elucidate. The belief is that the diseases are transmitted via water and enter the oysters during filter feeding. Other than isolating new commercial beds from other infected populations, control attempts have proven futile or equally deadly to the oysters.

The small snail, *Boonea impressa,* resides just inside the shell edge of an oyster where it uses a piercing mouthpart to suck body fluids from the mantle tissue. This snail may transmit infective stages of Dermo disease similar to the way a blood-sucking mosquito transmits malaria.

Blue Crabs: The Beautiful Swimmer That Is Tasty

Blue Crabs (*Callinectes sapidus*) cannot be mistaken for any other crab. The bright blue color for which they are named is most evident on the claws and is more intense in older individuals. They can also be greenish and brownish on the carapace with touches of red on the tips of their claws. Blue Crabs search the soft-bottom sediments of estuaries and tidal flats for their next meal. They are skilled predators, particularly upon Soft-Shell Clams. They are equally comfortable scavenging upon dead fish or any other meat they can find. They have a large **crusher claw** used to overcome the defensive shells of snails and bivalves and a fine cutter claw suited for removing meat from the crushed shells of prey. As all crabbers know, Blue Crabs are lightning fast and are not shy about using their claws to protect themselves. The name *Callinectes sapidus* literally means "the beautiful swimmer who is tasty." As with all members of the swimming crab family, the fifth pair of legs is shaped like flattened paddles that can be used to propel the crab through the water. The carapace, or top shell, features distinctive elongated spines on either side. A crab with "points" is almost certainly a Blue.

Newly molted soft-shell crab and its shed carapace positioned on top of new carapace to show the increase in body size
SCOTT SHUMWAY

Blue Crabs are found throughout most of the Atlantic, Gulf, and Caribbean coasts, but are uncommon north of Cape Cod. Chesapeake Bay is home to more Blue Crabs than any other place on earth and is where the greatest numbers are harvested.

All crustaceans must periodically shed their rigid external skeleton and secrete a new larger skeleton in order to accommodate further growth. The fishers who make their living off crabs have a keen understanding of the timing of the various stages of the life cycle, some of which fetch more money than others. Aside from truly large crabs, the most desirable is the soft-shell stage of the life cycle. This is the period immediately after molting when the new skeleton has yet to harden. Consumption by humans usually involves pan frying the soft-shell crab for a few minutes, placing it between two pieces of bread, and eating the entire thing eyestalks and all—a slightly crunchy, yet flavorful experience.

Once a female crab molts to maturity, she is ready for her only opportunity to breed. As she nears her final molt, a female crab emits pheromones designed to attract potential mates. Males seek out these females, as mating can only occur while the new shell is still soft. Upon finding and subduing a mate, the male uses his legs to form a cage around her. He guards his mate from rival males while waiting for the chance to pass on his sperm. Packets of sperm are transferred immediately after the female has molted. The male guards his mate until her shell has had sufficient time to harden. At this point he leaves her to fend for herself and will probably never see her again.

Mate-guarding behavior protects the newly molted, and helpless, female from fish predators and cannibalistic crabs. Guarding also prevents other males from subsequently mating with the female and fertilizing her eggs. Therefore, most females mate with only one male in their lifetime. The female's new shell takes seventy-two hours to harden. If the goal is to protect her from predation, then males

Male and female Blue Crabs showing differences in shape of the abdomen. The abdomen of male crabs has the outline of the Washington Monument while females have the outline of the Capitol dome.   SCOTT SHUMWAY

should only guard her until her shell has hardened. In reality males will guard their females for three times longer than this in order to prevent her from mating again.

Confused about how to tell a male crab from a female? Folks from Washington, D.C., determine crab gender by using the following mantra regarding abdomen shape: "Males have the Washington Monument and females have the Capitol dome". In crabs the abdomen is folded beneath the carapace in order to place the center of gravity beneath the walking legs. Males have narrow elongated abdomens, longer than they are wide. Adult females, on the other hand, have much wider abdomens that are designed to hold large masses of developing eggs. In young females the abdomen is shaped like a triangle while in sexually mature females the sides of the triangle become rounded.

In late summer, soon after mating, Chesapeake females begin a long migration to deeper waters at the mouth of the bay. Here they either commence spawning or overwinter and postpone spawning until the next spring. Spawning involves moving fertilized eggs to an external position beneath the female's extensible abdomen where they are brooded for a period of time. (Crabs taken in traps at this stage are used to make she-crab soup.) Females are able to store sperm and will only allow eggs to be fertilized upon reaching the spawning grounds, either that winter or the next spring. The number of broods of eggs that a female can produce in her lifetime is still a mystery to scientists, and it is believed that some of the sperm can be stored for an additional year and used for a second season of spawning.

As the eggs mature, they expand in size and the abdominal flap is pushed farther out from the body. Constant waving of the flap helps bring fresh aerated water to the eggs and carries away any waste. During late fall or early spring, the females on the spawning grounds release their fertilized eggs into the water. The eggs hatch into tiny waterborne **zoea larvae** that metamorphose within a few weeks into a bottom-dwelling **megalops.** This second stage resembles a miniature crab with an elongated posterior tail.

Eventually it molts into a juvenile crab that, if it has not already been carried up the estuary by tidal currents, must begin an arduous journey to the upper parts of the estuary where the water is warm and shallow, food is abundant, and large predators are scarce. Despite their small size, crabs are capable of impressive long-distance movement. Adult crabs marked by scientists in the upper Chesapeake Bay have been recovered 118 miles (190 km) away. Migrating females have been clocked at bottom speeds of 262 yards (240 m) per hour or more than two football-field lengths in an hour. At this rate it will take them thirty-four days to reach the spawning grounds, providing they don't end up in a crab trap.

Female Blue Crabs with extended abdomens bearing eggs   SCOTT SHUMWAY

Crab Molting

The arthropod **molting** process may be divided into several stages but in reality represents a continuous process. The need to molt is stimulated by the crab running out of room to grow within its existing external skeleton. Once this state has been reached, the crab will begin to resorb valuable calcium carbonate from its existing shell and begin forming a new cuticle (or shell) beneath the old one (premolt). Next the old shell will be shed (molt or ecdysis). This is not an easy task and leaves the crab completely defenseless against predators. In order to pop off the old shell, the crab will begin to fill the new one with water causing it to expand. Previously the new cuticle had been folded, allowing the crab to have a larger new skeleton stored within the smaller old one. After the old shell has been shed, the next task is to completely expand the new shell and harden it off with calcium carbonate (postmolt). Actual growth of muscle tissues and internal organs can now resume (intermolt).

Horseshoe Crabs

The **American Horseshoe Crab** (*Limulus polyphemus*) may be found from the sandy shores of estuaries where it lays its eggs to the continental shelf 100 miles (161 km) offshore. Horseshoe Crabs are more closely related to spiders than to true crabs. Dr. Carl Shuster Jr., for whom a Horseshoe Crab sanctuary has been named, began a 2003 seminal book on the biology of this species with a series of questions that include "What animal: Has ten eyes? Needs a book to breathe? Looks and moves like a tank? Has a tail that was used as a spear? Walked with the dinosaurs? Chews with its legs? Can fertilize corn? Has blue blood? Is called a living fossil?" The answer in each case is, of course, the American Horseshoe Crab. Three of its ten light receptors are readily apparent. The two compound eyes located where you would expect to find a pair of eyes on such an organism are each made up of 1,000 individual photoreceptors called ommatidia. They are the largest photoreceptors in the animal kingdom and research on them has revealed much about light sensing in our own eyes. Two centrally located eyes, the median ocelli, earned the Horseshoe Crab the Latin name *polyphemus* after the one-eyed Cyclops from Homer's *Odyssey*. The gills form a series of flaps resembling the pages of a book, hence the name book gills. The comparison to a tank may be unfair. True they move with stubborn determination, but the overall shape is more like the aerodynamic form of a Porsche 911 moving in reverse. Younger individuals or those that have recently

American Horseshoe Crabs (Limulus polyphemus) *mating*   SCOTT SHUMWAY

Underside of male Horseshoe Crab showing hooklike first legs used for grasping females during mating   SCOTT SHUMWAY

molted have smooth protective shells free of fouling organisms while the carapaces of older crabs are covered with algae, barnacles, bryozoans, and any combination of the thirty-eight known species of hitchhikers. Native Americans reportedly used the telson, or tail spine, as a spearhead.

Horseshoe Crabs crawl over the bottom on five pairs of walking legs, each of which is tipped with a pair of pincers (except for the first pair in males). An additional pair of smaller pincers is found anterior to the walking legs. None of these pincers has appreciable crushing power. Instead they are used to move food toward the mouth. The bases of each pair of legs are hardened and meet at the center. These gnathobases are used to grind food and, through a series of spikes, move it toward the mouth. Favored prey are worms and small bivalves, such as Gem, Soft-Shell, Baltic, and Razor Clams. Prey are generally passed into the mouth, shell and all. In the case of Blue Mussels and surf clams, the gnathobases are used to steadily chip the shell margins, and then the meat is removed by the pincers prior to ingestion.

Delaware Bay contains more Horseshoe Crabs than any other place on earth. Crabs arrive by the thousands on the Jersey and Delaware shores to mate and lay eggs every May. The scenario is repeated in many other locations, but in smaller numbers. Males and females crawl up the beach already locked together in mating position, looking like an ancient tandem trailer truck. The security of this position is made possible by modifications of the male's front legs. Whereas the female has weak pincers at the end of her front legs, males have a hooklike device that looks somewhat like a boxing glove or the hook on the end of a construction crane. He uses the hook to lock onto the back of a female and will hang on until egg laying is complete.

Females excavate a shallow nest in the sand prior to laying eggs. Presumably intertidal sand is chosen in order to escape the hungry predators lurking subtidally. Given the number of gulls and shorebirds that prey upon newly laid eggs (see the next section), the chances of surviving subtidally must be near zero. Eggs hatch a few weeks later and larvae are dispersed by the tides. After egg laying the adults retreat to deeper regions of the estuary and may travel extensively over the continental shelf.

Once Horseshoe Crabs reach adult size, they have few natural predators to fear. Only when molting or flipped upside down on a beach are they vulnerable to predators. There are two major exceptions to this. The first are Loggerhead Sea Turtles that enter the Chesapeake and other bays to feed on crabs from May to November. With fewer than 200 years' experience preying upon Horseshoe Crabs, human beings are proving to be the most formidable threat in the 300-million-year evolutionary history of the crab.

Soon after arriving in the New World, colonists began using Horseshoe Crabs as fertilizer and as food for hogs and poultry. By the mid-1800s a thriving fertilizer industry had grown up on the shores of Delaware Bay. From 1870 to 1920 an average of 1.5 million crabs were harvested each year to be ground up into fertilizer. Most were caught in weirs and pounds constructed along bayside beaches while others were simply picked up as they came ashore to lay eggs. Captured "king crabs," as they were called locally, were transferred to holding pens where up to 300,000 crabs would be left to dry. The resulting stench was ultimately declared a health nuisance, but not before millions of crabs gave their lives. Several factories ground up the crabs to produce a fertilizer known as cancerine (remember *cancer* means "crab"). The fertilizer industry was in decline by the 1930s and the last factory closed in 1966. The advent of modern chemical fertilizers, decreased catches, and the incompatibility of expanded housing development with pens of rotting Horseshoe Crabs brought an end to the industry. The crab population fortunately began to make a strong recovery. At some point, no one really knows for sure, the Horseshoe Crabs of Delaware Bay became an important part of the food chain for thousands of shorebirds on their annual northward migrations.

Shorebirds and Horseshoe Crabs in Delaware Bay

The shorebirds of the Americas engage in an annual migration that brings them from nesting grounds in Hudson Bay and other parts of North America to "wintering" grounds in Central and South America. While scientists are not completely sure of the reason for these ultra-long-distance migrations, it seems to be centered on the need for a huge number of birds to consume a huge amount of food in order to survive and to successfully bear young. Each spring the **Red Knot,** a plump shorebird with

Semipalmated Sandpipers make up 30–70 percent of the migratory shorebirds landing on the shores of Delaware Bay each spring.
DENNIS DONOHUE—WWW.THROUGH-MY-LENS.COM

Shorebirds at the Delaware Bay stopover site during spring migration   SCOTT SHUMWAY

Sanderlings on Delaware Bay   SCOTT SHUMWAY

a red breast like that of an American Robin, begins a marathon migration spanning 9,400 miles (15,127 km) from Patagonia at the southern tip of Argentina to the Canadian Arctic. It makes the journey with fewer stops than a modern jetliner would take and, like the jetliner, is dependent upon working runways with large supplies of fuel. For these birds, stored body fat is their version of jet fuel. Red Knots, as well as **Semipalmated Sandpipers, Ruddy Turnstones,** and **Sanderlings,** fly nonstop over the Atlantic Ocean from staging sites in Brazil and Suriname to the shores of Delaware Bay—a distance of nearly 7,000 miles (11,265 km). Their main target is about 50 miles (80 km) of Delaware and New Jersey shoreline. Once they land, they must feed. They have fewer than two weeks to put on enough fat to get them through the remaining 2,400 miles

Laughing Gulls and Red Knots on Reeds Beach, New Jersey   SCOTT SHUMWAY

(3,862 km). If they can't get enough food, then they won't be able to complete the journey. If they stay too long, then the best nest sites will already be occupied. They feed ravenously on eggs of Horseshoe Crabs. The arrival of the shorebirds coincides with the annual Horseshoe Crab mating and egg-laying orgy. It is as if there were only one McDonald's restaurant in the world and all the customers could eat were Egg McCrab. The sign out front would read OVER ONE MILLION SERVED EACH SPRING.

During May and June Horseshoe Crabs emerge en masse on protected shores to mate and lay eggs during high tide. The statistics are phenomenal. In the 1980s up to a quarter million crabs were counted on a single beach with each female capable of laying 80,000 eggs. Up to a million eggs may be buried below a square yard (.8 sq m) of sand. The top 2 inches (5 cm), where the bills of hungry shore-birds probe, may be more egg than sand. The modern-day Horseshoe Crab popu-lation of Delaware Bay has been estimated at one to four million crabs. The numbers of shorebirds landing in the bay are equally staggering. During the six-week migration period, up to 600,000 birds feed on the bay beaches while another 700,000 frequent nearby salt marshes. Semipalmated Sandpipers (30–70 percent), Ruddy Turnstones (20–35 percent), Red Knots (15–20 percent), and Sanderlings (4–6 percent) make up the majority of the migratory birds found feeding on the beaches. Each bird must double its body weight before departing. Resident Laugh-

Laughing Gulls, Red Knots, Sanderlings, and Ruddy Turnstones feeding on Delaware Bay.
SCOTT SHUMWAY

ing Gulls also join in the feast. The odds seem against the Horseshoe Crabs; but the birds do not eat all of the eggs, and the egg-laying period extends beyond the peak migration period.

Humans, however, are once again presenting a much larger threat to the survival of the crabs, and hence their avian predators. Horseshoe Crabs are of no interest to humans as a food source, but for decades fisherman have used them in limited numbers to bait eel and whelk traps. In recent years an insatiable demand for eel in Asia has resulted in rapid growth of the fishery. The previously limited harvest of Horseshoe Crabs for bait skyrocketed to a catch of 900,000 crabs in 1996—perhaps a third of the Delaware Bay crab population. Repeated shoreline censuses revealed a 90 percent decrease in Horseshoe Crab egg densities from 1990 to 1996. A dramatic drop in the numbers of migratory shorebirds was observed over this same time interval. Today the numbers continue to drop, Red Knots are rare, and part of the offshore waters of Delaware Bay are designated a Horseshoe Crab sanctuary where harvest is prohibited.

There are other threats to Delaware Bay, most of which are common to all large estuarine ecosystems. Delaware Bay is the leading entry port for oil on the East Coast with 12.25 billion gallons (46 million liters) of oil passing through on container ships in 1990 alone. An oil spill during critical mating and feeding weeks of May would be catastrophic. Industrial plants and agricultural lands along the northern shores have been a source of chemical pollution for years. PCBs and DDT are present and have entered the avian food chain with unknown long-term effects. Finally, flocks of humans gathering each spring to view the natural spectacle of birds and crabs may unintentionally harm the shorebirds. In order to lessen the impact, bird-watchers are now restricted to roped-off viewing areas during the migration season.

In 1986 Delaware Bay was declared part of the Western Hemisphere Shorebird Reserve Network, an organization devoted to the promotion of monitoring and conservation management of important migration stopover sites throughout the Americas. Other designated sites include the Bay of Fundy, Monomoy National Wildlife Refuge (Massachusetts), Great Marsh (Massachusetts), Forsythe NWR (New Jersey), and the barrier islands of Maryland and Virginia.

Recently Horseshoe Crabs have assumed a surprising role in modern medicine. Their blue-pigmented blood coagulates around gram-negative bacteria. These disease-causing bacteria may be deadly contaminants of vaccines. Extracts of Limulus amebocyte lysate (LAL) are used to screen vaccines and other pharmaceuticals for bacteria. LAL is obtained by collecting blood samples from live crabs that are subsequently released. Theoretically this is a sustainable practice that has much less of an impact on crab and bird populations than either grinding crabs up for fertilizer or using them as eel bait. Horseshoe Crabs are worth an astounding $260 million annually to the Delaware Bay economy with $222 million due to the LAL industry. Another $15 million is brought in by migrating bird-watchers who flock to the Jersey and Delaware shores to witness the crab-shorebird event.

Fish

Only a few of the fish found in estuaries are permanent residents. The rest are migrants either passing through on their way to or from freshwater, congregating for spawning, or seeking a place to develop as larvae or juveniles. While the total number of different species residing in estuaries is often low, the **abundance** and **biomass** of certain species is very large. In Narragansett Bay, ten fish species out of a total of ninety-nine account for 90 percent of all fish.

Estuaries and meandering salt-marsh creeks are valuable **nursery grounds** for juvenile fish. The abundance of nutrients, plankton, and benthic invertebrates provides a great resource for developing fish, some of which double in size each month that they spend in the estuary. The shallow depths of estuaries exclude large predators. Shallow creeks, salt-marsh grasses, Eelgrass beds, and oyster beds provide refuges where small fish can hide from their predators. Juvenile predatory fish, such a Striped Bass, Tautog, and Bluefish, in turn feed upon the young of other fish. The food chain in which marsh detritus and estuarine phytoplankton are consumed by juvenile fish that are either themselves consumed or mature and migrate out to sea provides an important transfer of energy from the estuarine ecosystem to larger offshore ecosystems.

Some fishes spend most of their lives at sea, but migrate up estuaries on their way to freshwater rivers and ponds to spawn. These **anadromous** fish include Alewife, shad, Striped Bass, Rainbow Smelt, and Atlantic Salmon. They reportedly migrate upstream to the same location where they hatched months or years earlier. **Alewife** *(Alosa pseudoharengus)* and **shad** *(Alosa spp.)* are members of the herring family known for their spring "runs" up estuaries and associated rivers. High densities of fish can be observed along their runs starting in May, at about the

Focus on the Chesapeake

Chesapeake Bay and its tributaries form the largest estuary in North America. It is also the largest source of commercially harvested Blue Crabs and a major source of Soft-Shell Clams and oysters. The Chesapeake originated 12,000 years ago when the Susquehanna River was flooded as glaciers melted and sea level rose. The result is a large partially enclosed main channel open to the sea at its southern end. The deep central portion reflects the original channel of the Susquehanna. The bay is fed by 19 freshwater rivers and at least 400 smaller creeks and streams. The large rivers each form their own subestuary, a smaller version of the larger system. The largest input comes from the Susquehanna River to the north and Potomac and James Rivers from the west. The western shore of the bay features the major rivers that have their origins in the Appalachian Mountains. The eastern shore, in comparison, features miles of flat marshland and meandering creeks. For such a large body of water, the Chesapeake is surprisingly shallow with an average depth of less than 30 feet (9 m). Extensive tidal flats and shallow subtidal regions provide excellent habitat for oysters, Soft-Shell Clams, and Eelgrass.

Because of its large size and the differences between the western and eastern shores, the Chesapeake contains a diversity of habitats. Sand beaches similar to those of the open coast, minus breaking waves, line a small portion of the bay. The bay contains extensive shallow subtidal habitat with a mud or sand bottom. Beds of Eelgrass and Widgeon Grass are found scattered throughout the bay. Much of the 4,600-mile (7,400-km) shoreline, particularly the eastern shore of Maryland, supports extensive salt- and freshwater marshes, as well as extensive intertidal mud and sand flats. Extensive oyster beds once lined the shallow waters of the bay. The center of the bay, particularly as it nears the mouth, is much deeper and is often deficient in oxygen, yet it still supports schooling fish such as Menhaden.

Historically, the Chesapeake Bay has been a highly productive ecosystem, fueled by phytoplankton, salt-marsh detritus, and Eelgrass beds. Then along came humans capable of devising ingenious ways of harvesting the seemingly inexhaustible supply of fish and shellfish. Initially the impact was minimal, but by 1900 this began to change as the human population increased. Fish, clams, oysters, and crabs that were once only available to the local inhabitants because of their propensity to spoil rapidly were suddenly in demand in restaurants and fish markets in Philadelphia and New York. Faster boats and the arrival of the railroad created a market for fresh seafood far from the point of origin. Crabs were harvested using improved traps and by dragging nets across the previously undisturbed bottom. Oysters were either "tonged" with long rakes or dredged using large metal devices towed behind a moving boat. Oyster-reef habitat began to disappear as well as the old shells that oyster larvae settle on. Today Soft-Shell Clams are "dug" by hydraulic harvesters that use a jet of water to remove the soft sediment surrounding the clams before scraping them up in a giant net. These practices are highly destructive to the food chain and the structural integrity of the ecosystem. Over the last fifty years, matters have become much worse as the human population has increased tremendously along the shores of the bay and its tributaries. With humans come effluent from sewage treatment plants. Agricultural runoff brings in fertilizers, pesticides, and livestock waste. These contaminants lead to eutrophication, toxic algal blooms, and outbreaks of pathogens. The result is an ecosystem that attracts thousands of tourists to its shores each year and is still beautiful to behold, yet is severely degraded relative to a hundred years ago. The stocks of crabs, clams, and oysters that seemed inexhaustible to the previous generation of shellfishermen are now threatened by these changes. The future of the Chesapeake ecosystem is dependent upon changes in fishing practices to achieve a sustainable yield over the long term. The once extensive oyster beds must be restored, as the ecosystem is dependent upon their water filtration services. Toxic inputs from agriculture, power generation, industry, and sewage must be reduced or eliminated. Development along the shore must be regulated so that important buffering of terrestrial and estuarine processes is not disturbed.

same time that a small tree comes into bloom. Not surprisingly, the tree growing near streams and sporting delicate white flowers for a few weeks each May is called the shadbush *(Amelanchier)*. Once the fish reach their destinations, they deposit eggs and then swim back to sea. Soon after hatching, the larvae migrate downstream into the estuary where they spend the next few months feeding and increasing in size. Sadly many historic runs have been altered or degraded to the point where fish are no longer able to swim upstream, spawn, or successfully support young.

Striped Bass *(Morone saxatilis)* spawn almost exclusively in the upper reaches of Chesapeake Bay. They later migrate up and down the East Coast, stopping in estuaries to forage. Their seasonal arrival in various estuaries and offshore locations supports a popular recreational fishery.

Another group of fish swims from freshwater to salt water in order to spawn in large oceanic gyres. This small group of **catadromous** fishes is composed of **freshwater eels.**

Winter Flounder *(Pleuronectes americanus)* are **estuarine spawners.** They spend most of their time on the mud and sand bottoms of nearshore waters where they are one of the most abundant species of fish. Between January and May they migrate into estuaries to spawn. Unlike other flounders that spawn at sea, Winter Flounder lay non-buoyant eggs that sink and stick to the bottom, thereby preventing them from being carried away by outgoing tides. The young spend their first two years in the estuary where they feed on benthic bivalves and worms, as well as plank-

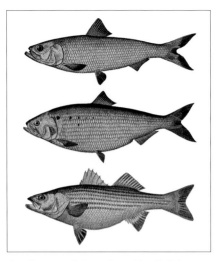

Anadromous fish, such as Alewife (Alosa pseudoharengus), Shad (Alosa spp.), and Striped Bass (Morone saxatilis), *pass through estuaries on their way to freshwater spawning grounds.*   NOAA PHOTO LIBRARY – NATIONAL MARINE FISHERIES HISTORIC IMAGE COLLECTION

Striped Bass support a popular recreational fishery.   SCOTT SHUMWAY

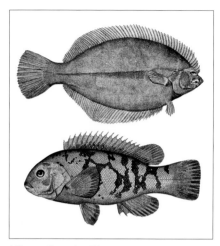

Winter Flounder (Pleuronectes americanus) and Tautog (Tautoga onitis) spawn in estuaries.   NOAA PHOTO LIBRARY—NATIONAL MARINE FISHERIES HISTORIC IMAGE COLLECTION

tonic amphipods and copepods. As flounder approach adulthood, the extended siphons of clams become one of their favorite foods. They can live up to twelve years, during which time they make repeated annual spawning migrations to nearby estuaries. The main predators of Winter Flounder are Ospreys and humans.

Tautog (*Tautoga onitis*) also live just offshore and utilize estuaries as spawning and nursery grounds. Tautog is a predator on molluscs, crustaceans, and worms as well as being a highly valued sport fish.

Most fish species **spawn offshore** while their larvae and juveniles migrate into estuaries. Carefully controlled vertical migration in the water column enables larval fish to exploit tidal currents to carry them up the mouths of estuaries. Metamorphosis into swimming juveniles takes place soon after they enter an estuary. Menhaden, mullets, Scup (Porgy), and most other species of flounder are common marine spawning fish that spend their juvenile stages in estuaries.

Economically, **Menhaden** (*Brevoortia tyrannus*) are perhaps the most valuable estuarine finfish. Overfishing and large fluctuations in population size have plagued this species, which was at one time the most important finfish in the United States. Rather than being consumed directly by humans, this oil-rich fish is ground up and used in domestic animal feed.

Bluefish (*Pomatomus saltatrix*) are voracious predators that spawn offshore. The juveniles migrate into estuaries to take advantage of the large numbers of small fish prey. The presence of predators like Bluefish and Striped Bass is often revealed by schools of smaller fish, such as Menhaden, liter-

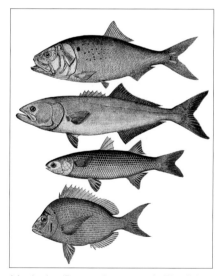

Menhaden (Brevoortia tyrannus), *Bluefish* (Pomatomus saltatrix), *Striped Mullet* (Mugil cephalus), *and Scup* (Stenotomus chrysops) *spawn offshore, but their young utilize estuaries as nursery grounds (fish are not to scale).* NOAA PHOTO LIBRARY –NATIONAL MARINE FISHERIES HISTORIC IMAGE COLLECTION

View from the reported throne of Wampanoag Indian Chief Metacomet overlooking Mount Hope Bay, Rhode Island   SCOTT SHUMWAY

ally erupting from the surface in an attempt to avoid being eaten.

A small number of fish species are **permanent residents** that spawn, spend their childhood, and live their adult lives within the confines of an estuary. Most of these are closely associated with salt marshes and the creeks that run from marsh to surrounding estuary. They include the **sticklebacks, killifish, Mummichogs, and silversides** that are found in great abundance in marsh creeks.

Salt Marshes

The grasses and other flowering plants that live in salt marshes appear to be no different than typical terrestrial species, except that they grow with their roots in waterlogged saline soils and are regularly submerged and uncovered by tides. Salt marshes are transitional areas between the marine and terrestrial realms. Lush green expanses of salt marsh grasslands line the protected shores of estuaries and the back sides of barrier beaches from Newfoundland to Florida and along the Gulf Coast.

Only a handful of salt-tolerant plant species are able to grow in salt marshes, but this low diversity belies the ecological importance of these communities. They are the lifeblood of the larger estuarine ecosystem. The grasses, in particular Salt Marsh Cordgrass, are responsible for salt marshes being one of the most productive of all ecosystems.

John and Mildred Teal summed up the secret of the importance of salt marshes in the title of their classic book *Life and Death of the Salt Marsh,* for it is through death that the marsh plants support almost all life in the marsh and estuarine ecosystems. From March to September the marsh plants grow in size, flower, and set seed. When autumn arrives, the plants begin to turn brown and death sets in. However, the underground portion of the plants remains alive, and energy stored in underground rhizomes enables them to be reborn each spring.

Meanwhile, the dead stems fall to the ground or are sheared off by rising tides or winter ice rafting. Some will accumulate on the marsh as piles of dead plant parts known as wrack, while the rest will be swept out into surrounding creeks and bays. The subsequent process of decay is the essential step in releasing the energy and nutrients stored in the marsh grasses, enabling them to be passed up the food chain.

Salt marshes form wherever the shoreline is protected from wave action. Marshes are generally small north of Cape Cod where shorelines are rocky and the fine sediments needed to build up a marsh are in short supply. Farther south, ample sediments are available, and marshes are extensive.

The grasses themselves promote marsh expansion by slowing the movement of water over them, resulting in deposition of sediment. The roots and rhizomes of the grasses infiltrate newly deposited sediment, contributing to seaward spread of the marsh. The marsh also expands landward as sea level rises, something it has been doing since the end of the Pleistocene glaciations.

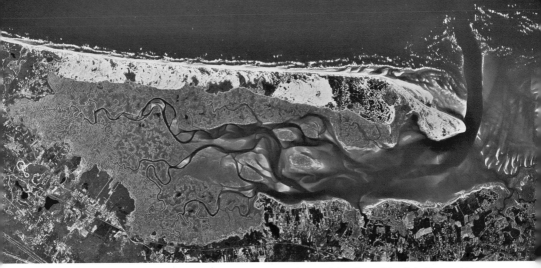

Aerial view of the Sandy Neck barrier beach, tidal inlet, and the Great Marsh in Barnstable, Massachusetts. The following two pictures were taken in this salt marsh. Note the meandering creeks and straight as an arrow mosquito ditches throughout the salt marsh. USGS

As the roots and rhizomes of the marsh plants die and slowly decompose, they form an organic soil known as peat. Salt marsh peat provides very firm footing, but creeks and unvegetated pools called "pannes" may have soft mud in which you can sink up to your thigh. Avoid these last two areas unless you are prepared to deal with the unpleasant consequences! (See the photograph of the author and one of his students!)

The Salt Marsh Food Chain

Through the process of **photosynthesis,** the marsh grasses remove carbon dioxide from the air and, by harnessing the sun's energy, split water molecules and bind carbon molecules together to form sugars. (Sugars are also known as carbohydrates—a word that in itself tells you that the main ingredients are carbon and water). The marsh grasses either use these carbohydrates to build the plant body or store them for use as future energy to drive the metabolic needs of the plant. When these sugars are broken down, energy is released and used to generate ATP, the ultimate energy molecule used to drive almost all biochemical reactions on earth. Plants, including salt marsh grasses, and other photosynthesizers (cyanobacteria and algae) are able to make their own energy-rich carbohydrates and are known as autotrophs (literally "self-feeders") or **primary producers.**

In most food chains the energy captured by primary producers is transferred to herbivores that feed directly on the producers. The energy transfer continues as the herbivores are consumed by carnivores. In the process the energy originally harvested from the sun is passed up the food chain bit by bit or bite by bite.

In salt marsh food chains, the situation is different. In salt marshes, plants are densely packed and primary production is very high, yet very few animals feed directly on the grasses. Instead, passing energy up the food chain depends on the action of **decomposers,** bacteria and fungi, which break down the dead vegetation.

Zooplankton, snails, and tiny crustaceans consume the bacteria and fungi. These animals may in turn be consumed by small fish, which may be consumed by larger fish. The tides also flush out dissolved and particulate organic matter released by the decomposers, passing this material onto phytoplankton and filter feeders (mostly molluscs and worms) inhabiting the surrounding estuary and tidal flats.

Microbes of Marsh Sediments

Bacteria in the sediments play an essential role in the decomposition of dead marsh grasses and the cycling of nutrients. As microbial decomposers break down dead plant roots, they deplete the oxygen supply in the soil. Anoxic (oxygen-depleted) mud and peat are deficient in oxygen needed for cellular respiration and accumulate toxic hydrogen sulfide that then inhibits nutrient uptake by living plant roots.

Bacteria are often lumped together based on their biochemical or metabolic processes, rather than being referred to by species names. Many salt marsh bacteria transform various sulfur compounds during their metabolism. **Sulfate reducers** cannot be seen, but

Creek and Salt Marsh Cordgrass in the Great Marsh (Barnstable, Massachusetts)
SCOTT SHUMWAY

The author and one of his college students stuck in a marsh creek
BATHRAM KRISHNAMOORTHY

anyone who visits a marsh can certainly experience the rotten-eggs smell of the hydrogen sulfide that these bacteria generate as part of breaking down marsh grasses. **Photosynthetic sulfur bacteria** utilize hydrogen sulfide during photosynthesis. Large numbers on the surface of the marsh or in pannes are red or pink in color and visible to the naked eye. Another group known as **sulfur oxidizers** store sulfur granules in their bodies and form oozing white masses along creek banks.

Marsh grasses die in place each fall. With time the leaves become leaky, and soluble chemical compounds leach out into the water. Eventually gravity, flood tides, or winter ice movement sheer off the dead stems, and a complex process of decay feeds microbes and releases nutrients back to the marsh.

The dead stems are quickly colonized by bacteria and fungi that begin to break them down. At the same time **detritivores** (snails and amphipods) consume the decaying plant material and the associated microbes. It is, after all, the microbes that are really being sought out by the "detritivores," who simply grind up the detritus into smaller pieces and then defecate it back to the environment for recolonization and further breakdown by more microbes.

More than half of a marsh grass plant lies belowground. The roots and rhizomes eventually die of old age and decompose in the same location where they grew. Decomposition belowground is carried out by sulfate-reducing bacteria. Sulfate is one of the most abundant ions in seawater and marsh sediments. These anaerobic bacteria reduce sulfate and generate hydrogen sulfide as a waste product as part of the biochemical reactions that enable them to break down the organic molecules that make up dead plant parts.

Thanks to the slow release by decomposition and the constant influx from tides, most nutrients required for plant growth are plentiful in salt marshes. However, they are not necessarily accessible by marsh plants. Low availability of oxygen in the soil and toxic effects of hydrogen sulfide inhibit the uptake of nutrients. As a result plant growth can be nitrogen limited, despite a seemingly sufficient supply in the soil.

Salt Marsh Plants, Adaptations, and Patterns

Soils that are saline and deficient in oxygen present the greatest obstacle to plant survival in a salt marsh. The soil conditions undoubtedly explain why so few species are found growing here. Highly specialized adaptations make it possible for certain plants to survive in the marsh.

Marsh grasses are often called salt-loving plants, or **halophytes,** yet they are really salt-tolerant plants. Too much salt is toxic to plant cells, and salt in the soil makes it difficult for roots to take up sufficient quantities of water. Some marsh grasses can discriminate against salt at the roots, preventing it from entering the plant in the first place.

Most marsh grasses also have specialized salt glands that remove excess salt from their sap and excrete it as crystals on the outside of the leaves. These crystals can be seen or felt upon the outside of the grass blades. Excreting salt, however, requires energy that could otherwise be used for growth. For this reason most marsh plants, even though tolerant of saline conditions, grow better under reduced salinities. However, they are prevented from growing in the nonsaline areas surrounding marshes by superior competitors. It is also important to remember that these plants have limits to just how much salinity they can handle and that there are differences among plant species within the marsh.

The rhizomes and stems of marsh grasses contain many hollow air spaces that form a specialized tissue called **aerenchyma.** These spaces provide a conduit for oxygen to diffuse from the atmosphere down to the roots and rhizomes, enabling them to grow and take up nutrients in the otherwise anoxic soil.

The different species of salt marsh plants inhabit distinct zones within the marsh. These zones can be seen clearly as differences in coloration, plant height, and leaf width. Each zone forms a band running parallel to the tide line and reflects increasing elevation from the marsh edge to the terrestrial border of the marsh.

Salt Marsh Cordgrass (Spartina alterniflora)
SCOTT SHUMWAY

This change in elevation is subtle and may not be readily apparent to the casual observer. Low elevation areas are more deeply flooded while the highest elevations may not be covered by any but the highest monthly tides. Because these elevation changes are slight, a total of a few centimeters, the movement of the tide over the marsh is rapid and can be observed over a matter of minutes. These small elevation differences have severe consequences for plant growth and play an important role in setting the plant distribution patterns within a marsh.

Salt Marsh Cordgrass *(Spartina alterniflora)* grows at the lowest elevations along marsh creeks and the seaward edges of marshes. All marsh grasses grow as a series of upright shoots (ramets) connected by a horizontal rhizome that spreads underground. Cordgrass shoots can reach 6 feet (2 m) in height in a single growing season. Most of the wrack or plant litter seen in a marsh is made up of dead cordgrass stems.

Marsh Hay (Spartina patens)   SCOTT SHUMWAY

Cordgrass has large amounts of aerenchyma that enable it to survive in the most heavily waterlogged and anoxic part of the marsh. Cordgrass near creek banks often reaches the same height as a full-grown human. A few feet away, soil conditions may prevent it from ever growing more than a few inches in height.

Salt Marsh Hay or **Salt Meadow Grass** *(Spartina patens)* occupies the next higher vegetation zone. Marsh Hay rarely exceeds 2 feet (61 cm) in height and has

Black Rush (Juncus gerardi) *in flower*
SCOTT SHUMWAY

Blue-green blades of Spike Grass (Distichlis spicata) and succulent stems of Glasswort (Salicornia europea). SCOTT SHUMWAY

thin stems. The bright color of Marsh Hay during the summer sets the standard for "grass green." Because the stems are thin with little ability to support themselves, they often lean against their neighbors for support, giving the species a distinctive cowlick appearance. Spacing of shoots along the rhizome is extremely compact, resulting in a turflike morphology and formation of dense peat.

Marsh Hay was once harvested for animal fodder. In colonial times grazing livestock were simply let loose upon coastal marshes. Today you can still purchase Marsh Hay for use as garden mulch.

Black Rush (*Juncus gerardi*) occupies a zone immediately above the Marsh Hay. The taller **Needle Rush** (*Juncus roemarianus*) becomes common south of Maryland. Grasses and rushes are superficially similar, but upon close inspection it is easy to distinguish these two plant families. Flowers in both families are wind pollinated and possess elaborate feathery stigmas designed to capture tiny pollen grains floating in the wind. Rush flowers resemble miniature lilies and have all the same parts as a lily flower. Grass flowers, however, are more complicated, consisting of a series of paperlike coverings that partially enclose the sexual parts of the flower. Each rush flower matures into a capsule that releases numerous tiny seeds, whereas a single grass flower can only produce a single seed.

Spike Grass (*Distichlis spicata*) grows scattered throughout the Marsh Hay and Black Rush zones. Stepping on a new shoot in bare feet provides an unforgettable understanding of its common name. Under normal circumstances it does not form its own zone because it is forced to hide out as a fugitive due to its weak competitive ability. However, should something happen to kill off its neighbors, Spike Grass rises to the occasion. For example, high tides can dump large piles of wrack onto the marsh. If it does not decay fast enough, the wrack pile kills the underlying vegetation creating a **bare patch.** Because Spike Grass consists of widely spaced shoots on a rapidly spreading rhizome, it can capitalize on such disturbances and become the first species to colonize a bare patch.

Bare patch   SCOTT SHUMWAY

These bare patches become hypersaline as high tides leave behind a thin film of salt water that evaporates in the hot summer sun, causing salt to accumulate on the surface. Despite being salt-tolerant plants, marsh species have limits to how much salt they can put up with, and bare patches often exceed this limit. Spike Grass is the most salt-tolerant marsh grass and can often be identified by the presence of a fine coating of salt crystals along its blue-green leaf blades.

So not only can it grow quickly into disturbed areas, but Spike Grass can use its superior salt tolerance to thrive in hypersaline patches where other plants cannot grow. During the process of recolonizing disturbed areas, known as **ecological succession,** Spike Grass is the first species to arrive. Over time, however, the plants shade the surface of the patch and soil salinities drop. Only then can the less-tolerant Marsh Hay or Black Rush begin to spread into these areas. This process by which an early colonizer prepares the way for another species to invade an area is known as facilitation. Marsh Hay and Black Rush do not show any appreciation for the facilitative effects of Spike Grass colonization and quickly outcompete it, relegating it to fugitive status once again. In some areas that are frequently disturbed by wrack deposition, Spike Grass may persist for many years as a monoculture. In other cases its rise to glory and subsequent replacement may only take fewer than three years.

Marsh Elder *(Iva frutescens)* is a woody shrub that grows nearest the terrestrial upland. A member of the aster family, this shrub grows about 6 feet (1.8 m) tall and often appears sickly with many dead branches. As you might predict, it is even less tolerant of anoxia and waterlogging than any of the other marsh plants. Another shrub in the aster family, **Groundsel Tree** *(Baccharis halimifolia)* may also be found in this location and can be distinguished in late summer when its feathery white flowers are visible.

Marsh Elder (Iva frutescens) *and Song Sparrow*   GARRY KESSLER

Marsh Heather (Limonium nashii)
SCOTT SHUMWAY

Marsh Elder, Groundsel Tree, Seaside Goldenrod, and perhaps other plants of the high marsh may be covered with a bright orange spaghetti-like mass. This mass is **dodder** *(Cuscuta),* a parasitic plant distinguished by its creeping orange stems, lack of leaves, small white flowers, and habit of mooching off other plants. Only the seedlings are green and photosynthetic. In order to survive, dodder must quickly contact another plant and anchor into its vascular tissues. It then has no need for its own chlorophyll and meets all of its energy needs by drawing carbohydrates from the host plant.

There are about a dozen other marsh species that are sparsely scattered throughout the marsh and can thrive in bare patches where competition is reduced. A few, such as **Glasswort** *(Salicornia europea)* and **Orach** or Goosefoot *(Atriplex patula),* are annuals and must grow from seed each year. The annual Glasswort and its perennial relative *S. virginica* are even more salt tolerant than Spike Grass. They grow as green succulent stems that are often densely packed in bare patches. The seeds of Glasswort have hairlike barbs, not unlike Velcro hooks, which latch onto wrack for a free ride to the next bare patch.

Other species are perennials that rely upon bare patches for their initial establishment from seed and then stubbornly persist for many years. Included in this group are the plants whose flowers add muted color to the swards of green grass. **Marsh Heather** (*Limonium nashii* and *L. carolinianum*), **Seaside Goldenrod** (*Solidago*

Common Reed (Phragmites australis) *growing at the edge of a salt marsh*   SCOTT SHUMWAY

sempervirens), **Salt Marsh Aster** *(Aster tenuifolia),* **Seaside Gerardia** *(Gerardia maritima),* **Salt Marsh Fleabane** *(Pluchea purpurascens),* and **Sea Oxeye** *(Borrichia frutescens)* produce showy flowers that light up the marsh in later summer with shades of lavender, yellow, and white. **Narrow-leaved Cattail** *(Typha angustifolia)* grows at the edges of marshes where freshwater seeps across the surface from adjacent upland.

Last but not least of the marsh grasses is **Common Reed Grass** *(Phragmites australis),* or simply "Phrag" to scientists working to control its monopolization of marshes. The robust 6–13-foot-high (1.8–4m) stems and inch-wide (2.5-cm) blue-green leaf blades are a stark contrast to the other marsh grasses. Large, feathery, purplish flower spikes top off the stems. The success of this plant, like other marsh grasses, lies in its spreading rhizome. Establishment of new plants from seed is rare and can only take place on disturbed ground where potential competition with neighbors has been eliminated. However, once a plant becomes established, it has enormous potential to use its rhizomes to spread and dominate brackish marshes.

Phragmites has the dubious distinction of being a highly invasive native alien! It is both a native species and an alien invader, or what is known as a **cryptic invader.** Fossil evidence reveals that *Phragmites* has occupied New England marshes for at least 4,000 years. Throughout most of that time, however, it has been a minor player. Only over the past hundred years has it become one of the most abundant species in coastal and freshwater wetlands.

By using the tools of molecular biology to trace the ancestral history of present-day and hundred-year-old dried museum specimens of *Phragmites,* scientists have been able to document two genetically distinct varieties. One is native to North America. The other is native to Europe and Asia and is believed to have arrived in North America during the nineteenth century.

The earliest reports of large-scale spread of *Phragmites* were associated with shipping ports where ballast, in the form of rock, soil, and stowaway *Phragmites* rhizomes or seeds, was dumped onshore. Today the native variety is extremely rare while the European variety is everywhere. Apparently the European variety is highly invasive while the native one is not.

Human alterations of salt marsh ecosystems have enhanced the success of this invasive plant. Shoreline development has created the disturbed ground that *Phragmites* seeds need for germination. *Phragmites* does poorly under normal conditions where seawater regularly floods the marsh. Alteration of natural tidal flows with tide gates, dikes, and roadways has provided the brackish conditions under which *Phragmites* readily spreads. Destruction of upland vegetation has removed the filter that intercepts fertilizer and other nutrient-rich runoff before it enters a marsh. As marshes become enriched with nutrients, a final limitation on *Phragmites'* growth is removed, and it spreads rapidly.

How does *Phragmites* outcompete existing plants in marshes? The native plants are simply unable to grow in the shade cast by the much larger *Phragmites.* Most, if not all, East Coast marshes contain some *Phragmites,* and many have been completely taken over.

Much effort and expense has been devoted to controlling the spread of Phrag and to restoring marshes to preinvasion conditions. The most effective control is to restore natural tidal flow and the high salinities that favor native species. Mowing, burning, herbiciding, replanting native species, and sometimes all four together have also been tried but with only moderate success.

Marsh Plant Zonation

Marsh plants exhibit a clearly recognizable zonation pattern, with Salt Marsh Cordgrass, Marsh Hay, Black Rush (or Needle Rush), and Marsh Elder each forming a discrete zone that reflects a change in elevation from the seaward to the terrestrial edge of the marsh. With this change in elevation comes a change in soil conditions caused by the frequency of flooding by high tides.

The **low marsh,** occupied by cordgrass, is flooded twice a day by high tides. The soils here are the most saline, most waterlogged, and most anoxic of all the areas in a marsh. **Tall Cordgrass** lives immediately next to marsh creeks while Stunted, or **Short-Form Cordgrass,** lives slightly above. Depending on geographic location and marsh slope, the cordgrass zone may be a few feet deep or run for hundreds of yards.

The Plant That Ate the Wetlands

Somtimes called "the plant that ate the wetlands" **Purple Loosestrife** *(Lythrum salicaria),* an alien species imported from Europe in the nineteenth century, is a perennial known for its showy red-purple flowers. Its shoots originate from a persistent rootstock that sends up an increasing number of new shoots each year. Purple Loosestrife is only found at the landward edges of salt marshes, where seepage of freshwater from the surrounding upland changes the soil conditions from salty to brackish or freshwater wetland. This is the same habitat where several rare plant species struggle to survive.

The secret of Purple Loosestrife's success is its ability to produce phenomenal numbers of tiny seeds that can either germinate immediately or remain dormant in the soil for years. A single stem can produce up to 1,000 flowers, each of which matures into a seed capsule. Each capsule produces approximately 100 seeds, and each plant typically consists of 20 to 50 stems. An average plant can easily produce more than 2.5 million seeds in a single season, which are dispersed by water or on the feet of waterfowl. Once seedlings sprout, their growth rates can approach .4 inches (1 cm) per day. The high density of the plants, rapid growth, huge seed production, and 6-foot (2 m) height combine to make Purple Loosestrife a formidable competitor as it takes over wetlands.

Purple Loosestrife (Lythrum salicaria)
SCOTT SHUMWAY

Once numerous plants become established, Purple Loosestrife is impossible to control using any known methods, including cutting, burning, and herbicides.

Marsh Hay grows in the next higher zone followed by **Black Rush** above that. **Marsh Elder** shrubs, and sometimes **Groundsel,** grow at the upper reaches of the marsh. The frequency of tidal flooding decreases with increases in elevation. This area is known as the **high marsh** and may only be flooded for a few days every month. The soils here are less saline and better oxygenated.

The borders between zones are distinct, with little overlap of plant species. These borders are set by the differing abilities of the plant species to tolerate the stressful soil conditions at lower elevations as well as by their differing competitive abilities. Higher elevations represent prime real estate for the plants, but only the superior competitor will be able to inhabit this more desirable or less-stressful area. The lowest elevation that any of the major marsh plants can inhabit is determined by tidal flooding, and the highest elevation where the plant can be found is determined by the next best competitor.

Animals of the Marsh

Most of the marsh animals depend directly or indirectly upon detritus as a food source. Amphipods and snails graze upon detritus. Other snails feed on microscopic algae that cover the marsh surface. Fiddler crabs ingest mud in order to extract the abundant detritus while mussels are filter feeders that extract detritus from the water column. These species are all fair game for predatory crabs, fish, and birds.

Crabs

The creek banks and surface of the low marsh are pockmarked with holes about an inch (2.5 cm) in diameter. These holes are the burrows of **fiddler crabs,** which can be present in densities of up to one hundred per square yard (120 per sq m). Three species occur within our range, the **Mud Fiddler** *(Uca pugnax)*, **Sand Fiddler** *(U. pugilator)*, and **Red-Jointed Fiddler** *(U. minax)*. The Latin names *pugnax, pugilator,* and *minax* translate into the "fighter," "boxer," and "threatener," providing a good introduction to the most noteworthy behaviors of the males. Observing these crabs can be a challenge, as the slightest shadow will send hundreds of them scurrying for the protection of their burrows.

Fiddler crabs earn their living as deposit feeders, scooping sediment into their mouths. While appearing to eat dirt, they are really consuming diatoms and other organic matter found in the mud. They reach out with their small claws, pinch the sediment, and shovel tiny amounts into their mouths, often running frantically from feeding stop to feeding stop. They also glean diatoms from the surface of cordgrass stems.

The name Fiddler refers to the large claw of the males. This oversized claw evolved not from its survival benefit, as do most traits, but through its ability to attract females. Physical or behavioral traits that appear to function solely in obtaining mates and leaving offspring are said to be the results of **sexual selection** (as opposed to natural selection). Often times sexually selected traits appear to be absurd when viewed outside of the context of mate acquisition and may otherwise be a liability. Such is the case with the large claw of male fiddlers.

Males either move the claw in a side-to-side sawing motion or wave it up and down in an effort to attract the attention of a female and to lure her into the privacy of his burrow. Once a female enters his burrow, the male quickly seals the opening with mud and presumably mates with her (only they know for sure!). Sealing the burrow openings prevents water from entering at high tide but more importantly blocks access by rival males.

The other function of the large claw is to do battle with other males also intent on attracting the attention of interested females. Much of the battle involves ritualized fighting in which the loser retreats before any physical harm occurs. In other cases the loser may be dismembered. It is not uncommon for fiddler crabs to sacrifice a claw to avoid further damage by a rival suitor or to escape from a predator. If you capture a male fiddler crab and he manages to pinch you, chances are that you will be left with only a claw attached to your hand. The escaped crab will slowly regenerate the lost limb.

Fiddler crabs forage for food at low tide and are highly vulnerable to predators, especially shorebirds, herons, egrets, and crows. It is advantageous for them to eat quickly and return to the protection of a burrow as soon as possible. Females have

Mud Fiddler Crabs (Uca pugnax) *foraging in a salt marsh*   SCOTT SHUMWAY

two small claws that they use to shovel sediment into their mouths. Males on the other hand are burdened with a giant claw that is useless for feeding and are forced to use only one claw to feed, leaving them exposed for twice as long as females. Males are therefore more likely to encounter a predator than females. The severity of this liability is debatable, as lab-based feeding experiments have demonstrated that White Ibis, a species of wading bird, actively avoids feeding on males. When the large claw was removed before the start of the experiment, birds preyed upon males and females with equal frequency, so perhaps the claw has a survival benefit after all.

Red-Jointed Fiddler Crab (Uca Minax) *male showing small feeding claw and large display claw*   SCOTT SHUMWAY

While nowhere near as numerous as the fiddlers, Mud, Marsh, Green, and Blue Crabs are also found in salt marsh creeks. Blue Crabs will even follow rising tides to search for food, especially snails, on the surface of the marsh.

Amphipod Crustaceans

Legions of **amphipods** *(Gammarus, Orchestia, Ulorchestia),* crustaceans commonly referred to as "scud," crawl and hop over the marsh surface. They are barely an inch (2.5 cm) in length and resemble a shrimp with a curved back that has been flattened from side to side. Amphipods feed upon detritus on the marsh surface as well as on fungi coating the stems of grasses.

Ribbed Mussels

Creek banks are home to large numbers of **Ribbed Mussels** *(Geukenisa demissa).* The dark ribbed shells of these 4-inch-long (10-cm) bivalves are anchored to marsh peat by beardlike byssal threads. Breaking one open reveals bright yellow tissues that are revolting enough to erase the urge to ask if these mussels are considered suitable for human consumption.

Ribbed Mussels (Geukensia demissa) *growing in a marsh creek bank*   SCOTT SHUMWAY

Ribbed Mussels are filter feeders that consume phytoplankton. They are prodigious filterers. In some cases they are reported to be able to filter the equivalent of all of the tidal water transported into a marsh each day!

They also generate an equally impressive amount of nitrogen-rich feces. This nitrogen provides fertilizer for cordgrass and is one reason why plants growing along creeks grow so tall. The mussels in turn use cordgrass roots as attachment points for their byssal threads. The masses of mussels and anchoring threads play an important role in holding the edges of the marsh together and in preventing the marsh grasses from eroding away due to daily water movement, storms, and winter ice scour.

Fiddler crabs are also engaged in a mutually beneficial relationship with the cordgrass. The network of fine grass roots acts like tiny reinforcement rods that prevent the soft mud from collapsing around the fiddler crab burrows. The burrows serve as conduits for oxygen and help aerate the soils, resulting in increased cordgrass growth.

Snails

Creek banks are littered with **Mud Snails** *(Nassarius obsoleta)* and **Common and Marsh Periwinkles** *(Littorina littorea* and *L. irrorata)*. The **Marsh Periwinkle** is found south of Maryland where it grazes algae and fungi from the stems of cordgrass. The Marsh Periwinkle plays a surprisingly important role in regulating the productivity of marsh grasses. As it grazes, the feeding radula of the periwinkle leaves behind scars on the grass stems. These wounds are subsequently colonized by fungi that provide additional food for the snails. As snail densities increase, so does the scarring inflicted upon the grass stems and leaves. The grasses become susceptible to infection and may die. It has become increasingly common for

Common Periwinkles (Littorina littorea) *feeding on roots and rhizomes of Salt Marsh Cordgrass*   SCOTT SHUMWAY

the grazing by snails to reduce a productive stand of cordgrass to a barren mudflat.

Historically the population size of Marsh Periwinkles was controlled through predation by Blue Crabs, Diamondback Terrapins, and fish. Human activities have significantly reduced all of these predators. Overharvest of Blue Crabs over the past fifty years is thought to be the major reason for the high densities of periwinkles currently plaguing Mid-Atlantic marshes. Ecologists now refer to this type of

Coffee Bean Snails   SCOTT SHUMWAY

interaction as a "trophic cascade" in which high-level predators are indirectly responsible for regulating populations several rungs down the food chain. The removal of such "top-down" control is having a devastating effect on some southern marshes. These revelations are also forcing scientists to rethink classic views that salt marsh ecosystems are under "bottom-up" control in which grass productivity is regulated by soil oxygenation, salinity, and nutrient availability rather than by herbivory.

Coffee Bean or Salt Marsh Snails *(Melampus bidentatus)* graze algae and detritus from the marsh surface and from the bases of grasses. At high tide these small brown snails climb up grass stems to avoid being inundated. It may seem odd for a snail to crawl out of the water, but this is an air-breathing or pulmonate snail, unlike most snails that breath underwater using gills. Coffee Bean Snails are a favored snack for migrant **Black Ducks** *(Anas rubripes)*.

Insects

Insects, both herbivores and bloodsuckers, are the most common animals in the salt marsh. The most common insect species can be divided into those that feed on plants and those that feed on mammals. **Bright Green Grasshoppers** *(Conocephalus spartinae)* appear when the grasses flower and proceed to chew on flowers and developing seeds. The grasshoppers consume enough pollen to effectively lower the amount of seeds the grasses can set, no mean feat given the ability of wind-pollinated grasses to produce an overabundance of pollen. **Plant Hoppers** *(Prokelisia marginata)* use piercing mouthparts to tap into plant stems and suck the sap out of them.

The lack of insect diversity is more than compensated for by the abundance of some of the world's most annoying insects that feed on mammals such as humans. Salt marshes are notorious for their swarms of biting insects whose females seek out humans and other unfortunate mammals for a blood meal. The protein gained from feeding on blood provides a female with essential nourishment for her developing eggs. Mosquitoes, gnats, and horseflies all use the marsh as a place to lay eggs and as a nursery ground for their larvae. **Salt Marsh Mosquitoes** *(Aedes sollicitans)* lay their eggs in the high marsh. The eggs wait until a flood tide to hatch, resulting in the sudden arrival of swarms of hungry bloodsuckers.

Biting midges *(Culicoides)* are commonly called **"no-see-ums"** because their bites are felt before the specklike insects are seen. At less than a 0.0625 inch (1.5

Insect Control

Most efforts to control biting flies are targeted at mosquitoes because of their ability to transmit disease to humans. Larvicides are applied to marsh pools while aerosol insecticides are sprayed at night. There are no good controls for the other species of biting flies. The mud surfaces where their larvae live are simply too extensive for control to be effective. Flying adults may be killed by sprays, but they are soon replaced by newly metamorphosed individuals. Blue box traps baited with pheromones and deployed in salt marshes are somewhat successful at reducing Greenhead populations.

Recognizing the importance of standing water for the life cycles of mosquitoes, humans have constructed miles of ditches in an attempt to drain marshes of standing water and eliminate larval habitat. It is difficult to find a salt marsh anywhere in the eastern United States that does not have a series of straight ditches running through it. It is important not to confuse these straight-as-an-arrow structures with the naturally occurring meandering and never-straight creeks. We now realize that at high tide the tiny fish inhabiting marsh creeks enter pannes where they are ravenous consumers of mosquito larvae. This knowledge calls into question the wisdom of constructing ditches in marshes, particularly in the low marsh where mosquitoes do not lay eggs due to the threat of predation. Regardless of their effectiveness the ditches constructed during the early half of the twentieth century are likely to persist for the remainder of the following century.

mm) in length, no-see-ums can travel straight through standard sixteen-mesh window screening! A single bite can easily be ignored, but on a windless day scores of hungry females attack marsh visitors, driving them back inside or to the brink of insanity.

Known as **Greenheads** (*Tabanus conterminus*) after their large bright green eyes, salt marsh horseflies inflict painful bites. Their sharp mouthparts easily slice open human skin and quickly inject an anticoagulant that causes fresh blood to flow. **Deerflies** (*Chrysops*) are brown and slightly smaller than Greenheads, but no less annoying. Insect repellants don't seem to be much of a deterrent to either of these flies. Horsefly and midge larvae develop in the moist marsh mud. The larvae of **Biting Houseflies** develop within piles of decaying seaweed. While most of these biting flies originate from salt marshes, the flying adults readily travel to nearby sand dunes, beaches, and backyards where they terrorize helpless humans.

Fish

Salt marsh creeks are inhabited by thousands of minnow-sized fish, the most numerous of which are **Atlantic Silversides** *(Menidia menidia)* and **Mummichogs** *(Fundulus heteroclitus)*, followed by other species of killifish *(Fundulus* species), sticklebacks *(Gasterosteus, Pungitius, Apeltes),* and Sheepshead Minnow *(Cyprinodon variegatus).* These fish consume plankton, some detritus, and soft-bodied invertebrates, including insect larvae. By living in marsh creeks, they avoid exposure to larger predators, which are unable to navigate the shallows of the marsh. High tides connect isolated pannes to nearby creeks. Mummichogs travel in and out of pannes at this time to take advantage of the refuge from predators. Eels sometimes find their way into creeks and pannes where they prey on the smaller Mummichogs.

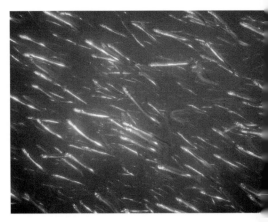

Atlantic Silversides (Menidia menidia)
R. WAHLE

Mummichog (Fundulus heteroclitus)
SCOTT SHUMWAY

Turtles

Diamondback Terrapins *(Malaclemys terrapin)* are turtles that inhabit salt marsh creeks from Cape Cod to the Gulf of Mexico. Adults spend their time in the low-marsh and marsh creeks where they feed upon periwinkles, Coffee Bean Snails, crabs, fish, and worms. With luck you might spot a turtle head at the surface of the water just before it ducks back under, or you might spot terrapins sunning themselves on creek banks at low tide.

Terrapin females are considerably larger than males (9 vs. 5.5 inches long [23 vs. 14 cm]). A mated female will ride in on a daytime high tide, crawl out of the marsh and over a sand dune where she will dig a nest hole and lay four to eighteen eggs before making the exhausting trip back to the marsh. If you look carefully in June and July, you might find terrapin tracks in the sand dunes or a female search-ing for a good nest site. The tracks look like those of a miniature tricycle with two rows of tracks left by the feet (look for claw marks) and a center track created by the tail as it drags in the sand. The tracks may go on for considerable distance before turning around, either because the eggs have been laid in a nest or because the turtle was frightened by a potential predator. Never uncover turtle eggs, as predators may later follow your scent to the nest; and never disturb a female, as she will abandon her nesting attempt.

The eggs hatch from August to October. During the incubation period the temperature in the nest determines the sex of the young. Below 79° F (26° C) all babies are male, above 86° F (30° C) they are female, and between these temperatures the sex ratio varies. Once the young hatch, they must crawl out of the nest, over the dunes, and into the salt marsh. The whereabouts and activities of juvenile Diamondback Terrapins remain a mystery.

Diamondback Terrapins (Malaclemys terrapin) *live in salt-marsh creeks and leave the marsh only to dig nests and lay eggs in nearby sand dunes.*   SCOTT SHUMWAY

Most predation on terrapins occurs at the egg, hatchling, or juvenile stage. Red Fox and raccoons excavate nests at night and consume most of the eggs that they find. Gulls and crows then finish off any eggs that remain exposed. Gulls will even watch over a nesting female and then swoop down to steal a few eggs while she is still in the process of laying her clutch. In a bizarre twist of fate, the roots of American Beachgrass sometimes infiltrate a nest and take up nutrients from the eggs! Raccoons sometimes prey upon nesting females. Otherwise the greatest threat to survival of adults comes from humans.

The species was nearly wiped out during the 1920s when turtle meat was valued for making soup. Since then populations south of New York were thought to be recovering, but they now face new threats, including crab traps. Traffic fatalities are common because roadways often cross terrapin migration routes. Please remember to yield for turtles!

Birds

A mix of bird species nest in the marsh, feed there all summer long, or only visit during migration. Nesting birds include loud conspicuous species like **Boat-Tailed Grackle** and **Red-Winged Blackbird** as well as secretive species like **Clapper Rail, Willet, Marsh Wren, Saltmarsh Sharp-Tailed Sparrow,** and **Seaside Sparrow. Rails** are chickenlike in size and shape, but rarely show

Saltmarsh Sharp-Tailed Sparrow (Ammodramus cauducutus) *is a shy secretive sparrow that seems determined to challenge birdwatchers with its habit of disappearing almost as soon as it is spotted.*
DENNIS DONOHUE— WWW.THROUGH-MY-LENS.COM

Willet (Catoptrophorus semipalmatus)
DENNIS DONOHUE—WWW.THROUGH-MY-LENS.COM

Black Skimmer
DENNIS DONOHUE—WWW.THROUGH-MY-LENS.COM

themselves. When spotted, they can swiftly disappear into the grasses. **Willets** give off loud warning calls when you approach too closely and can be identified by the white "W" pattern revealed on their wings when they take flight. **Sparrows** perch on the tops of cordgrass only momentarily and seem to fly away the instant they are noticed.

Herons and **egrets** stand patiently at the edges of creeks or wade into flooded pools in search of fish, while **terns** drop out of the air and dive into the water to seize prey.

For a few weeks every spring and fall, hordes of migrating shorebirds descend upon salt marshes and tidal flats to load up on food to fuel the next stage of their journey (see "Estuaries" chapter). A few bird species are worth mentioning in greater detail.

The most unusual foraging tactic is employed by **Black Skimmers** *(Rynchops niger)*. They fly the length of creeks with mouth open and lower mandible skimming through the surface of the water. It is not uncommon to see several skimmers foraging close together in a balletlike scene reminiscent of Disney's *Fantasia.*

During the winter flocks of **Snow Geese** *(Chen caerulescens)* descend upon marshes and feed heavily on cordgrass rhizomes. Snow Geese are one of the few species to feed directly on the tissues of living marsh grass and can take a heavy toll on the plants. Because of the extreme inefficiency of the goose digestive system and their tendency to defecate four times per minute, much of what they consume is quickly returned to the ecosystem chewed up but with little having actually been digested.

One of the most thrilling sights is that of an **Osprey** *(Pandion haliaetus)* plunging feet first into the water and then flying away with a fish in its talons. Ospreys are large birds of prey (5–6-foot [1.5–1.8-m] wingspan), easily recognized by their dark brown back and upper wings that are offset by being mostly white underneath and on the head. A distinguishing dark band runs through the eyes down to the back of the neck. Females have a faint brown necklace adorning their breast. Viewed in flight, the wings have a characteristic bend at the wrist accompanied by a dark wrist patch on the otherwise mostly white undersurface. Ospreys breed throughout coastal regions of the eastern United States, as well as across Canada, part of the west coast of the United States, and some inland locations.

Osprey chicks   ANDREW K. HOWARD

They are the only raptors with a diet that relies almost exclusively on fish. A male supporting a mate and family of three chicks needs to spend about 195 minutes each day hunting for fish. Ospreys forage by flying over the water with their white head focused on the water below. They pause and hover briefly before swooping down feet first into the water. If successful, the Osprey then flies with a fish clutched in its talons to a nearby perch where it consumes its prey. Remarkably, the birds can take off from the water with a heavy load that is then oriented headfirst to reduce drag during flight. Foot-long (30-cm) Winter Flounder, herring, Menhaden, smelt, and Pollock are the most frequently taken prey.

East Coast birds migrate to Central and South America for the winter. They return in March and quickly set about mating, preparing nests, and incubating eggs. The male engages in an impressive mating display or sky dance that involves fluttering around a female while carrying a fish in his talons and emitting a loud mating scream. Eventually the female may accept the fish as a gift and become a faithful partner for at least the rest of the season.

Osprey nests are big messy affairs composed mostly of sticks. Unlike most other birds Ospreys reuse nests year after year, with the same birds often returning to the same site. Because they commonly live ten to twelve years, and up to twenty years, there is ample opportunity to reuse nests. A well-constructed nest represents a huge investment in time and energy; so rather than starting from scratch each year, Ospreys simply make improvements to existing nests. Another real advantage to this strategy is that the birds can get around to laying eggs much sooner if they don't have to spend time building a new nest. Typically the males bring sticks and other building materials that the female then arranges in the nest. As home improvement progresses and egg laying begins, layers of seaweed are added to soften the nest as well as various plastic items and other flotsam. Over time a nest may become as large as 13 feet (4 m) deep and 6.5 feet (2 m) in diameter.

The ideal nest site is raised off the ground and surrounded by water. The water provides an effective barrier against marauding raccoons and other predators. Ospreys are fairly tolerant of humans and seem to get used to having automobiles,

Osprey Conservation Lessons

Because they feed at the top of the food chain, Ospreys are likely to be exposed to high concentrations of dangerous chemicals. In the 1960s this exposure almost brought about their extinction.

Beginning in the 1940s, **DDT** became the pesticide of choice for most farmers. It has a low toxicity to humans and does a great job of killing insect pests. It also persists in the environment for a long time, often ending up in aquatic habitats where it enters the local food chain. Tiny phytoplankton simply absorb DDT from the water. Zooplankton consume the phytoplankton and are then eaten by small fish that get eaten by larger fish that may ultimately become Osprey food. Because DDT and its persistent breakdown product DDE are stored in oily and fatty tissues but not excreted, they get passed along from one level of the food chain to the next. While the amounts present in the tissues of the phytoplankton are miniscule, the zooplankton consume large quantities of phytoplankton and accumulate larger amounts of DDE. At each higher level of the food chain, the concentration of DDE becomes higher by at least an order of magnitude. By the time it reaches the top predators, such as Ospreys and eagles, the concentrations are up to ten million times higher than the amount in the water and are biologically significant.

The insidious thing about **bioaccumulation** of DDE is that it interferes with calcium deposition in bird eggs. As a result birds lay eggs with shells too thin to sustain the weight of an incubating parent. The impact on Osprey populations is best illustrated from studies conducted on eastern Long Island where the number of nests plummeted from 500 in 1940 to 74 in 1970. Osprey populations throughout the East Coast experienced a 90 percent reduction during this time, almost entirely due to DDT exposure. Bald Eagles, Peregrine Falcons, and other raptors also experienced drastic declines. Largely due to data collected on these birds, the use of DDT was banned in the United States in 1972. Populations of these birds have since increased.

Osprey recovery has been accelerated by the willingness of the birds to use artificial nest substrates. Dead trees at the perimeters of waterways, on islands, or in beaver ponds are the natural locations for Osprey nest construction. Coastal development and trapping of beavers has decreased the abundance of these structures. Osprey will readily build nests on high platforms placed in salt marshes. These platforms have been so successful that mating populations have increased dramatically. In some areas, over 90 percent of the Osprey nests are located on artificial sites. Thanks to these nest platforms it is relatively easy to locate and observe Ospreys and their young.

boats, and fisherman nearby. However, it is not advisable to approach a nest too closely. The parents use high-pitched alarm calls to announce that an intruder has been spotted. In extreme cases dive-bombing and grazing with sharp talons may ensue. In any case a bird screaming at you to go away is diverting valuable time and energy from raising its precious young. Once the young hatch, the parents, primarily the male, bring fish to the nest for the mother bird to tear apart with her hooked bill and distribute to the babies.

Mammals

Only a few mammals venture into marshes from the surrounding uplands. The most common are two species of rodent. The **Meadow Vole** *(Microtus pennsylvanicus)* cuts marsh stems to feed on their tender bases while the **White-Footed Mouse** *(Peromyscus leucopus)* feeds on seeds. Voles are the more frequent visitors of the two and leave behind foraging trails or tunnels beneath the grass canopy. Their presence, in turn, attracts raptors such as Northern Harriers.

Winter

Winter brings a new set of stresses to northern marshes. Water in creek banks may freeze, entombing Ribbed Mussels, grass roots, and entire sections of bank in the frozen ice. When creeks flood during high tides, large blocks of ice float upward, bringing with them chunks of peat, roots and rhizomes, and mussels. The power of this ice rafting should not be underestimated. Sections of creek bank the size of a small car can be torn away and deposited into the creek. Blocks of marsh peat

Marsh in early spring showing dead remains of plants from previous year   SCOTT SHUMWAY

Life and Death of Salt Marshes—Is Death Gaining the Upper Hand?

A recent review of the current health of salt marshes signals an ominous warning that "danger lies ahead for all salt marshes." Salt marshes are important suppliers of energy and nutrients into estuaries. They are buffers between the sea and land, nurseries for commercially important fish and shellfish, and areas of great aesthetic value. Yet, for most of the past three centuries, marshes have been viewed as areas to be exploited and altered.

What is the story of human impact on salt marshes? Marsh Hay was harvested; and the water flow through marshes, altered to increase Marsh Hay habitat. Marshes were ditched to drain off water, promoting the growth of Marsh Hay while inhibiting the success of mosquitoes. Marshes were viewed as potential land that could be reclaimed by filling. The Back Bay of Boston as well as Logan Airport in Boston and Kennedy Airport in New York are all reclaimed salt marshes. The marshes were dredged to provide better navigation channels for commercial ships, and the dredge spoils were used to fill other marsh areas.

Development of virtually all uplands adjacent to marshes increased the flow of nitrogen-rich runoff and removed the potential for the marshes' landward expansion as sea level rises. As nutrients have become more abundant and freshwater runoff has increased, highly aggressive *Phragmites* has invaded. As sea levels continue to rise due to climate change, cordgrass expands its range to higher elevations at the same time that *Phragmites* spreads from the landward edge of the marsh. The high marsh zones previously dominated by Marsh Hay and Black Rush are being squeezed into an ever-shrinking habitat.

3–6 feet (1–2 m) on a side can be transported onto the high marsh. They can be seen in the summer when square mounds of cordgrass with dead mussels embedded in the sides are found sitting on top of the Marsh Hay zone. Winter is also the time when wrack is most abundant and transported in large piles to parts of the marsh.

Tidal Flats

As the tide recedes from estuaries and salt marshes, expanses of tidal flat are uncovered. Common names for these areas reflect the type of substrate or the reason people visit such places: So tidal flats may be referred as mudflats, sand flats, clam flats, or even oyster flats. Worm, diatom, and snail flats would be equally appropriate, but not likely to catch on. Mudflats are messy places. The fine-grained mud is only loosely held in place at the surface. Human visitors slip and sink as they walk across the flats. Rubber boots are recommended footwear and will come back with a tenacious stinky coating. The wonderful aroma of the exposed flats is an olfactory clue to the importance of sulfur compounds for the bacteria that thrive in the oxygen-deficient mud. What initially look like barren expanses of mud are, upon closer inspection and with the use of a shovel, three-dimensional habitats that provide a home for crawling snails and burrowing worms, clams, and crustaceans. Even closer study with a microscope reveals a hidden world of single-celled algae, animals not much bigger than a sand grain, and millions of bacteria. One of the biggest attractions of tidal flats is the opportunity to hunt for edible clams, either with bare feet or metal rakes. Bird-watchers are also attracted to these areas as some of the largest and most beautiful birds in North America come here to search for food. A bonus comes during spring and late-summer migration when shorebirds arrive by the thousands.

Tidal flats are important ecologically as links between salt marshes and adjacent estuarine ecosystems. Tidal flats are home to clams and bait worms that form the basis of some of our most valuable coastal fisheries. They are part of the estuarine nursery ground for valuable finfish, including Menhaden and flounder. Disruption of tidal-flat ecology has widespread and devastating impacts on natural communities as well as coastal economies. These areas are highly threatened by human activities, such as dredging, filling, pollution, and overharvesting.

Intertidal mud and sand flats form in sheltered areas where wave energy is low and currents are slow. Low tides leave flats exposed to the air. Downeast Maine has the most extreme tidal range and the most extensive tidal flats on the East Coast.

Some tidal flats are covered with coarse sand while others are made up of very fine particles and are rich in organic material. Most will be somewhere in between depending on waves, currents, and locally available sediment and detritus. Only in slow-moving water do fine particles have the opportunity to settle to the bottom. This is why wave-swept beaches are covered by coarse sand and pebbles while the

Sandy tidal flats in Brewster, Massachusetts   SCOTT SHUMWAY

back sides of barrier beaches, protected embayments, the shores of estuaries, and salt marsh creeks are covered in fine sand or mud.

In the Gulf of Maine where the overall landscape is rocky, the primary source of tidal flat sediments is mud transported by rivers, whereas Mid-Atlantic flats are fortified with an abundance of sand left behind by melting glaciers. Within an estuary there is a gradient in sediment composition. Farther inland where rivers transport sediments that have run off of the land, tidal flats are composed of mud, whereas at the mouth of an estuary, strong tidal currents result in sandier sediments.

Water movement, sediment grain size, temperature, and exposure time determine what species can inhabit tidal flats, and of those species, whether they reside on sandy or muddy substrates. Tidal flat sediments exhibit drastic changes in oxygenation with depth. On mudflats with fine-grained particles, well-oxygenated sediments extend only a fraction of an inch below the surface. As you dig down into the mud, a sharp transition to oxygen-deficient, or anoxic, sediments is evident as a color shift from brown to black that is accompanied by the unmistakable rotten eggs smell of hydrogen sulfide. The black color signifies the presence of iron sulfides formed by bacteria that thrive in the anoxic mud. A different group of bacteria may form iron pyrite in deeper sediments and impart a gray coloration. On sand flats the oxygenated layer extends much deeper because the larger grain size permits the percolation of aerated water. Despite the poorly oxygenated sediments, tidal flats are occupied by numerous bivalves and worms, each with its own connection to the surface.

The Tidal Flat Food Chain

Millions of single-celled algae, such as diatoms, ooze their way over the surface of tidal flats. While they are invisible to us without the aid of a microscope, their photosynthetic activity (primary production) provides a rich food source that helps fuel the food chain. This high productivity is further supplemented by the breakdown of dead grasses (detritus) that have washed off of adjacent salt marshes. As the mostly invisible pieces of detritus are broken down by microbes, they become an essential food source for deposit- and filter-feeding invertebrates. Over time the dead grasses are broken down into smaller and smaller pieces, each of which is covered by microbes. While these decomposers render the marsh grasses palatable to a wide range of invertebrates, they also serve as an important food source for these animals. Most detritus feeders are actually consuming the bacteria and fungi covering bits of detritus.

Bottom-Dwelling Animal Life

Often the only clues to the existence of the many different life-forms buried in tidal flat sediments are mysterious holes, volcano-like mounds, spaghetti-like piles of fecal matter, tubes that barely project above the surface, and squirting jets of water. Most tidal flat animals spend their lives buried in the sediment (infauna) while a few, primarily snails and crabs, crawl about on the surface (epifauna). Many microscopic animals (meiofauna), such as harpacticoid copepods, seed shrimp (ostracods), and roundworms (nematodes), live between, and are not much larger than, the grains of the sediment. The exact assemblage of species varies geographically (with latitude) and with substrate type (mud vs. sand).

Burrowing, or infaunal, species are represented by polychaete worms, bivalve molluscs, and amphipod crustaceans. Most are either **deposit feeders** that ingest sediment or **suspension feeders** that filter food particles out of the water column.

Suspension feeding bivalves draw in water rich in phytoplankton and dissolved organic material through one siphon and shoot filtered water and wastes out through another. A suspension-feeding clam living in fine sediment would be at great risk of having its intake siphon clogged. Therefore such filter feeders are more abundant in coarser grained sediments.

Fine-grained muddy sediment favors deposit feeders. These areas are rich in organic particles, which are really tiny pieces of partially decomposed dead bodies, mostly those of salt marsh grasses. These organic particles are very small and weigh very little. They are easily suspended in the water column and only deposited in areas of very little water movement. Mud rich in organic particles represents a bonanza for deposit-feeding worms and other invertebrates that ingest sediment, digest the organic material, and defecate the rest. Deposit feeders constantly rework the surface sediments and leave behind a landscape littered with elongated strings and tiny volcano-like mounds of fecal material that will be smoothed out by the rising tide.

Worms and Wormlike Creatures

Tiny **mud worms,** also called spionids, are often the most numerous species on mudflats. They are very skinny and rarely more than 1–3 inches (2.5–7.6 cm) in length. They live in soft mud burrows at the surface and are distinguished by two long tentacles that they use to glean food particles from the sediment surface.

Other deposit feeders like the **Ice Cream Cone Worm** (*Pectinaria gouldii*) ingest food in a conveyer-belt style, taking in sediment with their head oriented downward and depositing waste materials at the surface. It lives in a cone-shaped tube created by cementing sand grains together. The wider head end is oriented down into the sediment while the narrow end barely pokes out of the mud. It excavates sediment using shiny golden combs that look more like pieces of jewelry than mud shovels.

Another group of conveyer-belt feeders commonly known as **Bamboo Worms** (*Clymenella torquata*) live in tubes resembling a cluster of drinking straws poking out of the mud.

Terebellid Worms (*Amphitrite johnstoni*) live in mud tubes. They have numerous spaghetti-like sticky tentacles on the head that when waved over the sediment trap food particles.

Worm casts on tidal flat   SCOTT SHUMWAY

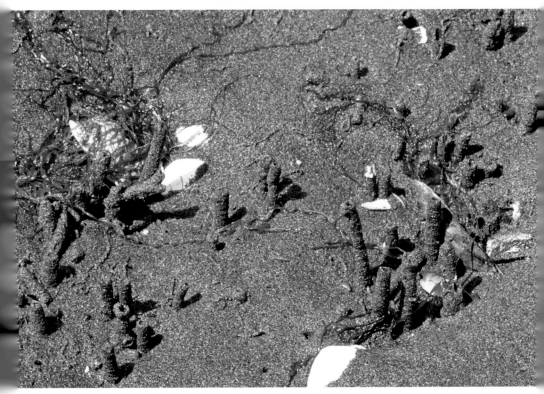

Tubes created by Bamboo Worms (Clymenella)   SCOTT SHUMWAY

The **Plumed Worm** *(Diopatra cuprea)* is a deceptive sedentary predator that lives in parchmentlike tubes about the diameter of an index finger and up to a foot (30 cm) long. The vertical tubes protrude above the surface and are camouflaged with brownish clumps of sand, grass blades, seaweed, and shells. The various decorations disguise the fact that this is the home of a predator that waits patiently for prey items to come within reach. It is possible to excavate an entire tube by digging deeply with a shovel. If you are lucky you will see the head of the worm cowering in the tube.

The most commonly encountered **mobile worms** are the **bloodworms** *(Glycera)* and **clam worms** or **sandworms** *(Nereis),* both of which are harvested commercially for use as fishing bait. These mobile predators have many paddle-shaped parapodia for crawling and formidable jaws that they use to capture soft-bodied prey, including other worms. Bloodworms are easily wounded, hence the name.

Other wormlike creatures lack segmentation and belong to several different phyla. **Roundworms,** or nematodes, are numerous, but rarely observed due to their microscopic sizes. Ribbonlike **nemertean worms** move through mud in search of prey. **Sipunculid worms** lack segments and are classified in their own phylum. There are even burrowing **sea cucumbers** that have wormlike bodies. Their volcano-like waste piles are often the only signs of their presence.

Clam Worm (Nereis) *showing well-developed pairs of parapodia typical of a crawling polychaete and Blood Worm* (Glycera)   GARRY KESSLER AND SCOTT SHUMWAY

Worms

Most segmented worms found in the marine environment are polychaetes, and the best place to find them is on tidal flats. Their elongated bodies consist of many independently controlled segments. The two anterior-most segments contain the mouth, eyes, and sensory structures. The exterior of the remaining segments is often identical with each segment supporting a pair of paddlelike appendages called parapodia. The name polychaete comes from the Greek words meaning "many hairs" and refers to the small bristles along each parapodium. The many different species of worms differ in the ways that their parapodia have been modified.

Polychaete worms are either mobile or sedentary. Mobile species crawl over the surface or burrow tunnels in the sediment using their paddlelike parapodia to propel them. What looks like mad writhing on the part of the worm, is actually a highly coordinated movement of oarlike parapodia and body wall muscles that move the worm from side to side. The lowly worm is really exceptionally coordinated. Burrowing worms can contract different sets of muscles to cause individual segments to either swell up, making

Polychaete worms from a Maine mudflat

them short and fat, or to extend, making segments long and narrow. The result is that some segments act like anchors to hold the worm in place while other segments push their way into the mud and move the worm forward.

Sedentary worms spend all or most of their lives anchored in one location. Some inhabit burrows and can reburrow should they become dislodged, while others reside in permanent tubes of their own making. Sedentary worms have highly reduced parapodia as they are not needed for locomotion. Instead their parapodia are often designed to circulate water through borrows or tubes.

Plumed Worm (Diopatra) *tube exhumed from sediment*   SCOTT SHUMWAY

Clams

Whereas most clams are suspension feeders, **Macoma Clams** *(Macoma baltica)* are deposit feeders. Macoma have incurrent and excurrent siphons that are separate from one another, unlike most clams where they are fused. These small clams (1.5-inch [3.8-cm]) wave their incurrent siphon over mud surfaces where it sucks up food particles like a vacuum cleaner wand. Undigested particles are shot out of the excurrent siphon.

No bigger than a quarter of an inch, Amethyst Gem Clams often carpet the surface of sandy tidal flats.   SCOTT SHUMWAY

Suspension feeders are primarily bivalve molluscs that make their living filtering algae and organic particles from the water column. The most abundant of these is the tiny 0.125 inch (3 mm) **Amethyst Gem Clam** *(Gemma gemma).* The common name refers to blue or purplish regions on the shell. Up to 240,000 gem clams can be found close to the surface on a square yard of sand flat.

Soft-Shell Clams *(Mya arenaria)* burrow deep in sand flats and extend a long siphon to feed. Their presence is often revealed when they periodically squirt jets of water out of their excurrent siphon. The shells are oval shaped and chalky white. The hinge of the left valve has a spoon-shaped projection (chondrophore), which is accommodated by a pit in the opposite valve. They can grow to be 14 inches (36 cm) in length. The edges of the valves do not meet completely as the siphon is too large to be completely withdrawn, hence the common name "Long Neck." These are the Steamer Clams that we love to dip in melted butter and slurp by the dozens. If left alone, they can live up to ten or twelve years, but current harvesting practices limit them to a two-year lifespan in many areas. The specific name *arenaria* means "sand dweller."

Soft-Shell Clam (Mya arenaria)   GARRY KESSLER

The other commercially important tidal-flat clam is the Hard-Shell Clam or **Quahog** *(Mercenaria mercenaria)*. The name preferred by New Englanders is Quahog and is correctly pronounced "KO-hog." They are found primarily on sand flats south of Cape Cod.

Quahogs grow to 4 inches (10 cm) in length, although larger specimens may be found in areas closed to shellfishing. The dark gray outer surface belies the inner beauty of its shells. Native Americans used the thick shells with their shiny white and purple insides to fashion wampum. Native

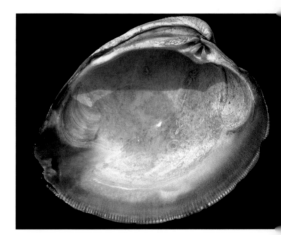

Inner suface of a Quahog (Mercenaria mercenaria) *shell showing purple*   SCOTT SHUMWAY

Americans and succeeding generations of North Americans have valued Quahogs for food.

Common names and uses vary with overall size. The smallest at less than 1.5 inches (3.8 cm) in length are called Littlenecks; up to 2 inches (5 cm), they are known as Cherrystones; and over 3 inches (7.5 cm), Chowder Clams. Smaller clams are more tender than larger ones, explaining why you will never see chowder-sized clams served up at a raw bar. It is also why Littlenecks are priced higher at the market.

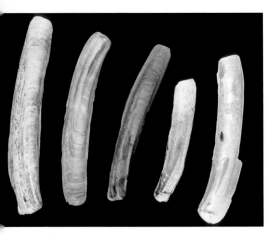

Razor Clam (Ensis directus) *shells*
SCOTT SHUMWAY

The champion burrower on sand flats is the **Razor Clam** or Jacknife Clam *(Ensis directus)*. Up to 10 inches (25 cm) in length and rarely 1 inch (2.5 cm) wide, the shells of this elongated clam resemble an old-fashioned straightedge razor. Their locations are revealed at low tide by a characteristic oval depression. Take care digging them up as they are quite fragile and surprisingly long. If repositioned foot down in the sand, they will quickly bury themselves with a jerking motion. Razor Clams are reported to be every bit as tasty as Soft-Shells.

Mobile Surface Dwellers

The mobile surface dwellers are made up of snails and arthropods. Thousands of Mud Snails and periwinkles litter tidal flats at low tide. The homely looking **Mud Snail** *(Nassarius obsoletus)* grazes on the film of microbes and diatoms coating the surface of tidal flats. It will also quickly scavenge any recent inputs of detritus or carrion. Because of their ability to detect concentrated patches of food, Mud Snails are often found in dense clusters.

The **Common Periwinkle** *(Littorina littorea)* and **Rough Periwinkle** *(Littorina saxatilis)* also graze here. The Common Periwinkle is an introduced species that

Hard-Substrate Oases in a Soft-Bottom Habitat

Mussel beds sometimes form on New England tidal flats resulting in a dense accumulation of **Blue Mussels** *(Mytilus edulis),* a species more characteristic of rocky shores. Rocks or shells nucleate the settlement of mussels, which in turn serve as an attachment site for more mussels. The mussels secrete anchoring byssal threads that bind them to one another and any available shells or stones. Over time a large area of tidal flat may become covered by mussel bed. Worms, molluscs, crustaceans, barnacles, and other species more commonly associated with hard surfaces make their homes within the mussel bed. South of New England beds of oysters form islands of hard substrate within otherwise soft-bottom habitat.

over the course of its 165-year residence in North America has had a negative impact on Mud Snails by displacing them from the best feeding locations and by consuming their egg masses. Mud Snails actively avoid periwinkles and will delay egg laying in their presence.

Hydrobia totteni is one of the most plentiful residents of tidal flats. However, at only 0.125 inch (2–4 mm) in length, it is easily overlooked. This snail also grazes on microalgae. It in turn gets displaced by the much larger Mud Snails (these two species are sometimes referred to as the American and Eastern Mud Snails).

Moon snails are predators that use their large muscular foot to plow through sediments in search of buried bivalves. The foot is so large that it partially obscures the shell when it is extended. Soft-Shell Clams are their preferred food source. Once a buried clam has been located, the snail will use its radula in combination with acid secretions to bore a small hole through the shell (boring details are described in "Rocky Shores" chapter). This is followed by secretion of enzymes that digest the clam in its own shell. The semidigested clam meat is then slurped up by the snail. Clamshells bearing a circular hole with a beveled edge were victims of moon snails.

The **Lobed Moon Snail** *(Polinices duplicatus)* prefers sand flats and is

Mud Snails (Nassarius obsoletus) *are the most abundant snails on many tidal flats.*
SCOTT SHUMWAY

Northern Moon Snail (Lunatia heros) *showing off its large foot as it plows through the sediment in search of a bivalve to drill for dinner.*
GARRY KESSLER

more common south of Cape Cod while the **Northern Moon Snail** *(Lunatia heros)* is common north of Long Island with a preference for subtidal habitats. The Northern Moon Snail reaches a larger size (4 vs. 3 inches [10 vs. 7.5 cm]) and has an open space, called an umbilicus, beneath the whorls of its shell. The Lobed Moon Snail is often called Sharkeye because of a shiny brown covering that obscures the opening.

Predatory crabs forage on flooded tidal flats during high tides, only to retreat as the tide recedes. Depending on the species, these predators are capable of using their claws to crush mollusc shells, capture soft prey, nip at extended siphons, and excavate buried bivalves. **Green** *(Carcinus maenas)* and **Blue** *(Callinectes sapidus)* **Crabs** prey heavily on molluscs and worms. Green Crabs dig through the upper layers of sediment in search of Soft-Shell Clams *(Mya arenaria),* Razor Clams *(Ensis directus),* and small Hard-Shell Clams *(Mercenaria mercenaria).* In New England they have been implicated as a contributing factor to the crash in the Soft-Shell Clam industry, which went from a 14.7 million pound harvest in 1938 to a 2.3 million pound harvest in 1959 and has continued to decline over the past thirty years.

Lady Crab (Ovalipes ocellatus)
SANDRA E. SHUMWAY

Horseshoe Crabs *(Limulus polyphemus)* also forage for bivalves and polychaetes, leaving excavation pits several inches deep. **Hermit crabs** *(Pagurus),* **Lady Crabs** *(Ovalipes ocellatus),* and **spider crabs** *(Libinia)* forage here, as do deposit-feeding fiddler crabs.

Sand Shrimp (Crangon septemspinosus)
GARRY KESSLER

Grass *(Palaemonetes pugio)* and **Sand Shrimp** *(Crangon septemspinosus)* may be found over tidal flats at high tide. They are small (up to 2.5 inches [6 cm]) and well camouflaged. Grass Shrimp are translucent and nearly invisible in the water, while Sand Shrimp are various shades of brown that exquisitely match a sandy or muddy background. They are, in turn, important prey for several fish species.

Fish

Numerous **fish** forage over the flats at high tide. As the water is quite shallow, these predators are mostly small or flat. Many are juveniles that migrate into estuaries from the open ocean or whose parents migrate to estuaries to spawn. Shallow, food-rich waters lacking large predators provide an ideal nursery ground. The flooded tidal flats at the fringes of these estuaries provide areas where these small fish can feed without worrying about competing with, or becoming a meal for, larger fish. The pulses of large numbers of juvenile fish feeding on tidal flats can cause localized crashes in the population sizes of many invertebrate species.

The collection of fish in estuaries and tidal flats varies seasonally with the life cycles and migration patterns of each species. **Winter Flounder** *(Pleuronectes americanus)* and **skates** *(Raja)* prey heavily on bottom-dwelling invertebrates. Their flat bodies are ideally suited for swimming in shallow water. Skates excavate prey by undulating their flattened triangular bodies in order to loosen up the substrate and expose buried clams, crustaceans, and worms. The resulting burrow pits are sometimes visible at low tide.

Summer migrants such as **Summer Flounder** *(Paralichthys dentatus),* **Black Sea Bass** *(Centropristis striata),* and **Kingfish** *(Menticirrhus saxatilis)* move northward as water temperatures rise. **Sand Lance** *(Ammodytes americanus)* are found on shallow sand flats only during the summer. They have the disconcerting ability to burrow into sand and disappear almost instantaneously.

Mummichogs *(Fundulus heteroclitus)* are finger-sized fish that are year-round residents of marsh creeks and tidal flats. They burrow into mud and enter a state of torpor for the winter. They emerge in early spring to start feeding on everything from algae to molluscs before the part-time residents arrive. These tough fish can also survive in the warm, oxygen-depleted waters of midsummer.

Birds: Satisfied Customers of the All-You-Can-Eat Tidal Flat Buffet

Birds visit tidal flats much like humans visit restaurants. Sometimes we are in the mood for a high-quality meal, but other times fast food is the goal, while most times we face the daily grind of eating to survive. Birds seem to fit these various categories. Long-legged waders like herons and egrets patiently prowl knee-deep water in search of fish and crabs. Gulls and terns seem to be constantly searching for fish and invertebrates. Every spring and fall thousands of migratory shorebirds descend upon tidal flats in search of fast food that will pack on fat to fuel them for long-distance migrations (see "Estuaries" chapter). Within a few days or weeks, these migrants can deplete a tidal flat of much of its invertebrate biomass. Fortunately, the birds don't stick around long and most invertebrates produce huge numbers of larvae that help populations rebound after such a feeding frenzy.

Rather than driving tidal flat invertebrates to extinction and lowering species diversity, shorebirds appear to concentrate their feeding on the most abundant species. This focus actually promotes the well-being of less abundant species by easing competition from neighbors. One of the ways that shorebird species differ from one another is in the length of their bills and how they use them to capture prey. These differences in feeding techniques and bill sizes enable shorebirds to divide up the food resources such that they can exploit many different food types without completely decimating any single one. The results are less competition among migrating birds that must quickly fill up on food and a dispersal of preda-

History of Shorebird Exploitation

Herons and egrets, as well as many gulls, terns, sandpipers, and plovers, were nearly driven to extinction in the late 1800s and early 1900s. Market hunting brought thousands of shorebirds and sea ducks to market where they were sold for food. Eggs were collected for food and natural history collections. However, it was a bizarre fad in women's fashion apparel that almost wiped out these birds for good.

For several decades in the late 1800s, it was fashionable for women to wear hats adorned with the breeding plumes of egrets, herons, and other birds. While this might be understandable, as adornment with feathers is part of many human cultures, the runaway fad soon led to women wearing entire dead birds upon their heads.

Several things happened to prevent the extinction of these birds. As news of their decline began to spread, some high society women developed a strong environmental ethic and rallied to stop the hat craze. The result was the formation of the Massachusetts Audubon Society, followed by other local organizations and eventually the National Audubon Society. The agencies organized hat boycotts, lobbied hard to put an end to plume hunting, and fought to set aside areas, particularly the Florida Everglades, as wildlife refuges.

In 1914 a new fashion craze emerged when actress Irene Castle appeared on stage with a bobbed haircut. Fans loved it and soon women everywhere were sporting new hairstyles that couldn't hold up a hat weighed down by a stuffed bird. The United States enacted the Lacey Act of 1899 and the Migratory Bird Treaty Act of 1917 that closely regulated any hunting of shorebirds, ducks, and songbirds.

Over the next ninety years, many of these birds returned from the brink of extinction to breed, once again, throughout their historic range. For many species, however, population sizes are still below historic levels. Some, such as Piping Plovers, Roseate Terns, and Least Terns, remain rare.

tion effects among the various invertebrates. Tidal flats are important stopover sites, or staging areas, where migrating birds rest and refuel. Without these sites migratory shorebirds would be unable to reach their wintering grounds or complete the return flight to their breeding grounds.

Herons and egrets are the largest and most graceful birds that feed on the shore. **Wading birds** have long legs, long pointed beaks, and long sinuous necks that aid them in foraging for fish along tidal flats and marsh creeks. From largest (52 inches [130 cm]) to smallest (22 inches [55 cm]), these birds include the **Great Blue Heron** *(Ardea herodias)*, **Great Egret** *(A. alba)*, **Snowy Egret** *(Egretta thula)*, **Yellow- and Black-Crowned Night Herons** *(Nyctanassa violacea* and *Nycticorax nycticorax)*, **Tricolored Heron** *(E. tricolor)*, **Little Blue Heron** *(E. caerulea)*, and **Green Heron** *(Butorides virescens)*.

Their primary food is fish, which they usually hunt while standing motionless while knee-deep in water. They use a quick stabbing or grabbing motion with their beak to capture fish and crustaceans. They carefully consume fish headfirst to avoid the problem of dorsal spines catching in the throat. They often feed in groups. Presumably the movements of many feet create disturbances that expose and possibly confuse prey, making it easier for the birds to capture them. Estuarine tidal flats, salt marsh creeks, and salt marsh pools are favored foraging locations.

Herons and egrets tend to nest communally, often in mixed species groups. They construct nests of sticks in trees located near a body of water. The birds prefer islands, which keep the young safe from snakes and mammalian predators. Nesting sites and even the nests themselves may be reused for many years, but not necessarily by the same birds.

Most wading birds are migratory to some degree. Those breeding to the north where feeding ponds and coastlines freeze for the winter have no choice but to migrate. Some southern birds stay put for the winter while others head to Central America.

The **Great Blue Heron** *(Ardea herodias)* is the largest heron in North America, standing 5 feet (1.6 m) tall. Its size and overall gray coloration with streaks of white, black, and brown distinguish it from other species. When it is in flight, its neck is tucked into an S-shape and its wing beats are long and slow. Its longer legs enable it to forage in deeper water than other birds.

Herons have elaborate courtship displays in which the two birds approach closely with heads up, necks stretched out, breeding plumes erect, and wings spread. In many cases the

Great Blue Heron (Ardea herodias)
SCOTT SHUMWAY

male will pick up a stick, shake it about, and pass it to the female. They also use a variety of displays to ward off invaders from feeding territories. In general a bird making unusual head and neck movements is probably trying to convey a message to a rival that it should move away.

Herons may reuse their nests for many years, making them as much as 3 feet (1 m) deep over time. Both parents bring food to the chicks. Great Blue Herons are sensitive to nest-site disturbance and should be given a wide berth during nesting season.

The **Great Egret** *(Ardea alba)* is white with a yellow bill and black legs and feet. Elongated plumes or aigrettes are produced during the breeding season. The breeding plumes of Great and Snowy Egrets were the most desirable of all feathers during the ladies hat craze of the late 1800s. The Great Egret became the poster child of the conservation movement that eventually saved these birds, and even today it can be seen on the emblem of the National Audubon Society.

In the past this bird was known as the American Egret, a suitable name for a stately bird that breeds from Maine to Central America. However, the range of the bird extends far beyond the Americas with breeding colonies in Europe, Siberia, China, Japan, India, New Zealand, and parts of Africa. So the preferred European name of Great Egret has been adopted as the official common name.

Snowy Egrets *(Egretta thula)* are the most animated of the common wading

Great Egret (Ardea alba)   SCOTT SHUMWAY

birds. They are bright white with a black bill and black legs that lead to absurd yellow feet. These golden slippers on black legs are unique to the Snowy Egret. The birds forage by shuffling their feet over the bottom to free up prey items. Their food-finding abilities must be well respected by others, because they will often attract birds of the same and different species to productive foraging areas.

Snowy Egret (Egretta thula)
DENNIS DONOHUE—WWW.THROUGH-MY-LENS.COM

Plume hunting exterminated breeding colonies from North Carolina to Long Island. Once hunting stopped, the birds recovered well. In fact they expanded their breeding range as far north as Maine. In recent decades population sizes have dropped by half in New York and New Jersey. Between 1995 and 1996 a colony in Avalon, New Jersey, experienced a 99 percent decline, most likely in response to competition for nest sites with Black-Crowned Night-Herons. The overall cause of decline is unknown. Snowy Egrets are particularly vulnerable to predation by raccoons, feral cats, and other opportunistic predators that do well around human habitations.

Eelgrass meadow JOANN M. BURKHOLDER

Seagrass Meadows

Dense growths of seagrasses form underwater grasslands known as **seagrass meadows.** The best way to experience a seagrass meadow is by snorkeling or scuba diving over the dense tangle of seagrass while ignoring the blades that tickle your face. Because they are in shallow water, it is sometimes impossible to swim above, rather than within, the canopy. The blades are covered with life and merit close, careful observation at a slow pace. If you are lucky, you will discover a "blade" that is really a pipefish and have fun trying to outswim one of the slowest fish in the sea. You might also return home with a tasty meal as Bay Scallops reside here.

Seagrasses are flowering plants that carry out all the same life processes as any other flowering plant, just that they do it underwater. Any botanist would tell you that seagrasses are not really grasses, as their flowers in no way resemble those of plants in the grass family. They do, however, have elongated, flattened, grasslike leaves. Seagrass blades grow rapidly with plants continuously producing new blades as old ones are shed. As a result there is always fresh food for those species that graze upon live seagrass blades. Even more importantly, there is a constant source of decaying leaves that fuel a detritus food chain.

There are two species of seagrass that are common in our area, **Eelgrass** *(Zostera marina)* and **Widgeon Grass** *(Ruppia maritima).* Eelgrass is by far the more abundant of the two, and this chapter will focus on Eelgrass and the ecosystem that it creates. Eelgrass forms dense meadows in shallow estuaries. These Eelgrass meadows, or beds, provide a three-dimensional structure that provides habitat for many other species, trap sediment and nutrients, and stabilize the substrate. The Eelgrass blades slow down the movement of currents passing over a meadow. This influences how nutrients and energy move in and out of seagrass meadows, as well as their availability to the species that live there. Whenever water slows down, the particles trapped in it are allowed to settle to the bottom. Eelgrass meadows, therefore, slowly accumulate sediments. Nutrients also build up, providing food for filter-feeding invertebrates and fertilizing the substrate that is mined for nutrients by the roots of the seagrasses.

A Detrital Food Chain

The **energy** captured by photosynthesizing Eelgrass is passed up the food chain in two ways. The most obvious is by consumption of living blades by herbivores, yet few species feed directly on Eelgrass. Instead, most of the material passed up the food chain enters as **detritus.** Eelgrass constantly sheds aging blades. Decomposing bacteria break them down into smaller and smaller pieces. The resulting **particulate organic matter** is consumed by filter feeders and detritivores. Much of this material remains within the meadow and is recycled locally.

The mechanical and biochemical decomposition of Eelgrass detritus and eventual movement of nutrients and energy up the food chain is complex, involving numerous players and chemical reactions. Initially **water-soluble organic compounds** leach out of the dead grass blades. These dissolved compounds serve as fertilizer for the **bacteria** that grow and feed upon the pieces of detritus. A single gram of dried detritus may support up to ten billion bacterial cells. Some small animals are able to selectively graze on these microscopic food sources. Most detritus feeders, however, ingest entire pieces of detritus or randomly scrape away at the surface coating. The detritus itself is not what is being sought after for food. Detritus-feeding snails, bivalves, and amphipods are really digesting the rich coating of bacteria, protozoa, and microalgae while the actual detritus passes through the digestive system virtually unchanged. The resulting fecal pellets are once again open for colonization by bacteria and are quickly recycled.

The Biology of Eelgrass and Widgeon Grass

Eelgrass is the most abundant seagrass in the cold waters of the North Atlantic. It grows in estuaries and protected embayments from Nova Scotia to the Carolinas, as well as along the shores of Europe and the North Pacific. Eelgrass is able to tolerate a wide range of salinities from full seawater to nearly fresh. Sunlight availability limits the maximum depth at which Eelgrass can grow. In New England plants grow at depths of 33 feet (10 m) whereas in highly turbid estuaries, such as the Chesapeake, plants are restricted to depths of less than 6 feet (2 m). Minimum depth is determined by tides, with plants growing up to the lower limit of the intertidal zone.

Eelgrass plants consist of upright shoots that produce thin flattened blades (up to 0.4 inch [1 cm] wide) each with a rounded tip. Each shoot includes a basal sheath from which two to five leaf blades are produced. Leaves grow quickly, and overall productivity

Eelgrass (Zostera marina)   GARRY KESSLER

Eelgrass Reproduction

Eelgrass is a long-lived perennial that produces flowers as it sees fit in response to cues that scientists have yet to fully comprehend. A shoot will produce many small flowers on a small rodlike structure called a *spadix* that is partially obscured by a folded leaf or *spathe*. Pollination takes place underwater with sticky threads of pollen hopefully contacting a female flower. Self-pollination is inhibited by a spadix having male flower parts and releasing pollen only after the female parts have completed maturation.

Fertilized flowers produce seeds that sink to the bottom. Seeds may either germinate over the next year or remain dormant, but viable, for several years. They are often eaten by waterfowl and possibly dispersed by them as well.

of seagrass beds is high. New blades grow from the tip of the shoot while older blades are regularly shed from below. This conveyer-belt process ensures that the plant is constantly producing new blades while simultaneously ridding itself of old ones. The tempo of this process is mediated by seasonality and water temperature. The rate slows during the coldest winter months, as well as during the warmest summer months.

The many shoots of a single Eelgrass plant are connected underground by a rhizome that spreads horizontally through mud and sand. Rhizomes enable the plants to spread within the meadow, as well as to expand the margins of the meadow. As they spread, the rhizomes will send up new shoots. At the node where a shoot is produced, clusters of roots will extend down into the substrate where they will take up nutrients. The roots and rhizomes firmly anchor the seagrass in place and stabilize the mud or sand substrate.

The grass blades contain an extensive network of internal **air canals.** The trapped air provides buoyancy, keeping the blades oriented toward sunlight. The air canals, known as **aerenchyma**

Eelgrass (Zostera marina) *and Widgeon Grass* (Ruppia maritima)   JOANN M. BURKHOLDER

Wasting Disease

Between 1930 and 1931 nearly all of the Eelgrass on both sides of the Atlantic Ocean was destroyed by a pathogenic marine slime mold *(Labyrinthula zosterae)*. Scientists were stymied for decades about the actual cause of this **"wasting disease"** because the slime mold is found on seagrasses throughout the world and usually has no detectable negative effect. However when plants are stressed for some other reason, they become susceptible to the disease-causing capabilities of the slime mold. The exact trigger for the 1930s event remains a mystery.

Immediately after the 1930s wasting event, sediments previously anchored by Eelgrass began to wash away. Soft-bottom habitats and the invertebrates that lived there disappeared, leaving behind rock and cobble substrate. Sandy beaches previously protected from waves by the baffling effect of seagrass beds were eroded by waves, leaving behind rocky beaches and depositing new sandbars offshore.

Brant *(Branta bernicla),* a type of goose, relied heavily on Eelgrass as a source of food, and its numbers plummeted. Decades later the remaining Brant had switched their diets to Widgeon Grass and Sea Lettuce.

Eelgrass living in the most dilute parts of estuaries did not fall victim to wasting disease, presumably because the pathogen is unable to tolerate low salinities. Seeds dispersed from these survivors helped fuel the regeneration of Eelgrass beds over the ensuing decades. Many Eelgrass beds have recovered, but some are still far below pre-1930 levels. Local outbreaks of wasting disease occur periodically, but the widespread destruction of the 1930s has not been duplicated.

Brant are geese that feed heavily on Eelgrass and Widgeon Grass.
DENNIS DONOHUE—WWW.THROUGH-MY-LENS.COM

tissue, allow gases, particularly oxygen, to diffuse throughout the plant. Aeren-chyma tissues provide a conduit for oxygen produced in leaf tissue to travel to the rhizomes and roots, which occupy waterlogged sediment that is deficient in oxy-gen. Some of the oxygen diffuses out of the roots into the surrounding sediment. This oxygenated root zone enables the plants to take up nutrients that would be otherwise unavailable.

Widgeon Grass is less common than Eelgrass and grows interspersed with Eel-grass or by itself in brackish parts of estuaries and salt marsh pools. It can be dis-tinguished from Eelgrass by its narrower blades (less than .04 inch [1 mm]) with pointed tips. A widgeon is a kind of duck, and the common name of this seagrass reflects its value as a food source for migrating and overwintering waterfowl.

Other Inhabitants of Eelgrass Meadows: Epiphytes, Invertebrates, and Fish

The blades of seagrasses are typically fouled with epiphytic algae and invertebrates. In many cases the biomass of the **epiphytes** (literally plants that live on other plants) can exceed that of the blade itself. This has an obvious cost to the plant, as the epiphytes intercept valuable sunlight. In an environment of mud and sand, seagrasses are an oasis for species requiring a firm substrate. Over ninety-one species of microscopic algae, primarily diatoms, contribute to a feltlike covering on the surface of Eelgrass blades while an additional 120 species of red, green, and brown algae have been found growing on Eelgrass blades. Many of these epiphytes take up dissolved nutrients and organic carbon directly from the seagrass blades. At least 177 animal species also live here and serve as valuable food for numerous fish species. Sessile invertebrates, such as hydroids and bryozoans, are common on seagrass blades. Mobile amphipods and snails, such as the quarter-inch-long (6-mm) *Bittium* **snails,** move along the grass blades grazing heavily on epiphytes.

The importance of Eelgrass beds to other species can be seen in comparisons of species diversity and abundance between beds and surrounding unvegetated sediments. Most invertebrates are either found only in Eelgrass meadows or in much greater abundance there than in other parts of an estuary. **Quahog** clams *(Mercenaria mercenaria)* are threatened with predation by **whelks** and siphon-nip-ping fish, unless they are living within an Eelgrass meadow where whelks have a hard time excavating rhizome-laden sediments and fish cannot see through the maze of blades.

The **Bay Scallop** *(Argopecten irradians)* is a commercially harvested shellfish that is dependent upon Eelgrass beds. These are the "small" scallops found in the grocery store or heaped on a plate after being deep-fried. Juvenile scallops attach to Eelgrass blades where they are elevated out of reach of predatory crabs. Mature scallops later fall to the bottom, too big for crabs to handle and able to move about through bursts of jet propulsion. Seagrass beds concentrate phytoplankton as a result of dampening water currents. This is beneficial to the filter-feeding Bay

Bay Scallop (Argopecten irradians)
SANDRA E. SHUMWAY

Scallops, which can capture food more easily within seagrass beds than in other parts of the estuary. Bay Scallops only live for one to two years, so having a dependable Eelgrass bed habitat is essential for long-term survival of their populations. They suffered severe declines during the 1930s wasting event. Many estuaries experienced a resurgence in scallops following recovery of Eelgrass beds; however the Chesapeake fishery has yet to rebound.

Small fish are likewise more abundant within beds than outside. The dense growth of seagrass blades forms a junglelike tangle that is an ideal hiding and foraging habitat for larval and juvenile fishes, as well as crabs and shrimp. Few

Current Threats to Seagrass Survival

Many seagrass meadows are currently decreasing in area as turbidity and nutrient pollution increase. Seagrasses require high levels of sunlight for photosynthesis. Turbidity increases with higher amounts of sediment in the water and higher densities of phytoplankton. Poor land use in the surrounding watersheds results in higher sediment loads in rivers and estuaries. Sewage effluent and runoff of agricultural fertilizers contribute to nutrient pollution or eutrophication. Higher nutrient levels would initially seem beneficial to an aquatic plant, but this is not the case for seagrasses. They thrive under low-nutrient conditions. One way that they can do this successfully is by using their roots and spreading rhizomes to exploit the sediment nutrient pool in addition to what is available in the water. They grow better under low nutrients than their potential competitors, the phytoplankton and epiphytic algae. The table is turned, however, once nutrient levels rise. All of these species exhibit more rapid growth in response to more nutrients, but the increase by phytoplankton and epiphytes far outstrips the modest response by seagrasses. The higher density of phytoplankton intercepts sunlight. The epiphytic algae that cover seagrass blades respond rapidly to nutrient increases and further deplete the availability of sunlight below what is needed for seagrass survival.

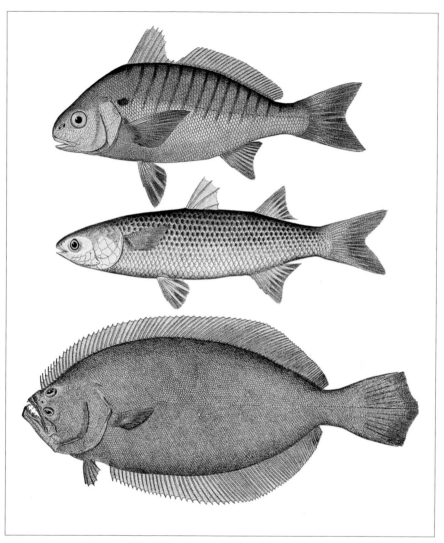

Mullet, Spot, and Summer Flounder are common part-time residents in Eelgrass meadows.
NOAA PHOTO LIBRARY–NATIONAL MARINE FISHERIES HISTORIC IMAGE COLLECTION

species of fish spend their entire lives in Eelgrass meadows, but many species use them as nursery grounds during their juvenile stages. **Mullet, silversides, Spot, Bluefish, Tautog, Summer Flounder,** and **Menhaden** are just some of the common part-time residents in Eelgrass meadows along the Atlantic coast.

Foraging **Cownose Rays** *(Rhinoptera bonasus)* excavate the sediment beneath Eelgrass in search of Soft-Shell Clams. They consume the clams and nearly all sizable invertebrates, leaving behind a bare patch. Over time seagrasses recolonize these disturbed areas through rhizome spread or seed dispersal.

Bufflehead   GARRY KESSLER

Various species of gulls, herons, and egrets feed selectively on invertebrates and fish, primarily during the summer. However, most birds associated with seagrass meadows are migrating shorebirds or wintering geese, swans, and dabbling ducks. The latter two groups are recognized by their characteristic feeding posture of head tipped down with tail and backside pointing up in the air. These herbivores can have a major impact on Eelgrass meadows as they crop the plants. **Bufflehead** (*Bucephala albeola*), in comparison, are ducks that feed heavily on snails and worms living in the meadows.

The Open Ocean

Just offshore lies a world that is a complete mystery to most of us, even though it covers nearly three-quarters of the planet. The open ocean, as it is called, is a deep vast area where life is often so spread out that it seems like a desert. This is in stark contrast to the shallow nearshore regions where life is highly concentrated. But the open ocean is not really a desert. Whales, Ocean Sunfish, Swordfish, tuna, and sharks roam for miles in search of food. The deep waters are filled with so many tiny flashlight fish that the sonar on military ships sometimes suggests a false bottom to the ocean. However, you are not likely to casually encounter any of these species. You must go out of your way to see them. Modern-day whale watches open up this offshore world to many ecotourists. While the whales get most of the attention, the open ocean is also home to some really big fish and millions of seabirds.

Most of our experience with the marine environment, and the focus of this book, involves shallow waters, the beach we walk upon, and the things that we can

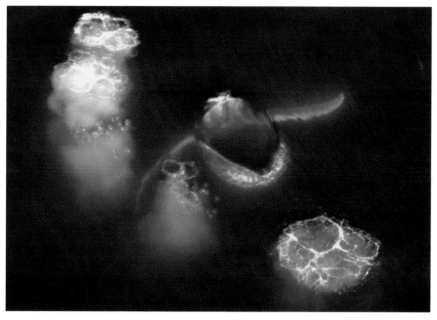

Humpback Whale bubble feeding. The enormous white flippers identify this as a Humpback.
TIM VOORHEIS/GULF OF MAINE PRODUCTIONS

185

observe while standing on the beach. Even if we SCUBA dive, we are still limited to relatively shallow waters. Indeed, the greatest abundance of marine life is found in this narrow band along the shore. Yet the vast majority of the ocean is located outside of this shallow area, and, just as most beachgoers have no experience with this region, much of its biology remains a mystery to scientists. Studying the open ocean is difficult, time consuming, and very expensive. The popularity of whale and dolphin watches has made it possible for most of us to visit this part of the ocean, albeit the part that is closest to shore.

On the east coast of North America, the **continental shelf,** the underwater extension of the continental landmass, is very broad, extending 80–200 miles (130–160 km) from shore. The edge of the shelf drops off into very deep water and is known as the **continental slope.** There are several consequences of these seafloor contours. First, a boat ride to the edge of the East Coast shelf takes several hours. Second, the extensive, and relatively shallow, shelf provides a rich foraging area for many species of fish and the humans who hunt them. Finally, these areas are also the feeding grounds of several species of great whale. These are the destinations of summer whale watches.

Where to Look and What to Look For

It is a waste of time to search the open ocean for whales or seabirds without first understanding what they eat and where their food is located. These animals do not roam the sea aimlessly. They go where their food is located, and so do the pilots of whaleboats and fishing boats. For an animal that must locate food in the open ocean, it is logical to focus efforts on highly concentrated patches of food. The amount of energy expended searching for single prey items would probably exceed the energy gained from eating those prey. Overall the most important food sources are **krill** and **schooling fish.** They occur in large concentrated masses, making them easy food for the lucky predator (or filter feeder) that finds them. Krill are shrimplike crustaceans, also known as euphausids. They are distinguished by having eight pairs of legs and feathery gills at the base of these legs. Even though individually they are less than 2.5 inches (6 cm) long, masses of krill can impart to ocean water a pink hue that is visible from ship or aircraft.

Large schools of fish can also discolor the water. The most important schooling fish are **mackerel, Sand Lance,** and various species of **herrings.** The herrings and mackerels have the added nutritional benefit of being very fatty. Whereas fat is bad for couch-potato humans, it is a rich energy source for fish, whales, and birds, which never seem to rest.

These schooling fish and krill are not at the base of the food chain. Instead they are the primary consumers that feed upon **zooplankton** and **phytoplankton.** Once again these food items are not randomly distributed in the ocean. They require large inputs of nutrients and are concentrated in parts of the ocean where, and at times of the year when, nutrients are plentiful in the surface waters. There

High densities of krill stain the water pink and attract foraging whales, fish, and seabirds.
TIM VOORHIES/GULF OF MAINE PRODUCTIONS

are areas offshore where deep waters encounter changes in topography, such as seamounts (extinct underwater volcanoes), extensive shallow areas (George's and Stellwagen Banks), and deep submarine canyons at the margins of the continental shelf (Hydrographer's and Hudson Canyons). At certain times of the year, deep waters rise up off these features bringing nutrients and cold water to the surface. It is at these upwelling areas that the greatest amounts of plankton, small fish, and their consumers are found.

Cetaceans

Cetaceans are mammals that have hair, breathe air, give birth to live young, feed milk to their young, and never leave the ocean. Several species of cetaceans may be found over the continental shelf of the East Coast. **Humpback, Fin,** and **Minke Whales** are the most commonly sighted "great whales". Other whale species that are much less common but still possible to see on a whale watch include **Northern Right, Blue, Killer, Sei, Sperm,** and **Pilot.** Dolphins and porpoises are smaller whales that are quite common in certain locations and can sometimes be seen from shore.

Whales, or cetaceans, originally evolved from land-dwelling mammals resembling hippos fifty-five million years ago and have since become exquisitely adapted to a marine existence. Their nostrils are no longer forward facing, but located on top of the head, useful for an animal that needs to maintain a horizontal swimming posture while taking a breath of air. Muscles clamp shut the nostrils, or

Minke Whale (Balaenoptera acestorostrata) *preparing to dive*   SCOTT SHUMWAY

blowholes, while the whale is diving. When the whale surfaces, as much as one hundred gallons of air are released in a short blast. The resulting spout, or blow, is from trapped water droplets and condensation as warm moist whale breath meets the cold ocean air. Whales take hundreds of gallons of water into their mouths as they swim. If we tried to fill our mouths with water while swimming, we would end up drowning. Whales avoid this problem by having their airways completely separate from their mouths and throats.

Feeding adaptations divide cetaceans into the baleen whales (Mysticetes) and the toothed whales (Odontocetes). **Baleen whales** lack teeth but instead have a series of long thin baleen plates hanging down from their upper jaws. Baleen is made up of keratin, the same material that makes up hair and fingernails. Arranged like giant combs, baleen plates are smooth on the outer side and bristly on the inside and can be up to 6 feet (2 m) long. The name Mysticetes translates into "mustached whales" and is based on the hanging baleen. Blue, Fin, Humpback, and Minke whales all have expandable pleated throats and are referred to as rorquals, which in Norwegian roughly translates into "whales with tubes," referring to the pleats. They gulp-feed by opening their mouths extra wide while expanding their throats and taking in huge quantities of water. Their long fatty tongues slide back to plug their throats and thereby prevent water from filling their stomachs. Next the mouth is partially closed and the water expelled by contracting the throat pleats and sliding the tongue forward again. Food, from tiny copepods up to small fish, is trapped by the baleen plates and subsequently licked up off the baleen bristles by the giant tongue and swallowed. When this happens in a large concentration of krill or a school of fish, tremendous amounts of food are ingested in a single gulp.

There are several variations on this basic feeding method. Some whales are believed to be able to corral their prey into dense aggregations prior to feeding.

One of the most bizarre methods involves whales creating a circular array of air bubbles rising to the surface. These *bubble nets* are used by Humpbacks to concentrate small fish and plankton, either by carrying them to the surface, frightening them into a tight cluster, disorienting them, or all three. The final assault comes when the whales surge up through the cloud of concentrated food and break the surface at high speed while taking gulps of water and prey. They will also use this lunge-feeding approach on natural aggregations of prey.

Other whale species will swim at the surface on their sides with their mouths open to capture prey. The critically endangered **Northern Right Whales** *(Eubalaena glacialis)* skim feed by swimming along the surface with their mouths open. Water enters at the front and exits along the sides of their mouths where baleen plates 6 feet (2 m) long filter out zooplankton from the continuous stream of water.

Northern Right Whale (Eubalaena glacialis) *skim feeding showing its large baleen plates.*
TIM VOORHEIS/GULF OF MAINE PRODUCTIONS

Fin Whale (Balaenoptera physalus) *is the second largest animal to ever inhabit the earth.*
TIM VOORHIES/GULF OF MAINE PRODUCTIONS

The 60-foot-long **Fin Whale** *(Balaenoptera physalus),* also known as Finback, is second in size only to the Blue Whale. At 100 feet (30 m) in length, the Blue Whale is the largest animal to ever walk or swim on planet earth—ever. We have responded by hunting both these species to the brink of oblivion. A floating Fin Whale barely breaks the surface of the water and looks like a steel gray tanker truck adorned with an oddly curved dorsal fin. In order to dive, it simply bends its front end down, and the huge mass that follows propels the leviathan downward with hardly a splash.

The antics of the **Humpback Whale** *(Megaptera novaeangliae)* are responsible for making whale watching a profitable ecotourist industry. At 35–50 feet (11–15 m) in length and thirty-five tons (thirty-two metric tons) in weight, the Hump-back is a highly entertaining giant. However, it seems to be unaware of its size and will regularly delight whale watchers by propelling its entire body out of the water only to crash back with the world's largest belly flop, a behavior known as breaching. Why Humpbacks breach is not known for sure. One hypothesis is that this behavior helps dislodge barnacles that settle on their skin. Another is that their impact with the water stuns nearby prey. Humpbacks will also roll onto their sides and slap their immense flippers on the surface of the water, perhaps in another attempt to stun prey. Their flippers, or pectoral fins, are bright white and 16 feet (4.9 m) in length. The scientific name *Megaptera novaeangliae,* refers to their flip-pers and literally means "big winged New Englander." As Humpbacks launch into a deep dive, they extend their tail fluke up out of the water, propelling the rest of the body downward.

Humpbacks feed primarily upon small fish such a Sand Lance, mackerel, and herring. Sand Lance are small elongated silvery fish with the uncanny ability to burrow into sediment with a few quick wiggles of their body. Humpbacks congregate in areas where these fish are plentiful. So long as the fish concentrations are high, Humpbacks will return repeatedly to the same feeding grounds. However, when fish populations drop, the Humpbacks go elsewhere in search of food.

Toothed whales (Odontocetes) are predators that use teeth to capture prey. The largest are the **Sperm Whale** and **Killer Whale** (Orca), but these are rarely seen in our region. Dolphins and porpoises, however, are abundant and commonly spotted from shore. These small, highly social whales feed primarily on fish. **Atlantic White-Sided Dolphin** *(Lagenorhynchus acutus)*, **Common Bottlenose Dolphin** *(Tursiops truncatus)* and **Short-Beaked Common Dolphin** *(Delphinus delphis)*, and **Harbor Porpoise** *(Phocoena phocoena)* are the most common. Whereas dolphins travel in groups, frequently leap out of the water, and come close to boats,

Humpback Whale (Megaptera novaengliae) *breaching*   SCOTT SHUMWAY

Whaling and Whale Conservation

Humans have been hunting whales for more than 1,000 years. For much of this time, the whales stood a fighting chance; but as technology provided faster ships and more formidable killing tools, they suffered an overwhelming defeat. Whales eat huge amounts of food and store huge amounts of fat, which keeps them warm in the cold ocean and enables them to migrate long distances between feeding and calving areas and to endure long time periods of not eating. Rendered whale fat provides valuable lubricating oils, superior candles, and cosmetic creams. The swollen head of the Sperm and other toothed whales contains spermaceti oil, a valuable industrial lubricant. The large teeth of Sperm Whales were once the preferred medium of scrimshaw artists. Whale meat is also valued as a subsistence food for some northern cultures and as a delicacy by others. Baleen was once used for corsets, buggy whips, and sleigh runners.

Whaling, particularly nineteenth-century Yankee whaling, has been highly romanticized in sea shanties, literature, paintings, and scrimshaw. In reality, very little was romantic about the life of a sailor aboard a whaling ship. Ships would leave Nantucket bound for whatever part of the sea had whales to offer up. The waters off Greenland, Antarctica, and the Southern Pacific were common destinations. Boats would not return until the holds were filled with whale oil and baleen—journeys commonly lasted several months. The cramped living quarters were below the try works, where whale blubber was boiled to render oil that was then stored in barrels below deck. The constant stench of dead whale, smoking vats of fat, and sweaty sailors—not to mention the low ceilings and rough seas—must have been difficult to bear. The danger of rowing a tiny whaleboat, tossing a harpoon while at the mercy of ocean swells, and then hanging on for a "Nantucket sleigh ride" while the wounded whale exhausted itself to death sounds anything but romantic. The killing would be followed by a genuine blood bath as the whale was "processed" alongside the ship. All of this work was done by hearty souls who were often cheated out of their anticipated wages by the wealthy shipowners back on Nantucket. However, the industry not only continued but proliferated until there were hardly any great whales left to kill.

Whale hunting made a huge technological advance in 1868 with the invention of the exploding harpoon. This was followed by faster ships powered by steam and later diesel fuel. The battle was now one that the whale stood no chance of winning. As one whale species would disappear, the whalers would simply switch to another one or seek out a new part of the ocean. The first whales to go were the Northern Right, Pacific Gray, and others that lived close to shore and fueled shore-based whaling. "Modern" whalers went after Blue Whales; and when they were nearly extinct, switched to Fin, the next largest. Today only Minkes, the smallest of the baleen whales, are present in sufficient numbers to be considered for harvest.

In 1982 the International Whaling Commission (IWC), largely in response to pressure by environmental groups, voted to place a moratorium on all commercial whaling. However, some nations continue to kill whales, either for aboriginal hunting or under the guise of science. In the United States subsistence whaling is carried out by the Makah Tribe and Alaska Eskimos. A few nations ignore the IWC altogether. In Japan whales are "taken" in the name of science and then taken to market. Iceland and other prowhaling nations continue to lobby for the resumption of commercial whaling.

Even after the cessation of commercial whaling, some species of great whale continue to decline. The North Atlantic Right Whale seems doomed to extinction. Its population has dipped so low (fewer than 300) that it is unlikely to recover. Under such conditions the annual death toll from accidental collisions with ships is much more devastating than the seemingly low numbers would suggest. Blue Whales have not been hunted in the North Atlantic since the middle of the twentieth century, but they have not increased in abundance.

What, you might ask, were the population levels prior to modern whaling? We don't, and never will, know. We can make educated guesses based on old whaling records, but these are fraught with error. In 2003 biologists Joseph Roman and Stephen Palumbi took a different approach to estimating whale numbers prior to whaling and came up with sobering results. By using the genetic variation present in the DNA of a subset of modern-day whales, it is possible to estimate the size of the historic population that would have generated this level of diversity. The scientists conclude that prior to whaling there were "240,000 humpback, 360,000 fin, and 265,000 minke whales in the North Atlantic" and that the "current populations of 10,000 humpback, 56,000 fin, and 149,000 minke whales are a fraction of past numbers" Therefore we have a long way to go before we can claim to have safely returned whale populations to "normal" or even safe levels.

Humpback Whale raising fluke to dive,
showing scalloped trailing edges of fluke
GREGORY SKOMAL

porpoises are rarely in groups, are not acrobatic, and avoid boats. Toothed whales are highly social and will remain in groups called pods for months at a time, often coordinating their foraging efforts. Baleen whales, in comparison, form smaller social groups that only last for a matter of hours.

Big Fish

The waters over the continental shelf are home to some really big fish. The most prized are **tuna.** These top predators are among the fastest fish in the sea with cruising speeds of 55 miles (88 km) per hour. They travel and forage in coordinated schools. Their speed is made possible by a streamlined body shape combined with other built-for-speed adaptations. The dorsal, pectoral, and pelvic fins can all be retracted into recessed grooves during high speed maneuvering in order to cut down on drag. A lunate, or half-moon-shaped, tail is connected to the body by a narrow peduncle. Strong musculature throughout the peduncle and body of the fish move the tail to generate rapid swimming. This tail shape in any fish translates into powerful swimming. Engineers study tuna biomechanics in hopes of applying what they learn to the design of future submarines.

The presence of a feeding school of tuna can be detected by the desperate attempts of prey species to escape by jumping out of the water. Mackerel, Bluefish, herring, and Sand Lance are favored prey.

Bluefin Tuna are perhaps the most valuable fish in the sea. The high fat content of their flesh makes them desirable for sushi. Tuna boats spend hours plying the ocean just searching for Bluefins. Sometimes helicopters are used to spot schools from the air and the locations are radioed to waiting boats that then speed off to intercept the fish. Tuna are then fished by using heavy-duty rod and reel. While monster-sized tuna are now rare, they can reach 15 feet (4.6 m) in length and exceed 1,400 lbs (635 kg) in weight. A hooked **North Atlantic Bluefin Tuna** (*Thunnus thynnus*) weighing a few hundred pounds may take hours to land, after which it may be rushed to an airplane for overnight delivery to the Tokyo fish market. In the early 1970s Bluefin sold for 5 cents per pound whereas in the 1990s it peaked near $80 per pound! In 2001 a single 445-pound fish fetched $173,853. The increase in demand and price has been accompanied by a decrease in tuna population numbers. Fisheries scientists are calling for a decrease in the numbers of fish harvested in order to allow the population to recover.

Bluefin Tuna (Thunnus thynnus) *are one of the fastest fish in the sea.*   GREGORY SKOMAL

One of the oddest fish in the sea is the **Ocean Sunfish** *(Mola mola)*. It has a large, gray, oval body that commonly reaches 5 feet (1.5 m) in length and 500 pounds (227 kg) in weight, although 10 feet (3 m) and 3,000 pounds (1360 kg) are possible. An Ocean Sunfish resembles a giant head with oversized dorsal and anal fins. Sunfish swim by flapping these fins. They appear to lack a tail fin and even look to be missing the rear half of their body. Sunfish spend much of their time drifting at the surface of the water, either with their dorsal fin sticking up like the fin of a shark or basking with their flattened bodies parallel to the surface of the water. They have a surprisingly small mouth that is used to capture jellyfish and comb jellies.

Sharks

Few groups of marine animals capture the imagination like sharks. Because they range over large areas of the ocean, more than twenty species of large predatory shark may be found off our coast. Some may even be found close to shore. The **Sandbar Shark** *(Carcharhinus plumbeus)* is the most common large shark in our region and uses the Chesapeake Bay as a nursery ground. Despite their reputations as man-eaters, sharks rarely attack humans, especially in our region. Worldwide millions of sharks die needlessly each year as bycatch or after having their fins severed for use in sharkfin soup.

Once despised by fishermen for ravaging other commercial species and destroying nets, the **Spiny Dogfish** *(Squalus acanthias)* is now fished for export to England where it is valued for fish and chips. Harvest of the 3-foot-long (1-m) Spiny Dogfish rose to such a high degree that in the 1990s the National Marine

Basking Sharks (Cetorhinus maximus) *are filter feeders that reportedly reach lengths of 50 feet!*   GREGORY SKOMAL

Fisheries Service completely closed some areas to fishing for this species. Its ability to recover from heavy fishing is hampered by the fact that it takes several years to reach sexual maturity, having an eighteen-month gestation period, and giving live birth to only a few babies at a time.

In contrast to these predators, the **Basking Shark** *(Cetorhinus maximus)* is a mere filter feeder whose primary diet is zooplankton. Capable of reaching 40 feet [12.2 m] in length, Basking Sharks are the world's second largest species of shark. Basking Sharks cruise the western Atlantic throughout the summer months when they may be seen "sunning" themselves, or basking, with fins exposed. Basking Sharks feed near the surface by swimming with their enormous mouths wide open. Gill rakers filter zooplankton from the water before it exits through the gill slits. One individual can filter up to 2,000 tons (1,800 metric tons) of water in an hour.

Seabirds

If you think about it, finding a bird over the open ocean does not make much sense. There are no perches to rest upon, no place to hide from predators, and no places to build a nest or raise helpless babies. And as in the "Rhyme of the Ancient Mariner," there's water everywhere, but none of it is drinkable. Yet, despite these huge obstacles, seabirds spend nearly their entire lives at sea and are among the most numerous birds in the world. Some highly specialized adaptations found nowhere else in the animal kingdom enable them to be successful in such a seemingly inhospitable habitat.

Some seabirds are capable of natural desalinization, enabling them to drink salt water without becoming dehydrated. Albatrosses, shearwaters, and petrels are commonly called "tube noses" because of a cylindrical protuberance along their bills. These are specialized nostrils that actively excrete salt.

Seabirds spend an inordinate amount of time flying over open ocean and are often referred to as "pelagic" species, a term usually reserved for creatures that swim in the ocean. They never set foot on land outside of the short breeding season. Disproportionately long, narrow wings, relative to the length and width of their bodies, enable seabirds to soar over the water while minimizing the amount of energy spent flapping their wings. This elongated wing design is also employed by aeronautics engineers in gliders and passenger jets. Seabirds use the strong winds of the open ocean to assist their flight and minimize energy expenditure. Wind speeds are somewhat lower next to the water's surface. Seabirds fly very low to the water. When they need a wind boost, they simply fly slightly higher and take advantage of the stronger winds. Making these shifts enables the birds to carry out soaring flight without devoting much energy to flapping their wings. Should the winds die down, the birds land on the water and wait for the winds to pick up. Specialized glands produce waterproof oil that seabirds spread over their feathers. This allows their bodies to stay dry and avoid losing heat while they sit on the cold ocean water, which is the only place for them to land.

Finding a suitable nest site remains a problem. Oceanic islands on which to construct nests are few and far between. As a result seabirds nest in huge colonies on certain islands. Thousands of birds will travel to an island to squeeze out a tiny piece of real estate on which to build a nest, incubate eggs, and raise young. Predators are rare on these islands for several reasons. First of all, four-legged predators and snakes have no way of getting to these offshore islands. Second, any approaching predator would be mobbed by thousands of large angry birds. Even if a predator goes after eggs or young, the risk to any one bird among the thousands is quite small. In addition crowded island life can increase the chances of finding a mate.

Names like shearwater, petrel, fulmar, kittiwake, jaeger, gannet, and alcid are foreign to most landlubbers, yet if you voyage out in a fishing or whale-watch boat, you will inevitably see at least a dozen and possibly hundreds of them. A few of the more common species are described here. Gannets and

The Greater Shearwater (Puffinus gravis) has a 42-inch wingspan and sometimes flies with a wing tip nearly touching the surface of the water. BLAIR NIKULA

puffins are described in greater detail as they are most easily seen close to shore and in large numbers.

Shearwaters have extremely long wings relative to their body. The Greater Shearwater, for example, has a 42-inch (107-cm) wingspan on a 19-inch-long (48-cm) body. Its name reflects its habit of flying with one wing angled downward and so close to the water that it appears to skim the surface with its wing tip. Sooty (*Puffinus griseus*), Greater (*P. gravis*), Manx (*P. puffinus*), and Cory's Shearwaters (*Calonextris diomedea*) are commonly encountered on whale watches. Storm Petrels are the smallest seabirds. They are often seen pattering the water with their feet while still airborne. The name petrel refers to the similarity of this behavior to the Biblical story in which St. Peter was supposedly summoned to walk on water. Wilson's Storm Petrel (*Oceanites oceanicus*) can sometimes be observed in large numbers close to shore. Despite being so common during our summers, Storm Petrels and shearwaters nest far away in the Antarctic. Parasitic and Pomarine Jaegers (*Stercorarius* spp.) are less common and are members of the gull family. They have the distinction of being the natural pirates of the open seas, harassing other birds until they drop their prey and then swooping down to steal the dropped meal. Black-Legged Kittiwakes (*Rissa tridactyla*) are small gulls that nest on the sides of cliffs and spend most of their time at sea. The Northern Fulmar

Wilson's Storm Petrel (Oceanites oceanicus) *is a small seabird that feeds by pattering on the surface of the water.*   BLAIR NIKULA

Seabird Conservation

Historically the numbers of seabirds was much higher than it is today. Birds nesting on offshore islands benefit greatly from the lack of predators. Perhaps this explains why they form nesting colonies that look unbearably over-crowded by our standards. However, animals that have little experience with predators are often fearless when approached by humans. History has shown that fearlessness of humans is deleterious to the survival of just about any species, especially if it tastes good. Early explorers and settlers of the North Atlantic readily plundered seabird-breeding colonies for eggs, meat, and feathers, causing severe declines in their numbers. We know from skeletal evidence that many islands were used for breeding in the past but are not used by seabirds today. Some island species evolve to become flightless, as in the case of penguins in the Antarctic. Everyone has heard of the unfortunate demise of the Dodo, a flightless bird endemic to the African island of Mauritius and fearless of the humans that clubbed them into extinction. The Great Auk of the North Atlantic suffered a similar fate. This 30-inch-tall (76-cm) relative of the puffin, Razorbill, and guillemot bred on a few islands in the North Atlantic with little to fear from predators and was not hampered by the fact that its stubby wings could not raise its big body into the air. This all changed when European explorers arrived and found Great Auks to be an easy source of food for the long trip home. By 1844 they became the first North American species to go extinct since European colonization. Most colonial nesting seabirds were similarly exploited, but have managed to escape extinction. Today most bird islands are protected and the species that nest there are increasing in numbers. They remain vulnerable to the introduction of preda-tors, such as rats. They also suffer from the expansion of predatory Great Black-Backed Gulls. Once these aggressive gulls set up nest sites on an island once used by seabirds, there is little chance of the other species ever returning. Global climate change threatens to alter the patterns of the currents that concentrate fish in the foraging waters of these birds. While the birds can probably fly to a new location to capture food, they do not have that option with their nesting grounds.

Northern Gannet (Morus bassinus) *adult in flight displaying bright white body with black wing tips*   BLAIR NIKULA

Immature Northern Gannet plunge diving
BLAIR NIKULA

(*Fulmarus glacialis*) resembles a gull in its outward appearance, but is really a close relative of the shearwaters and petrels. **Red** and **Red-Necked Phalaropes** (*Phalaropus* spp.) are sandpipers that nest in the Arctic, but spend winters at sea. They are sometimes found on the coast during the winter and are distinguished by their strange swimming behavior, which causes them to swim in circles, almost like a cat chasing its tail.

The **Northern Gannet** (*Morus bassanus*) is the largest seabird in the North Atlantic, and the one most likely to be seen from shore. Gannets have a 6-foot (2 m) wingspan. Their elongated bill and tail give their bodies the appearance of being pointed at both ends. Mature birds are nearly pure white with black wing tips. Birds with brown or patchy brown and white plumage are less than five years of age. From the deck of a boat on a sunny day, the bright white adult plumage is stunning. Even more impressive are the feeding behaviors.

Gannets are plunge divers. They drop out of the sky falling straight down with wings slightly folded back in the shape of an arrow. They splash into the water at 62 miles per hour (100 km/h) and travel 10–16 feet (3–5 m) deep in search of fish that they swallow while still submerged. They consume surface schooling fish with a preference for oil-rich species such as herring and mackerel.

Gannets in the western North Atlantic breed in massive colonies on six small islands in the Gulf of St. Lawrence and offshore from Newfoundland. The largest colony on Bonaventure Island, Quebec, has more than 36,936 breeding pairs. Once the birds pair with their mates, they are monogamous for life. This relationship is confirmed with a series of elaborate head and body movements each time the birds meet. Their nest is likely to be only 2.6 feet (80 cm) from the next nest. Once a pair has established a nest site, they will reuse it year after year. The couple will raise one chick per year. Adults will often travel 300 miles (500 km) from the breeding colony to find food for themselves and the chicks. Visits by tourists to breeding colonies on Bonaventure Island and Cape St. Mary's are possible but carefully regulated.

Gannets migrate south for the winter with large numbers of birds congregating off the Massachusetts coast. A spotting scope aimed from shore to the horizon will often reveal a flock of gannets in the form of white flashes dropping from the sky followed by splashes of water.

The **Atlantic Puffin** *(Fratercula arctica)* is probably the most charismatic of seabirds due to its black and white plumage offset by a gaudy, orange-patterned bill. Less than 1 foot (30 cm) in length, it is the bird equivalent of a circus clown dressed in a tuxedo! Puffins sometimes wander into the Gulf of Maine to feed, but for the most part, they remain far offshore.

Atlantic Puffins (Fratercula arctica) *resemble clowns in a tuxedos, nest in large colonies on offshore islands, and dive for fish.*   SCOTT SHUMWAY

Machias Seal Island, located in Maine or Canada, depending on whom you ask, has the closest breeding colony. During the breeding season Atlantic Puffins acquire a series of horny plates over the bill. The result is a larger and more brightly colored bill that seems to be good for attracting mates, but not much else; for once mating has been accomplished, the plates are soon shed.

Nests are located in burrows excavated on the ground on certain offshore islands. Over half of the puffins in North America gather at Witless Bay, Newfoundland, to breed. Burrowing is so extensive that every ten years or so large portions of the ground collapse in the nesting area. The birds typically forage for fish far offshore. Even in the winter they are rarely spotted south of the Gulf of Maine.

Sand Lance, Capelin, herring, White Hake and other small fish are their preferred food items. Puffins dive from the surface and swim through water in search of prey. They frequently capture several fish in one dive and return to the surface with them dangling from their bills. Puffins, like penguins and other members of the auk family (alcids), use their wings to swim and literally fly through the water while using their feet as rudders.

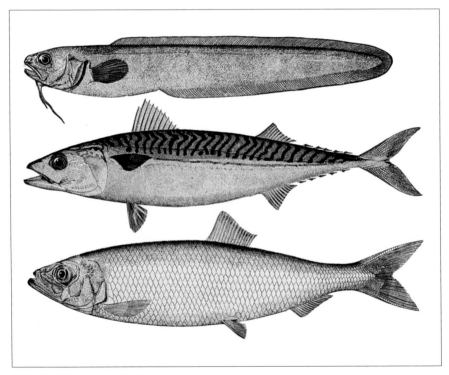

Schooling fish, such as Sand Lance (top), Mackerel, and herring are the preferred prey of many whales, seabirds, and larger fish.   NOAA PHOTO LIBRARY–NATIONAL MARINE FISHERIES HISTORIC IMAGE COLLECTION

The Beach in Winter

Most humans restrict their beach visits to the warm sunny days of summer, avoiding the short days of winter when the beach has been transformed into a bleak landscape of muted shades of tan and gray interspersed with snowy white. At this time of year, the winds and air temperatures combine to create a frigid, seemingly inhospitable place to visit, let alone live in full-time. Snow blankets the beach and dunes. Ice clings to intertidal rocks. Tide pools and even estuaries may freeze over. Rising tides

Frozen sand dune landscape, Sandy Neck (Barnstable, Massachusetts) SCOTT SHUMWAY

lift enormous chunks of ice from salt marsh creeks, displacing entombed mussels and marsh grasses with them. Plants of the marsh and sand dune are brown and lifeless. Despite this bleak backdrop, winter beaches are filled with the wonders of nature and feature a cast of characters that is quite different from the summer months. Despite the wind, waves, and temperatures, winter is not the time to avoid the beach. On the contrary it is time to bundle up and go bird-watching, seal watching, and beachcombing!

The winter ocean is characterized by very cold temperatures with rough and sometimes savage surf. Many resident animals respond by migrating to deeper water where they are sheltered from waves, bitter cold air temperatures, and the ravages of ice. Invertebrates enter a hibernation-like state in which their metabolism is lowered and feeding ceases. In contrast some algae take advantage of the paucity of herbivorous snails and do most of their growth and reproduction during winter.

In Maine ice scours intertidal rocks leaving behind swaths of bare rock where barnacles, mussels, and seaweed once thrived. In February tiny barnacle larvae will begin to settle on the newly cleared rocks.

The most extreme waves crash on the shore during winter storms and flood coastal areas when storm surges and high tides coincide. Waves can drastically reengineer beaches, carrying fine sand offshore and leaving behind stones to form what is called a "winter beach." Barrier spits may be breached by storm waves, sometimes forming a new island or burying a salt marsh with sand in a phenomenon known as an overwash event. Beach erosion forms offshore sandbars each winter, only to have much of this sand redeposited on the beach by summer waves.

A Beachcomber's Bonanza

Beachcombing is at a premium in winter. Not present are the masses of humanity that usually strip the beach of shells and take them home as souvenirs. The rough seas caused by winter storms rip mussels, snails, seaweeds, and other creatures from the comfort of their underwater homes and hurl them onto the beach. This is the best time of year to search for the large seaweeds that make up kelp beds, as well as the invertebrates that live in the dense tangle of the seaweed holdfast. The blades of kelps are covered by a rich community of invertebrates, including translucent vinelike colonies of hydroids, colonies of bryozoans that resemble lace doilies, and the small white curlicues of serpulid tube worms.

The molted shells of true crabs and juvenile Horseshoe Crabs are abundant during the winter. The wrack lines on sandy beaches, in comparison, are composed primarily of shed blades of Eelgrass whereas rocky beaches accumulate dislodged seaweeds. As the season progresses, the dead stems of marsh grasses are sheared from the ground and rafts of stems are carried away by high tides or dumped in large piles elsewhere in the marsh. These piles of wrack are often laden with the shells of Coffee Bean Snails, the skeletons of crabs, and beach fleas (amphipods).

Seal Sightings

Seals spend most of their time at sea, but groups will haul out on sand or rocky beaches to rest and to give birth. Seals are year-round residents of cold New England waters, but are more easily observed during the winter when they congregate closer to shore and slightly farther to the south. Of the nine species of earless seals found in the North Atlantic, only the Gray and Harbor Seals are likely to be found along our coastline. Earless seals differ from the sea lions of the West Coast by lacking external ear flaps, by having forelimbs that are unable to hold the body upright on land, and by being unable to shift their rear limbs beneath their bodies while on land. Because of these latter features, all movement on land is accomplished by dragging their bodies along the

Seals hauled out onshore
DENNIS DONOHUE—WWW.THROUGH-MY-LENS.COM

Harbor Seal (Phoca vitulina)   GARRY KESSLER

ground using only their forelimbs. As poor as they are at moving on land, they are consummate swimmers.

All seals are part of a group known as pinnipeds, which literally means "wing-footed." Their winglike body appendages propel them swiftly and skillfully through the water. In the case of the earless seals, the hind flippers provide much of the propulsive force while the forelimbs are used for steering. Dense fur and a thick layer of blubber provide insulation. They are carnivores that prey primarily on fish and squid. The reliance upon sight to locate prey and avoid sharks is evident in the large size of their eyes. Large sharks are their only nonhuman predators.

Gray Seals *(Halichoerus grypus)* have dense fur in various shades of gray. Males are large (up to 770 pounds [349 kg] vs. 440 pounds [200 kg] for females) and dark in color with light spots whereas females are light with dark spotting. The large head of male Gray Seals has earned them the nickname "horseheads."

Harbor Seals *(Phoca vitulina)* are smaller overall with males reaching 370 pounds (168 kg) and females 290 pounds (132 kg). They are also tan or silvery gray in color and covered with darker spots. Their head and snout are reminiscent of a cocker spaniel. Gray and Harbor Seals are often found together, and keeping track of the snout characteristics will help you tell them apart.

They can often be spotted just beyond breaking waves with their heads poking out of the water. They regularly haul out on remote sandy beaches or on offshore rocks where they are usually so still that it is hard to pick them out from the rocks. Historically both species have been hunted for food and fur. In the 1900s bounties were offered for killing these seals because they were considered competitors for commercial fish species. They are currently protected under the U.S. Marine Mammals Protection Act.

A Birder's Delight

Winter birding is a chilly but highly rewarding experience. Each habitat supports a particular set of bird species, and the winter visitors may be completely different from the summer residents. Long-distance migrants pass through in late summer and fall and may make another brief appearance in the spring. Most of these are shorebirds that don't stick around for the winter. Summer residents typically migrate to more southerly climates. As this shift takes place, thousands of sea ducks that breed as far north as the Arctic take up residence off the New England coast. Some even range as far south as Cape May and Cape Hatteras. Sea ducks, loons, grebes, geese, and cormorants gather just offshore and in protected bays where they alternate between intense feeding and resting. **American Black Ducks** and **Brants** poke along the shoreline for food or sit as still as a rock. Winter gulls hang out on sandy beaches along with a few summer stragglers. A few species of shorebird move in for the winter. **Purple Sandpipers** forage along intertidal rocks, **Sanderlings** comb sandy beaches, and **Dunlin** probe mudflats. **Snowy Owls** set up residence on dunes and salt marshes where they forage for rodents. **Snow Buntings** comb sand beaches for seeds while trying not to attract the attention of hungry birds of prey, such as **Merlins, Peregrine Falcons, Short-Eared Owls**, and **Northern Harriers.** Large flocks of **Snow Geese** feed in salt marshes. Strong winds associated with storms sometimes blow true seabirds unusually close to shore. Immediately after, or during, storms is the time to search for **Northern Gannets, Dovekies,**

Late-fall and winter bird-watching is very productive on sandy beaches, tidal flats, and dunes (South Beach, Chatham, Massachusetts).   SCOTT SHUMWAY

Razorbills, **Common** and **Thick-Billed Murres, Black Guillemots,** and even **Atlantic Puffins.** So grab a spotting scope and aim it out to sea. Only a few of the more common species are covered here.

Winter Gulls

Winter gulls are abundant on sandy beaches, but the gulls of winter are not necessarily the same species that were present during warmer months. Small numbers of summer gulls such as **Great Black-Backed, Herring,** and **Laughing** will stick around. Winter gulls are typically northern breeders that have migrated south to escape their frozen summer homes. **Ring-Billed Gulls** *(Larus delawarensis)* are usually the most abundant . This white-headed gull can be distinguished by its yellow legs and a black ring near the tip of the bill. One of the smallest gulls, **Bonaparte's Gull** *(Larus philadelphia),* is only found in our range during the winter. It is distinguished by its small size, white blaze on the wing, and white head with a dark blotch behind the eye. Large

Ring-Billed Gull (Larus delawarensis)
DENNIS DONOHUE—WWW.THROUGH-MY-LENS.COM

Immature Bonaparte's Gull (Larus philadelphia)
BLAIR NIKULA

floating flocks of "Bonies" congregate wherever there is an abundance of small fish. Less common species eagerly sought by bird-watchers include **Franklin's, Little, Common Black-Headed, Iceland, Lesser Black-Backed,** and **Glaucous Gulls.**

The **Black-Legged Kittiwake** *(Rissa tridactyla)* is a gull that breeds in large numbers on coastal rock ledges north of Newfoundland but winters at sea as far south as North Carolina. They may occasionally be viewed from shore, particularly following winter storms in the Gulf of Maine. At various times in the past, an unusually large abundance of Sand Lance, a small fish, has brought thousands of kittiwakes and other wintering gulls very close to shore. By the middle of April, most of these gulls will have left for their northern breeding grounds.

Sea Ducks

Sea ducks, as their name implies, are ducks that spend most of their lives at sea. The majority of these birds nest in northern coastal areas from the Gulf of Maine to the Canadian Arctic. It is difficult for me to think of the frigid coast of my native Massachusetts as a nice place to spend the winter, but that is just what these birds do. Some sea ducks are forced to migrate south as the waters near their breeding grounds become frozen over. Others form dense feeding flocks that track concentrations of fish, crustaceans, and other morsels of waterborne food. Most sea ducks spend all of their lives in or near salt water, yet some spend summer months in rivers and ponds. This switch from a freshwater to marine existence seems quite remarkable, until you consider the futility of searching for food in a frozen inland lake. These winter visitors arrive offshore in November and leave by the end of March. Viewing sea ducks can be a frustrating experience, as even with binoculars they are easily confused with lobster buoys bobbing on the water. However, peering through a powerful spotting scope will completely transform these birds from specks on the water into creatures of remarkable beauty. Clearly seasickness is not a problem for these birds as they are constantly bobbing up and down with the surf. Scoters, Common Eiders, and Harlequin Ducks paddle so close to breaking waves that you would predict drowning and fatal collisions with rocks to be common.

Careful observation of sea ducks will reveal that amorous activities are not inhibited by cold temperatures. They initiate courtship and carry out mate recognition behavior throughout the winter. Courting males will swim after females, raising themselves out of the water, bobbing their heads, and generally showing off in an attempt to either gain their attention or remind them of their marital status. Other behaviors make rival males aware that a female is already spoken for. Couples will even engage in brief copulations while acrobatically floating at sea.

Common winter ducks include the **American Black Duck** (a breeder whose numbers increase with seasonal migration, particularly in salt marshes), **Greater** and **Lesser Scaup, Common** and **King Eider, Harlequin Duck, Oldsquaw** (also called Long-Tailed Duck), three species of **scoter, Common Goldeneye** (Barrows is rare), **Bufflehead,** and **Red-Breasted Merganser.** Sea ducks are often accompanied by **Common** and **Red-Throated Loons, Horned Grebe, Great Cormorant** (Double-Crested Cormorants tend to head south), and **Brant.**

The **Common Eider** (*Somateria mollissima*) is the largest duck in North America. Eiders nest in large colonies in Canada and in smaller numbers along the New England coast. The superior insulating properties of their feathers have long been recognized by humans, particularly Europeans and

Male Red-Breasted Merganser (Mergus serrator)
DENNIS DONOHUE—WWW.THROUGH-MY-LENS.COM

Icelanders, who collect eiderdown from nests of these birds for use in quilts and jackets.

Males are easily recognized by their contrasting black wings and bright white backs. Their heads are mostly white with a black stripe at the top and a faint greenish wash to the nape. Females are almost all brown except for thin white wing stripes. Birds with plumage intermediate between these two are immature males. A large flock in flight forms a long line that may run the length of the horizon.

In winter eiders gather just offshore to forage for mussels, crustaceans, and green sea urchins. Rafts, as these floating feeding flocks are called, may contain over a thousand individuals. Eiders will feed intensively for a period of time and then spend 30–50 percent of their time resting while the accumulated food moves through their digestive system. They spend their days in a continuous cycle of stuffing themselves, resting, and then starting all over again, oftentimes with the entire flock appearing to coordinate bouts of feeding and resting. On a windless day their cooing calls sound like a herd of cattle calling from a distance.

Common Eider male (Somateria mollissima)
GARRY KESSLER

Large black ducks concentrated just beyond the breaking waves are probably **scoters.** They winter along the Atlantic and Pacific coasts of North America and build nests adjacent to inland water bodies in northern Canada and Alaska. Wintering scoters will form flocks ranging in size from a handful of birds to a few thousand. Scoters seem to have difficulty taking off from the water and will usually begin by running across the surface of the water while flapping their wings. They dive from the surface and use their feet to propel themselves to the bottom. They feed primarily on Blue Mussels and other molluscs that they pull up from the bottom and swallow whole. Flocks will sometimes dive synchronously, possibly as a way for flock members to locate mussel beds. Flocks of scoters tend to fly low over the ocean and often in lines. Wintering scoters congregate in bays and estuaries, as well as on the open coast. The Jersey Shore, Delaware Bay, and Chesapeake Bay have the largest concentrations.

Surf Scoter (Melanitta perspicillata)
GARRY KESSLER

Telling the three species of scoter apart is tricky. Females of all three species are generally dark brown with various patterns of lighter shading that differentiate each one. Males are all black, except for their distinguishing features described below. **Black Scoters** *(Melanitta nigra)* are identified by their bright orange bills. They are the only species likely to emit a whistling call while the other species are mostly silent. **Surf Scoters** *(M. perspicillata)* are the most colorful with a prominent white patch on the forehead and base of the head (nape) and a white, red, yellow, and black multicolored bill. Hunters sometimes refer to them as "Skunkhead Coot." **White-Winged Scoters** *(M. fusca)* are black with a small white teardrop around the eye and a large white patch on the wing. The white patch, or speculum, is not always visible. The birds can also be distinguished in flight. The white wing patch shows up well on both male and female White-Winged Scoters. When viewed from below, Black Scoters have two-toned wings of silver and black, whereas Surf Scoters are uniformly dark on the undersides of the wings.

The most colorful and animated of all the sea ducks is the **Harlequin Duck** *(Histrionicus histrionicus)*. Its name derives from the male's clownlike facial markings, which include a bold white stripe and crescent-shaped patch in front of the eye and smaller splotch of white to the rear, all across a blue-gray background. Blue and white striping run over a blue background on the breast and back while the sides are chestnut colored. When viewed at close range in good light, these birds are stunningly beautiful. Females, in comparison, have brown heads with a triangular white patch on the face.

The scientific name, *Histrionicus,* translates into "tricks," and indeed this bird performs incredible acrobatic feats as it swims and feeds in fast-moving streams

Harlequin Duck (Histrionicus histrionicus)   GARRY KESSLER

and crashing surf. Harlequins spend their summers in fast-moving Canadian streams and winter along the coast as far south as North Carolina. Most of the eastern North American population overwinters along the coast of Maine. Recent increases in numbers as far south as Cape Hatteras are due to rock jetties that mimic the areas where Harlequins naturally feed. They dive in shallow waters in search of mussels, snails, crabs, and other crustaceans. Foraging areas are near rocky shores in the midst of breaking waves. Somehow these brilliantly colored birds manage to get hit by waves and find food without getting smashed against the rocks. They are surprisingly vocal with a call sounding like the squeak of a mouse. Because they secure mates in the winter, we get to see them in their most spectacular plumage. They also exhibit interesting head nodding and rushing behavior as they either pair up for the first time, reestablish pair formation, or chase away rival males.

Other Overwintering Birds

Snow Buntings *(Plectrophenax nivalis)* nest in the high Arctic tundra in rock crevices, making them one of the northernmost nesting species of birds. During the frigid winter months, food is unavailable, and Snow Buntings migrate south where they form loose flocks ranging in size from a few dozen to a few hundred birds. Another Arctic bird, the **Lapland Longspur** *(Calcarius lapponicus),* sometimes travels with flocks of Snow Buntings. Both of these species have a long hind claw on each foot and leave behind readily identifiable tracks in sand and snow.

Snow Bunting (Plectrophenax nivalis).
CRAIG CATO

During winter Snow Buntings have black-and-white wings and white bellies with rufous streaks along the back and across the upper breast. They feed on coastal sand dunes, beaches, and salt marshes, as well as agricultural fields, as far south as the Delmarva Peninsula. They arrive in late October and stay until April. Seeds make up most of their diet, but in the winter they will also forage along the wrack line and water's edge in search of small crustaceans.

Snow Bunting flocks always seem to be in motion and at risk of burning up more energy flying than they gain from foraging. They have a swooping jerky flight pattern. The entire flock may suddenly land on a patch of sand, but will often erupt into flight almost immediately and certainly before any feeding can take place. When they do settle in to feed on seeds, it is possible to approach them closely. In fact, they blend in so well with beach sand that is possible to not see them and be startled when they rise up into the air.

Merlin (Falco columbarius)
DENNIS DONOHUE—WWW.THROUGH-MY-LENS.COM

Peregrine Falcon (Falco peregrinus)
BLAIR NIKULA

Aerial predators, such as Peregrine Falcons and Merlins, searching beaches for their next meal, probably explain the extreme nervous behavior of Snow Buntings. Whenever a flock takes off, there is the possibility that one of these falcons is in hot pursuit. **Merlins** *(Falco columbarius)* are small falcons that resemble pigeons in flight, earning them the nickname "Pigeon Hawk". They are boreal forest birds that spend time on the coast during winter migration. Shorebirds make up much of their winter diet. Merlins will often fly close to the ground in order to avoid being detected by flocks of shorebirds or Snow Buntings. By flying below the "radar" capabilities of their prey, Merlins are able to initiate surprise attacks. Snow Buntings will attempt to outfly an attacking Merlin. The result is a "ringing flight" in which both species fly higher and higher in a circular pattern. One of the benefits to being a member of a flock is that the swirling mass is confusing to predators who must hone in on a single individual to be successful. A bird that strays from the flock has sacrificed this layer of protection and is in clear and present danger of becoming a meal for an attacking falcon.

Peregrines are large falcons that have an overall bluish gray coloration with a distinct black moustache across either side of the face. Nearly wiped out by exposure to DDT, **Peregrine Falcons** *(Falco peregrinus)* are experiencing an impressive recovery partly due to their willingness to nest on window ledges of skyscrapers and do their part to reduce urban pigeon populations. They can be found on beaches during their fall migration as they stop to feed on birds and small mammals. The barrier beaches of Chincoteague and Assateague Islands are popular resting areas for migrating Peregrines. Any bird being followed by a hungry Peregrine is in a bad state indeed, as the Peregrine is one of the fastest animals on earth and considers 429 different species of bird fair game. Peregrines employ the same hunting styles as the Merlin but are best known for a midair tactic known as a "stoop." Peregrines will fly well above their intended prey and then fold their wings back and drop out of the sky as though they were hell bent on crashing into the ground. While employing a stoop, the falcon will reach velocities of up to 223 miles per hour (100 meters per second)! When attacking a bird or rodent on the ground, the Peregrine manages to pull out of the stoop at the last instant, grab the prey with its talons, and then roll along the ground in order to break the impact with the ground. In other instances the stooping falcon collides with its prey in midair at full speed. The duration of impact is less than 100 milliseconds during which time both feet grab and release the prey, delivering a lethal or near-lethal injury.

Thanks to Harry Potter's mail-delivering owl named Hedwig, nearly everyone these days knows what a **Snowy Owl** *(Bubo scandiacus)* looks like. They are almost all white with some brown barring on the head and breast with more promi-nent barring on females. They are the largest owl species in North America. Aside from Hedwig, Snowy Owls are restricted to the far north where they breed on open Arctic tundra. Their population size is closely tied to the availability of their favorite prey, rodents known as lemmings. A single Snowy Owl may consume up to 1,600 lemmings per year. In a year when lem-mings are abundant, a pair of owls may raise up to twelve young but forgoes egg laying altogether when prey are scarce. Lemming populations tend to follow a four-year cycle of boom and bust, and in years when lemming num-bers are exceptionally low, Snowy Owls are forced to migrate farther and wider

Snowy Owl (Bubo scandiacus)
DENNIS DONOHUE—WWW.THROUGH-MY-LENS.COM

in order to survive the winter. They are regular winter visitors to the Great Plains, but are generally scarce along the East Coast. During these years of food scarcity, Snowy Owls are present in much larger numbers (irruptions) on the coast.

They spend most of their time sitting on an elevated perch on a sand dune or salt marsh waiting for a rodent or rabbit to reveal its location. Exceptional powers of sight and hearing help them in detecting and capturing prey. Unlike most owls they forage by the light of day. Because they sit on dunes and fence posts out in the open, they are often easy to observe for long periods of time.

Sanderling (Calidris alba) *showing the bright white belly and head characteristic of this species in winter.* GARRY KESSLER

Dunlin (Calidris alpina) *in nonbreeding plumage* BLAIR NIKULA

Sanderlings *(Calidris alba)* are small sandpipers common along our coast during their winter migrations. They are perhaps best known for their foraging habit of running up and down sandy beaches just ahead of an incoming wave and then reversing direction as it recedes. Their activities mimic those of small children trying to stay as close to the water's edge without actually getting their feet wet. Bursts of running are interspersed with bill probing of the wet sand in search of crustaceans and bivalves. Mole Crabs and Horseshoe Crab eggs are favorite food items. Sanderlings can be distinguished from other small shorebirds or "peeps" by their white heads and bellies. They travel in small flocks that run up and down the shore together. They also fly in a frantic, but seemingly coordinated, manner alternately displaying flapping brown wings and bright white bellies. Surprisingly they are only part-time residents of the Atlantic coast. They nest in high Arctic tundra but spend little time in this location. Spring migration occurs in May, and southward migration takes place from July to October. Most birds overwinter in South America; however small numbers will overwinter along the Atlantic coast of the United States.

Large flocks of **Dunlin** *(Calidris alpina)* winter along coastal estuaries and are common from New Jersey south. These medium-sized sandpipers (9 inches [22 cm] in length) have a rufous back and black belly during breeding season. In winter they are much duller, brownish gray overall with a long black bill and black feet. Dunlin repeatedly probe the surface of mudflats with their bills in search of amphipods, molluscs, and worms. Merlins and other falcons take a large toll on wintering Dunlin.

AFTERWORD

One of my duties as a college professor is to assign homework. The assignment for the readers of this book is a simple, yet lifelong, task. **Go to the beach!**

See the world in a new way. Try to understand the world from the point of view of a snail, a whale, a blade of kelp, or any of the other species that live at the seashore. Each time that you visit the beach try to find a species that you have never seen before. Try to understand how the ecosystem functions, whether it be a wave-swept beach, estuary, or the open ocean.

Finally, work to protect these ecosystems and the species that live there. It is no longer possible to separate our actions from the well-being of these special places and unique species. No matter how far from the coast we might live, we have an impact either through the sewage we flush, the fertilizers that grow our crops, the greenhouse gasses we release by burning fossil fuels, or the seafood we buy in the grocery store. Humans have inserted themselves into these ecosystems, and we are now obligated to protect and care for them.

"Whatever attitude to human existence you fashion for yourself, know that it is valid only if it be the shadow of an attitude to Nature. As human life, so often likened to a spectacle upon a stage, is more justly a ritual. The ancient values of dignity, beauty, and poetry which sustain it are of Nature's inspiration: they are born of the mystery and beauty of the world. Do no dishonour to the earth lest you dishonour the spirit of man. Hold your hands out over the earth as over a flame. To all who love her, who open to her the doors of their veins, she gives of her strength, sustaining them with her own measureless tremor of dark life. Touch the earth, love the earth, honour the earth, her plains, her valleys, her hills, and her seas; rest your spirit in her solitary places. For the gifts of life are the earth's and they are given to all, and they are the songs of birds at daybreak, Orion and the Bear, and dawn over ocean from the beach."

— Henry Beston. (*The Outermost House: A Year of Life on the Great Beach of Cape Cod.* New York: Henry Holt and Company, 1928.)

REFERENCES

Introduction and The Coastline

Carlton, J. T. 1989. "Man's role in changing the face of the ocean: Biological invasions and implications for conservation of near-shore environments." *Conservation Biology* 3:265–273.

Chaplin, M. 2005. Water structure and behavior. www.lsbu.ac.uk/water/.

Conkling, P. W. 1995. *From Cape Cod to the Bay of Fundy: An Environmental Atlas of the Gulf of Maine.* Cambridge: MIT Press.

Davis, R. A. 1994. *The Evolving Coast.* New York: Scientific American Library.

Gosner, K. L. 1971. *Guide to Identification of Marine and Estuarine Invertebrates.* New York: Wiley.

Oldale, R. N. 1992. *Cape Cod and the Islands: The Geologic Story.* East Orleans, MA: Parnassus Imprints.

Ruiz et al. 2000. "Invasion of coastal marine communities in North America: Apparent patterns, processes, and biases." *Annual Review of Ecology and Systematics* 31: 481–531.

Food Chains and the Forgotten Plankton

Burkholder, J. M. 1999. "The lurking perils of Pfiesteria." *Scientific American* 281: 28–35.

Graham, L. E., and L. W. Wilcox. 2000. *Algae.* Saddle River, NJ: Prentice Hall.

The Harmful Algae Page, www.whoi.edu/redtide/.

Valiela, I. 1995. *Marine Ecological Processes.* New York: Springer-Verlag.

Rocky Shores

Acheson, J. M., and Steneck, R. S. 1997. "Bust and then boom in the Maine lobster industry: Perspectives of fishers and biologists." *North American Journal of Fisheries Management* 17: 826–847.

Behrens Yamada, S. 2001. *Global Invader: The European Green Crab.* Corvallis, OR: Oregon Sea Grant Publication ORESCU-B-01-001, Oregon State University.

Bertness, M. D. 1984. "Habitat and community modification by an introduced herbivorous snail." *Ecology* 65: 370–381.

Carriker, M. R., D. Van Zandt, and G. Charlton, 1967. "Gastropod *Urosalpinx:* pH of accessory boring organ while boring." *Science* 158: 920–922.

Franz, D. R., E. K. Worley, and A. S. Merrill, 1981. "Distribution patterns of common seastars of the middle Atlantic continental shelf of the northwest Atlantic (Gulf of Maine to Cape Hatteras)." *Biological Bulletin* 160: 394–418.

Galtstoff, P. S., H. F. Prytherch, and J. B. Engle. 1937. "Natural history and methods of controlling the common oyster drills (*Urosalpinx cinerea* Say and *Eupleura caudata* Say)." Fishery Circular No. 25, U.S. Department of Commerce, Bureau of Fisheries, pp. 1–24.

Graham, L. E., and L. W. Wilcox. 2000. *Algae.* Upper Saddle River, NJ: Prentice-Hall.

Jensen, G. C., P. S. McDonald, and D. A. Armstrong. 2002. "East meets west: Competitive interactions between green crab *Carcinus maenus,* and native and introduced shore crab *Hemigrapsus* spp." *Marine Ecology Progress Series* 225: 251–262.

Kingsbury, J., and P. Sze. 1997. *Seaweeds of Cape Cod and the Islands,* 2nd ed. Jersey Shore, PA: Bullbrier Press.

Lohrer, A. M. 2001. "The invasion by *Hemigrapsus sanguineus* in eastern North America: A review." *Aquatic Invaders* 12: 1–11.

Lohrer, A. M., and R. B. Whitlatch. 2002. "Relative impacts of two exotic brachyuran species on blue mussel populations in Long Island Sound." *Marine Ecology Progress Series* 227: 135–144.

Loosanoff, V. L. 1961. "Biology and methods of controlling the starfish, *Asterias forbesi* (DESOR)." Fishery Leaflet 520. Washington, DC: United States Department of the Interior, Fish and Wildlife Service Bureau of Commercial Fisheries.

Lubchenco, J. 1978. "Plant species diversity in a marine intertidal community: Importance of herbivore food preference and algal competitive abilities." *American Naturalist* 112: 23–39.

———. 1980. "Algal zonation in the New England rocky intertidal community: An experimental analysis." *Ecology* 61: 333–344.

———, and B. A. Menge. 1978. "Community development and persistence in a low rocky intertidal zone." *Ecological Monographs* 48: 67–94.

Maine Department of Marine Resources. 2006. Lobster Commercial Catch Statistics and 2005 Lobster Stock Assessment. www.maine.gov/dmr/rm/lobster/2005assessment.htm.

Menge, B. A. 1976. "Organization of the New England rocky intertidal community: Role of predation, competition, and environmental heterogeneity." *Ecological Monographs* 46: 355–393.

Petraitis, P. S., E. C. Rhile, and S. Dugeon. 2003. "Survivorship of juvenile barnacles and mussels: Spatial dependence and the origin of alternative communities." *Journal of Experimental Marine Biology and Ecology* 293: 217–236.

Steneck, R. S. 1982. "A limpet-coralline alga association: Adaptations and defenses between a selective herbivore and its prey." *Ecology* 63: 507–522.

Tubiash, H. S. 1966. "Ornamental Use of Starfishes." Circular 253. United States Department of the Interior, Washington, DC.

Wahle, R. A., and R. S. Steneck. 1992. "Habitat restrictions in early benthic life: Experiments on habitat selection and in situ predation with the American lobster." *Journal of Experimental Marine Biology and Ecology* 157: 91–114.

Williams, A. B., and J. J. McDermott. 1990. "An eastern United States record for the western Indo-Pacific crab *Hemigrapsus sanguineus* (Crustacea: Decapoda: Grapsidae)." *Proceedings of the Biological Society of Washington* 103: 108–109.

Whitman, J. D. 1985. "Refuges, biological disturbance, and rocky subtidal community structure in New England." *Ecological Monographs* 55: 421–445.

———. 1987. "Subtidal coexistence: Storms, grazing, mutualism, and the zonation of kelps and mussels." *Ecological Monographs* 57: 167–187.

Woodard, C. 2004. *The Lobster Coast: Rebels, Rusticators, and the Struggle for a Forgotten Frontier.* New York: Penguin Books.

Sandy Beaches

Burger, J. 1996. "Laughing Gull *(Larus atricilla)*." In *The Birds of North America*, No. 225 (A. Poole and F. Gill, eds.). Philadelphia: The Academy of Natural Sciences; Washington, DC: The American Ornithologists' Union.

Cargnelli, L. M., S. J. Griesbach, D. B. Packer, and E. Weissberger. 1999. "Essential fish habitat source document: Atlantic Surfclam, *Spisula solidissima*, life history and habitat characteristics." NOAA Technical Memorandum NMFS-NE-142, U.S. Department of Commerce.

Ellers, O. 1995a. "Behavioral control of swash-riding in the clam *Donax variabilis*." *Biological Bulletin* 189: 120–127.

_____. 1995. "Discrimination among wave-generated sounds by a swash-riding clam." *Biological Bulletin* 189: 128–137.

Ellis, R. 2003. *The Empty Ocean: Plundering the World's Marine Life*. Washington, DC: Island Press.

Good, T. P. 1998. "Great Black-backed Gull *(Larus marinus)*." In *The Birds of North America*, No. 330 (A. Poole and F. Gill, eds.). Philadelphia: The Birds of North America, Inc.

Gould, S. J. 1985. *The Flamingo's Smile: Reflections in Natural History*. New York: W.W. Norton & Company.

Haig, Susan M., and E. Elliott-Smith. (2004). "Piping Plover." In *The Birds of North America*, No. 2 (A. Poole, Ed.) Ithaca, NY: Cornell Laboratory of Ornithology.

Manning, L. M., and N. Lindquist. 2003. "Helpful inhabitant or pernicious passenger: Interactions between an infaunal bivalve, an epifaunal hydroid and three potential predators." *Oecologia* 134: 415–422.

McDermott, J. J. 1983. "Food web in the surf zone of an exposed sandy beach along the Mid-Atlantic coast of the United States." In A. McLachlan, and T. Erasmus, eds., *Sandy Beaches as Ecosystems*. The Hague, Netherlands: R W. Junk Publishers.

McLachlan, A. 1983. "Sandy beach ecology–A review." In A. McLachlan, and T. Erasmus, eds., *Sandy Beaches as Ecosystems*. The Hague, Netherlands: DR W. Junk Publishers.

Pierotti, R. J., and T. P. Good. 1994. "Herring Gull *(Larus argentatus)*." In The *Birds of North America*, No. 124 (A. Poole and F. Gill, Eds.). Philadelphia: The Academy of Natural Sciences; Washington, DC: The American Ornithologists' Union.

Ryder, J. P. 1993. "Ring-billed Gull." In *The Birds of North America*, No. 33 (A. Poole, P. Stettenheim, and F. Gill, Eds.). Philadelphia: The Academy of Natural Sciences; Washington, DC: The American Ornithologists' Union.

Thompson, B. C., J. A. Jackson, J. Burger, L. A. Hill, E. M. Kirsch, and J. L. Atwood. 1997. "Least Tern *(Sterna antillarum)*." In *The Birds of North America*, No. 290 (A. Poole and F. Gill, eds.). Philadelphia: The Academy of Natural Sciences; Washington, DC: The American Ornithologists' Union.

Turtle Expert Working Group. 2000. *Assessment Update for the Kemp's Ridley and Loggerhead Sea Turtle Populations in the Western North Atlantic*. U.S. Department of Commerce NOAA Technical Memo NMFS-SEFSC-444, 115 pp.

Wolcott, T. G. 1978. "Ecological role of Ghost Crabs, *Ocypode quadrata* (Fabricius) on an ocean beach: Scavengers or predators?" *Journal of Experimental Marine Biology and Ecology* 31: 67–82.

Yund, P. O., C. W. Cunnigham, and L. W. Buss. 1987. "Recruitment and postrecruitment interactions in a colonial hydroid." *Ecology* 68: 971–982.

Sand Dunes

Centers for Disease Control. 2005. Lyme Disease—Division of Vector-Borne Infectious Diseases, www.cdc.gov/ncidod/dvbid/lyme/index.htm.

Ehrenfeld, J. G. 1990. "Dynamics and processes of barrier island vegetation." *Reviews in Aquatic Sciences* 2: 437–480.

Nickerson, N. H., and F. R. Thibodeau. 1983. "Destruction of *Ammophila breviligulata* by pedestrian traffic: Quantification and control." *Biological Conservation* 27: 277–287.

Oldale, R. N. 1992. *Cape Cod and the Islands: The Geologic Story.* East Orleans, MA: Parnassus Imprints.

Shumway, S. W. 2000. "Facilitative effects of a sand dune shrub on species growing beneath the shrub canopy." *Oecologia* 124: 138–148.

_____, and C. Banks. 2001. "Species distributions in interdunal swale communities: The effects of soil waterlogging." *American Midland Naturalist* 145: 137–146.

Estuaries

Carlton, J. T., and J. A. Scanlon. 1985. "Progression and dispersal of an introduced alga: *Codium fragile* ssp. *tomentosoides* (Chlorophyta) on the Atlantic coast of North America." *Botanica Marina* 28: 155–165.

Gough. L. Personal communication. How to sex a crab.

Howes, B. L., and D. D. Goehringer. 1996. "Ecology of Buzzards Bay: An estuarine profile." *National Biological Service Biological Report* 31. 141 pp.

Jivoff, P. 1997a. "The relative roles of predation and sperm competition on the duration of the post-copulatory association between the sexes in the blue crab, *Callinectes sapidus.*" *Behavioral Ecology and Sociobiology* 40: 175–185.

_____. 1997b. "Sexual competition among male blue crab, *Callinectes sapidus.*" *Biological Bulletin* 193: 368–380.

Kennedy, V. S., R. I. E. Newell, and A. F. Eble, eds. 1996. *The Eastern Oyster* Crassostrea virginica. College Park: Maryland Seagrant College.

Ketchum, B. H., ed. 1983. *Estuaries and Enclosed Seas* (Ecosystems of the World, 26). New York: Elsevier.

Levin, L. A., D. F. Boesch, A. Covich, C. Dahm, C. Erséus, K. C. Ewel, R. T. Kneib, A. Moldenke, M. A. Palmer, P. Snelgrove, D. Strayer, and J. M. Weslawski. 2001. "The function of marine critical transition zones and the importance of sediment biodiversity." *Ecosystems* 4: 430–451.

Lippson, A. J., and R. L. Lippson. 1984. *Life in the Chesapeake Bay,* 2nd ed. Baltimore: The Johns Hopkins University Press.

Manomet. 2005. Western Hemisphere Shorebird Reserve Network, www.whsrn.org/.

Shuster, C. N., Jr., R. B. Barlow, and H. J. Brockmann. 2003. *The American Horseshoe Crab.* Cambridge, MA: Harvard University Press.

Turner, H. V., D. L. Wolcott, T. G. Wolcott, and A. J. Hines. 2003. "Post-mating behavior, intramolt growth, and onset of migration to Chesapeake Bay spawning grounds by adult female blue crabs, *Callinectes sapidus Rathbun.*" *Journal of Experimental Marine Biology and Ecology* 295: 107–130.

Warner, W. W. 1976. *Beautiful Swimmers: Watermen, Crabs and the Chesapeake Bay.* Boston: Little, Brown and Company.

Weidensaul, S. 1999. *Living on the Wind: Across the Hemisphere with Migratory Birds.* New York: North Point Press.

Salt Marshes

Auger, P. J., and P. Giovannone. 1979. "On the fringe of existence: Diamondback terrapins on Sandy Neck." *The Cape Naturalist* 8: 44–58.

Bertness, M. D. 1984. "Ribbed mussels and *Spartina alterniflora* production in a New England salt marsh." *Ecology* 65: 1794–1807.

_____. 1985. "Fiddler crab regulation of *Spartina alterniflora* production on a New England salt marsh." *Ecology* 66: 1042–1055.

_____. 1991a. "Interspecific interactions among high marsh perennials in a New England salt marsh." *Ecology* 72: 125–137.

_____. 1991b. "Zonation of *Spartina* patens and *Spartina alterniflora* in a New England salt marsh." *Ecology* 72: 138–148.

_____, and S.W. Shumway. 1992. Consumer driven pollen limitation of seed production in marsh grasses. *American Journal of Botany* 79: 288–293.

_____, B. R. Silliman, and R. Jefferies. 2004. "Salt marshes under siege." *American Scientist* 92: 54–61.

Bildstein, K. L., S. G. McDowell, and L. L. Brisbin. 1989. "Consequences of sexual dimorphism in sand fiddler crabs, *Uca pugilator:* Differential vulnerability to avian predation." *Animal Behavior* 37: 133–139.

Brennessel, B. 2006. *Diamonds in the Marsh: A Natural History of the Diamondback Terrapin.* Lebanon, NH: University Press of New England.

Christy, J. H., and M. Salmon. 1984. "Ecology and evolution of mating systems of fiddler crabs (genus Uca)." *Biological Review* 59: 483–509.

Ernst, C. H., J. E. Lovich, and R. W. Barbour. 1994. *Turtles of the United States and Canada.* Washington, DC: Smithsonian Institution Press.

Howes, B. L., and D. D. Goehringer. 1996. "Ecology of Buzzards Bay: An estuarine profile." *National Biological Services Biological Report* 33. 141 pp.

"Insect and Related Pests of Man and Animals: Some Important, Common and Potential Pests in the Southeastern United States." North Carolina Cooperative Extension Service. Publication AG-369.

Jordan, T. E., and I. Valiela. 1982. "The nitrogen budget of the ribbed mussel, *Geukensia demissa,* and its significance in nitrogen flow in a New England salt marsh." *Limnology and Oceanography* 27: 75–90.

Koeler, P. G., and F. M. Oi. 2003. "Biting Flies." Florida Cooperative Extension Service, Institute of Food and Agricultural Services, University of Florida. Publication ENY-220.

Mal, T. K. et al. 1992. "The biology of Canadian weeds. 100. *Lythrum salicaria.*" *Canadian Journal of Plant Science* 72: 1305–1330.

Malecki, R. A. 1993. "Biological control of purple loosestrife." *Bioscience* 43: 680–686.

Poole, A. F., R. O. Bierregaard, and M. S. Martell. 2002. "Osprey *(Pandion haliaetus)*." In *The Birds of North America,* No. 683 (A. Poole and F. Gill, eds.). Philadelphia: The Birds of North America, Inc.

Silliman, B. R., and M. D. Bertness. 2002. "A trophic cascade regulates salt marsh primary production." *Proceedings of the National Academy of Science* 99: 10500–10505.

Stegmann, E. W., R. B. Primack, and G. S. Ellmore. 1988. "Absorption of nutrient exudates from terrapin eggs by roots of *Ammophila breviligulata* (Gramineae)." *Canadian Journal of Botany* 66:714–718.

Stuckey, R. L. 1980. "Distributional history of *Lythrum salicaria* (purple loosestrife) in North America." *Bartonia* 47: 3–20.

Teal. J. M. 1986. "The ecology of regularly flooded salt marshes of New England: A community profile." U.S. Fish and Wildlife Service Biological Report 85(7.4). 61 pp.

———, and M. Teal. 1969. *Life and Death of the Salt Marsh.* New York: Ballantine Books.

Tidal Flats

Brousseau, D. J. 1978. "Spawning cycle, fecundity, and recruitment in a population of soft-shell clam, Mya arenaria, from Cape Ann, Massachusetts." *Fishery Bulletin* 76: 155–166.

Butler, R. W. 1992. "Great Blue Heron." In *The Birds of North America,* No. 25 (A. Poole, P. Stettenheim, and F. Gill, Eds.). Philadelphia: The Academy of Natural Sciences; Washington, DC: The American Ornithologists' Union.

Kelaher, B. P., J. S. Levinton, and M. J. Hoch. 2003. "Foraging by the mud snail, *Ilyanassa obsoleta* (Say), modulates spatial variation in benthic community structure." *Journal of Experimental Marine Biology and Ecology* 292: 139–157.

McCrimmon, D. A., Jr., J. C. Ogden, and G. T. Bancroft. 2001. "Great Egret *(Ardea alba)*." In *The Birds of North America,* No. 570 (A. Poole and F. Gill, eds.). Philadelphia: The Birds of North America, Inc.

Parsons, K. C., and T. L. Master. 2000. "Snowy Egret *(Egretta thula)*." In *The Birds of North America,* No. 489 (A. Poole and F. Gill, eds.). Philadelphia: The Birds of North America, Inc.

Smithsonian Institution. 1999. "The Feather Trade and the American Conservation Movement." http://americanhistory.si.edu/feather/.

Whitlatch, R. B. 1982. "The ecology of New England tidal flats: A community profile." Washington, DC: U.S. Fish and Wildlife Service, Biological Services Program, FWS/OBS-81/01. 125 pp.

Seagrass Meadows

Hemminga, M., and C. Duarte. 2000. *Seagrass Ecology.* Cambridge, UK: Cambridge University Press.

Rasmussen, E. 1977. "The wasting disease of Eelgrass *(Zostera marina)* and its effects on environmental factors and fauna." In C. P. McRoy, and C. Helfferich, eds., *Seagrass Ecosystems: A Scientific Perspective.* New York: Marcel Dekker.

Thayer, G. W., W. J. Kenworthy, and M. S. Fonseca. 1984. "The ecology of eelgrass meadows of the Atlantic coast: A community profile." U.S. Fish and Wildlife Service. FWS/OBS-84/02. 147 pp.

Open Ocean

Ellis, R. 2003. *The Empty Ocean: Plundering the World's Marine Life.* Washington, DC: Island Press.

Gaston, A. J. 2004. *Seabirds: A Natural History.* New Haven, CT: Yale University Press..

Lowther, P. E., A. W. Diamond, S. W. Kress, G. J. Robertson, and K. Russell. 2002. "Atlantic Puffin *(Fratercula arctica).*" In *The Birds of North America,* No. 709 (A. Poole, and F. Gill, eds.). Philadelphia : The Birds of North America, Inc.

Mowbray, T. B. 2002. "Northern Gannet *(Morus bassanus).*" In *The Birds of North America,* No. 693 (A. Poole and F. Gill, eds.). Philadelphia: The Birds of North America, Inc.

Nelson, B. 1979. *Seabirds: Their Biology and Ecology.* New York: A & W Publishers.

Reeves, R. R. et al. 2002. *Guide to Marine Mammals of the World.* New York: Chanticleer Press.

Roman, J., and S. R. Palumbi. 2003. "Whales before whaling in the North Atlantic." *Science* 301: 508–510.

Tove, M. H. 2000. *Guide to the Offshore Wildlife of the Northern Atlantic.* Austin: University of Texas Press.

Ward, N. 1995. *Stellwagen Bank: A Guide to the Whales, Sea Birds, and Marine Life of the Stellwagen Bank National Marine Sanctuary.* Camden, ME: Down East Books.

The Beach in Winter

Bordage, D., and J. L. Savard. 1995. "Black Scoter *(Melanitta nigra).*" In *The Birds of North America,* No. 177 (A. Poole and F. Gill, eds.). Philadelphia: The Academy of Natural Sciences; Washington, DC: The American Ornithologists' Union.

Brown, P. W., and L. H. Fredrickson. 1997. "White-winged Scoter *(Melanitta fusca).*" In The Birds of North America, No. 274 (A. Poole, and F. Gill, eds.). Philadelphia: The Academy of Natural Sciences; Washington, DC: The American Ornithologists' Union.

Goslow, Jr., G. E. 1971. "The attack and strike of some North American raptors." *Auk* 88: 815–827.

Goudie, R. I., G. J. Robertson, and A. Reed. 2000. "Common Eider *(Somateria mollissima).*" In *The Birds of North America,* No. 546 (A. Poole and F. Gill, eds.). Philadelphia: The Birds of North America, Inc.

Lyon, B., and R. Montgomerie. 1995. "Snow Bunting and McKay's Bunting (*Plectrophenax nivalis* and *Plectrophenax hyperboreus).*" In *The Birds of North America,* No. 198–199 (A. Poole, and F. Gill, eds.). Philadelphia: The Academy of Natural Sciences; Washington, DC: The American Ornithologists' Union.

MacWhirter, B., P. Austin-Smith, Jr., and D. Kroodsma. 2002. "Sanderling *(Calidris alba).*" In *The Birds of North America,* No. 653 (A. Poole and F. Gill, eds.). Philadelphia: The Birds of North America, Inc.

Parmelee, David. 1992. "Snowy Owl." In *The Birds of North America,* No. 10 (A. Poole, P. Stettenheim, and F. Gill, eds.). Philadelphia: The Academy of Natural Sciences; Washington, DC: The American Ornithologists' Union.

Robertson, G. J., and R. I. Goudie. 1999. "Harlequin Duck *(Histrionicus histrionicus).*" In *The Birds of North America,* No. 466 (Poole, A., and F. Gill, eds.). Philadelphia, PA: The Birds of North America, Inc.

Savard, J.-P. L., D. Bordage, and A. Reed. 1998. "Surf Scoter *(Melanitta perspicillata)*." In *The Birds of North America*, No. 363 (A. Poole and F. Gill, eds.). Philadelphia: The Birds of North America, Inc.

Tove, M. H. 2000. *Guide to the Offshore Wildlife of the Northern Atlantic.* Austin: University of Texas Press.

Viet, R. R., and W. R. Petersen. 1993. *Birds of Massachusetts.* Lincoln, MA: Massachusetts Audubon Society.

Warkentin, I. G., N. S. Sodhi, R. H. M. Espie, and A. F. Poole. (2005). "Merlin *(Falco columbarius)*." The Birds of North America Online. (A. Poole, ed.) Ithaca, NY: Cornell Laboratory of Ornithology.

Warnock, N. D., and R. E Gill. 1996. "Dunlin *(Calidris alpina)*." In *The Birds of North America*, No. 203 (A. Poole, and F. Gill, eds.). Philadelphia: The Academy of Natural Sciences; Washington, DC: The American Ornithologists' Union

General

Bigelow, H. B., and W. C. Schroeder. 1953. *Fishes of the Gulf of Maine. U.S. Fish and Wildlife Service Bulletin* 53(74): 1–577.

Gleason, H. A., and A. Cronquist. 1963. *Manual of Vascular Plants of Northeastern United States and Canada.* Boston: Willard Grant Press.

Gosner, K. L. 1971. *Guide to Identification of Marine and Estuarine Invertebrates.* New York: Wiley.

_____. 1978. *A Field Guide to the Atlantic Seashore from the Bay of Fundy to Cape Hatteras.* Boston: Houghton Mifflin.

Kaufman, K. 1996. *Lives of North American Birds.* Boston: Houghton Mifflin.

Martinez, A. J. 1994. *Marine Life of the North Atlantic.* Camden, ME: Downeast Books.

National Marine Fisheries Service. 1999. *Our Living Oceans. Report on the Status of U.S. Living Marine Resources.* U.S. Department of Commerce, NOAA Technical Memo. NMFS-F/SPO-41.

Pollack, L. W. 1998. *A Practical Guide to the Marine Animals of Northeastern North America.* New Brunswick, NJ: Rutgers University Press.

Poole, A. (editor). 2005. The Birds of North American Online: http://bna.birds.cornell.edu/BNA/. Ithaca, NY: Cornell Laboratory of Ornithology.

Sibley, D. A. 2000. *National Audubon Society: The Sibley Guide to Birds.* New York: Knopf.

Weiss, H. M. 1995. *Marine Animals of Southern New England and New York.* Hartford, CT: State Geological and Natural History Survey of Connecticut.

INDEX

A

adaptations, 9
Aedes sollicitans, 150
aerenchyma, 138, 179, 181
Agarum cribrosum, 67
Alewife, 129, 132
Alexandrium, 34
Alexandrium fundyense, 34
algal blooms, 32, 33–35
algal crust, 46
alien species, 6–7
Alosa pseudoharengus, 129, 132
Amelanchier, 132
American Beachgrass, 100–101
American Black Ducks, 131, 206, 208
American cranberry, 106
American Horseshoe Crab, 123–25
American Lobster, 69–71
American Oyster, 114–15
Amethyst Gem Clam, 166
Ammodytes americanus, 171
Ammophila breviligulata, 100–101
Amnesic shellfish poisoning (ASP), 33
amphipods, 78, 148, 204
Amphitrite johnstoni, 162
Anas rubripes, 150
animal plankton, 31–32
Apeltes, 152
Arbacia punctulata, 68
Arctostaphylos uva-ursi, 103
Arctic Tern, 92
Ardea alba, 173, 174
Ardea herodias, 173–74
Argopecten irradians, 181–82
Artemisia caudata, 103
Artemisia stelleriana, 103
Asian Shore Crab, 60–61
Asterias forbesii, 63, 117
Asterias vulgaris, 63
Aster tenuifolia, 143
Atlantic Puffins, 201–2, 207
Atlantic Silversides, 78, 134, 152, 183
Atlantic Surf Clam, 80
Atlantic White-Sided Dolphin, 191
Atriplex patula, 142
Aurelia aurita, 87
autotrophs, 136

B

Baccharis halimifolia, 141
backdunes, 100
Balaenoptera physalus, 187, 190
baleen whales, 188, 192, 193
Bamboo Worms, 162, 163
bar-built estuaries, 110
barnacles, 40, 50, 52
barrier beaches, 110
barrier islands, 18, 110
Basking Shark, 196
Bay of Fundy, 11, 12
Bay Scallop, 181–82
Beach Flea, 78, 204
Beach Heather, 102–3
Beach Hopper, 78
Beach Pea, 103
Beach Plum, 103
Bearberry, 103
bioaccumulation, 136
biodiversity, 7–9
biogeography, 2–3
biological species concept, 8
Biting Houseflies, 151
Biting midges, 150–51
Bittium snails, 181
Black-Bellied Plover, 94
Black-Crowned Night Heron, 173
Black Guillemot, 207
Black-Legged Kittiwake, 198, 207
Black Rush, 140, 146
Black Scoter, 210
Black Sea Bass, 171
Black Skimmer, 154
bloodworms, 164
Blue Crab, 117, 119–22, 170

Bluefin Tuna, 194, 195
Bluefish, 78, 133–34, 183
Blue Mussel, 53, 168
Blue Whales, 187, 190, 193
Boat-Tailed Grackle, 153
Bolinopsis infundibulum, 88
Boneparte's Gull, 207
Boonea impressa, 119
Boreal Region, 2
boring sponges, 82–83, 117, 119
Borrelia burgdorferi, 104
Borrichia frutescens, 143
Bottlenose Dolphin, 191
Branta bernicla, 180
Brant, 180, 206, 208
Brevoortia tyrannus, 133
brown seaweeds, 43
Bubo scandiacus, 206, 213
Bucephala albeola, 184
Bufflehead, 184, 208
Busycon carica, 85
Busycotypus canaliculatus, 85
Butorides virescens, 173
Buzzards Bay, 12

C

Cakile edentulata, 103
Calcarius lapponicus, 211
Calidris alba, 214
Calidris alpina, 214
Callinectes sapidus, 119–22, 170
Calonextris diomedea, 198
Calopogon pulchellus, 107
Canada Rush, 105
Cape Cod, 12
Carcharhinus plumbeus, 195
Carcinus maenus, 58–60, 170
Caretta caretta, 95–96
Catoptrophorus semipalmatus, 154
centric diatoms, 27–28
Centropristis striata, 171
cetaceans, 187–94
Cetorhinus maximus, 196
Chaetoceros, 27–28
Channeled Whelk, 85

Charadrius melodus, 92–93
Charadrius semipalmatus, 93
Chen caerulescens, 154
Chesapeake Bay, 13, 130–31
Chondrus crispus, 45, 47
Chrysops, 151
Chrysopsis falcata, 103
Chthamalus fragilis, 40
clams, 75, 146–48
clam worms, 164
Clapper Rail, 153
Clathromorphum circumscriptum,
    49–50
Cliona, 82–83, 117
Clymenella torquata, 162, 163
Cocklebur, 103
Codium fragile, 118
Coffee Bean Snail, 150
comb jellies, 87–88, 114
Common Atlantic Slippersnail, 80–82
Common Black-Headed Gull, 207
Common Eider, 208–9
Common Goldeneye, 208
Common Loon, 208
Common Murre, 207
Common Northern Comb Jelly, 88
Common Periwinkle, 6, 48, 49, 51, 64,
    65, 149, 168–69
Common Reed Grass, 143
Common Saltwort, 103
Common Sea Star, 63, 117
Common Tern, 92
Conocephalus spartinae, 150
continental shelf, 186
continental slope, 186
copepods, 31
Coquina, vi, 75–76
Corallina officinalis, 46
Coral Weed, 46, 64
Coriolis effect, 17
Cory's Shearwater, 198
Cownose Ray, 117, 183
crabs, 58–61, 76–78, 119–22, 146–48,
    170
Crangon septemspinosus, 78, 170

Crassostrea virginica, 114–15
Crepidula fornicata, 80–82
Ctenophore, 87–88
Culicoides, 150–51
currents, 18–20
Cuscuta, 142
Cyanea capillata, 87
cyanobacteria, 30, 136
Cyperus dentatus, 106
Cyprinodon variegatus, 152

D
DDT, 156
Dead Man's Fingers, 118
Deerflies, 151
Deer Tick, 104
Delmarva Peninsula, 13
Delphinus delphis, 191
deposit feeders, 162
Dermo, 119
Deschampsia flexuosa, 103
detritivores, 137–38
detritus, 25, 178
Diamondback Terrapin, 152–53
diatoms, 26–29, 113
Digging amphiphods, 75
dinoflagellates, 29–30, 33–34, 36
Diopatra cuprea, 164, 166
Distichlis spicata, 140–41
dodder, 142
Dogwinkle snails, 55–56, 57
dolphins, 187, 191
Donax variabilis, 75–76
Dovekie, 206
Drosera intermedia, 106
drowned river-valley estuaries, 110
Drumfish, 117
Dunlins, 94, 206, 214
Dusty Miller, 103

E
Echinarachnius parma, 85
ecological succession, 141
ecosystems, definition of, 4
Eelgrass, 176, 177–81, 182, 183, 184

eels, 132
egg cases, 86
egrets, 154, 173–75
Egretta caerulea, 173
Egretta thula, 173, 174–75
Egretta tricolor, 173
Emerita talpoida, 76, 78
Ensis directus, 168, 170
Enteromorpha intestinalis, 43, 64–65
epiphytes, 181

F
Falco columbarius, 206, 212
Falco peregrinus, 212–13
fiddler crabs, 146–48, 149
Fin Whale, 187, 190, 193
Flat-Clawed Hermit Crab, 84
flatworms, 117
food chains, 28–29
food web, 26
foredunes, 99–100
Forster's Tern, 92
Frankia, 102
Franklin's Gull, 207
Fratercula arctica, 201–2
Fucus, 44, 45
Fucus distichus, 44
Fucus spiralis, 44
Fucus vesiculosus, 44
Fulmarus glacialis, 198, 200
Fundulus heteroclitus, 152, 171

G
Gammarus, 148
Gasterosteus, 152
Gemma gemma, 166
Gerardia maritima, 143
Geukenisa demissa, 148–49
Ghost Crab, 77
Giant Kelp, 47
glacial activity, 23–24
Glasswort, 142
Glaucous Gull, 207
Glycera, 164
Goosefoot, 142

Grass Pink, 107
Grass Shrimp, 170
Gray Seal, 205
Great Black-Backed Gull, 88, 89, 90, 207
Great Blue Heron, 173–74
Great Cormorant, 208
Great Egret, 173, 174
Greater Shearwater, 197, 198
Greater Yellowlegs, 94
Great Scaup, 208
Green Crab, 6, 58–60, 170
Greene's Rush, 105–6
Green Fleece, 118
Greenheads, 151
Green Heron, 173
Green Sea Urchin, 66, 68
Groundsel, 146
Groundsel Tree, 141–42
Gulf of Maine, 11–12, 55, 71
Gulf Stream, 17
gulls, 88–91, 207

H

Hair Grass, 103
Halichoerus grypus, 205
Haliclystus, 87
Harbor Porpoise, 191
Harbor Seal, 205
Hard-Shell Clam, 167, 170
Harlequin Duck, 208, 210–11
haustorids, 75
Hemigrapsus sanguineus, 60–61
hermit crabs, 84–85, 170
herons, 154, 173–74
Herring Gull, 88, 89, 90, 207
Hildenbrandia rubra, 46
Histrionicus histrionicus, 210–11
Hollow-Stemmed Kelp, 67
Homarus americanus, 69–71
Homo sapiens, 9, 13–14
Horned Grebe, 208
Horse Mussel, 66
Horseshoe Crab, vi, 123–25, 127, 128, 129, 170
Horsetail Kelp, 66

Hudsonia tomentosa, 102–3
Humpback Whale, 182, 187, 190–91, 193
Hydractinia, 84
Hydrobia totteni, 169
Hydromedusae, 87

I

Ice Cream Cone Worm, 162
Iceland Gull, 207
Irish Moss, 45, 47, 64, 65
Iva frutescens, 141
Ixodes scapularis, 104

J

jellyfish, 86–88
Juncus canadensis, 105
Juncus gerardi, 140
Juncus greenei, 105
Juncus pelocarpus, 105
Juncus roemarianus, 140
Juniperus virginiana, 103

K

kelp beds, 66–67
Keyhole Urchin, 85
Killer Whale, 187, 191
killifish, 134, 152
King Eider, 208
Kingfish, 171
Knobbed Whelk, 85
Knotted Wrack, 44–45, 55
krill, 186, 187

L

Labrador Current, 17
Labyrinthula zosterae, 180
Lady Crab, vi, 78, 170
Lagenorhynchus acutus, 191
Laminaria, 66
Laminaria digitata, 66
Laminaria longicrurius, 67
Laminaria saccharina, 66–67
Lapland Longspurs, 211
Larus argentatus, 89
Larus atricilla, 89

Larus delawarensis, 207
Lathyrus japonicus, 103
Larus marinus, 88
Laughing Gull, 88, 89, 90, 207
Least Tern, 92
Leidy's Comb Jelly, 88
Leiostomus, 78
Lesser Black-Backed Gull, 207
Lesser Scaup, 208
Lesser Yellowlegs, 94
Libinia, 170
Limonium carolinianum, 142–43
Limonium nashii, 142–43
limpets, 49–50
Limulus polyphemus, 123–25, 170
Lion's Mane Jellyfish, 87
Little Blue Heron, 173
Little Gray Barnacle, 52
Littorina irrorata, 149–50
Littorina littorea, 48, 49, 51, 64, 65,
    149–50, 168
Littorina obtusata, 49
Littorina saxatilis, 48, 168
Lobed Moon Snail, 82, 169
lobsters, 69–71
Loggerhead Turtle, 95–96
Long-Billed Dowitcher, 94
Long-Clawed Hermit Crab, 84
Long Island, 12–13
longshore currents, 18
Longitudinal flagellum, 29
Long-Tailed Duck, 208
Lovenella gracilis, 76
Lunatia heros, 82, 169
Lyme disease, 104
Lythrum salicaria, 145

M

Macoma baltica, 166
Malaclemys terrapin, 152–53
Manx Shearwater, 198
Marbled Godwit, 94
Marsh Elder, 141–42, 146
Marsh Hay, 103, 139–40, 146, 158
Marsh Heather, 142–43

Marsh Periwinkle, 149–50
Marsh Wren, 153
Mastocarpus stellatus, 45–46
Meadow Vole, 157
Megaptera novaeangliae, 185, 187,
    190–91
meiofauna, 74
Melampus bidentatus, 150
Melanitta fusca, 210
Melanitta nigra, 210
Melanitta perspicillata, 209, 210
Mellita quinquiesperforata, 85
Menhaden, 133, 183
Menidia menidia, 78, 134, 152
Menticirrhus saxatilis, 78, 171
Mercenaria mercenaria, 167, 170, 181
Merlin, 206, 212
mermaids purse, 86
meroplankton, 32
Microrhopala vittata, 101
Microtus pennsylvanicus, 157
Minke Whale, 187, 188, 193
Mnemiopsis, 114
Mnemiopsis leidyi, 88
Modiolus modiolus, 66
Mola mola, 195
Mole Crab, vi, 76, 78
Moon Jelly, 87
moon snails, 57, 82, 169
Morone saxatilis, 132
Morus bassanus, 200–201
mosquitoes, 150
MSX, 119
Mud Crabs, 117
Mud Fiddler Crab, 146, 147
Mud Rush, 105
Mud Snail, 149, 168, 169
mud worms, 74–75, 119, 162
Mugil, 78
Mugil cephalus, 133
Mullet, 183
Mummichog, 134, 152, 171
Mushroom Cap Jellyfish, 87
mussels, 40, 53–55
Mya arenaria, 166–67, 170

Myrica cerifera, 102
Myrica pensylvanica, 101–2
Mysticetes, 188
Mytilus edulis, 53, 168

N
Narragansett Bay, 12
Narrow-leaved Cattail, 143
Nassarius obsoleta, 149, 168, 169
natural selection, 8
Needle Rush, 140
nematodes, 164
nemertean worms, 164
Nereis, 164
New York Harbor, 12–13
Nodding Ladies' Tresses, 107
North Atlantic Bluefin Tuna, 194
Northern Bayberry, 101–2
Northern Fulmar, 198, 200
Northern Gannet, 200–201, 206
Northern Harrier, 206
Northern Kingfish, 78
Northern Moon Snail, 82, 169
Northern Right Whale, 187, 189, 193
Northern Rock Barnacle, 40, 52
Northern Sea Star, 63
no-see-ums, 150–51
Nucella lapillus, 55–56
nutrient pollution, 113
Nutsedge, 106
Nyctanassa violacea, 173
Nycticorax nycticorax, 173

O
Oceanites oceanicus, 198
Ocean Sunfish, 195
Ocypode quadrata, 77
Odontocetes, 188, 191
Oldsquaw Duck, 208
Orach, 142
Orca, 191
Orchestia, 148
Osprey, 154–57
Ovalipes occellatus, 78, 170
overwash events, 98

Oyster, 114–19
oyster beds, 115–16
Oyster Drill, 56–58, 117

P
Pagurus, 170
Pagurus longicarpus, 84
Pagurus pollicaris, 84
Palaemonetes pugio, 170
Pandion haliaetus, 154–57
Panicum amarum, 103
Panopeus herbstii, 117
parabolic dunes, 97
Paralichthys dentatus, 117, 171, 183
Paralytic shellfish poisoning (PSP),
    33–34
Parasitic Jaeger, 198
Pea Crab, 119
Pectinaria gouldii, 162
pennate diatoms, 28
Peregrine Falcon, 206, 212–13
periwinkle snails, 48–49, 51
Peromyscus leucopus, 157
Pfiesteria piscicida, 34–35
Phalaropus, 200
Phoca vitulina, 205
Phocoena phocoena, 191
photic zone, 26
photosynthesis, 4, 25, 26, 136, 177–78
photosynthetic sulfur bacteria, 137
Phragmites australis, 143, 143–44, 158
Physalia physalia, 87
phytoplankton, 26, 32, 36, 113, 186
Pilot Whale, 187
Pinnotheris ostreum, 119
Piping Plover, 92, 93, 94
Plant Hopper, 150
Plectrophenax nivalis, 211
Pleurobrachia pileus, 88
Pleuronectes americanus, 132–33, 171
plovers, 92–94
Pluchea purpurascens, 143
Plumed Worm, 164, 166
Pogonia ophioglossoides, 107
Poison Ivy, 103

Polinices duplicatus, 82, 169
polychaetes, 165
Polydora, 119, 162
Polygonella articulata, 103
Polysiphonia Ianosa, 44–45
Pomarine Jaegers, 198
Pomatomus, 78
Pomatomus saltatrix, 133–134
Portuguese Man-of-War, 87
primary producers, 25, 136
Prokelisia marginata, 103, 150
Prunus maritima, 103
Pseudonitzschia pungens, 33
Puffinus gravis, 197, 198
Puffinus griseus, 198
Puffinus puffinus, 198
Pungitius, 152
Purple Loosestrife, 145
Purple Sandpiper, 94, 206
Purple Sea Urchin, 68

Q

Quahog, 167, 170, 181

R

Rails, 153–54
Raja, 86, 171
Ralfsia, 46
Razorbill, 207
Razor Clam, 168, 170
Red-Breasted Merganser, 208
Red Cedar, 103
Red-Jointed Fiddler Crab, 146, 148
Red Knot, 94, 125, 127, 128
Red-Necked Phalarope, 200
Red Phalarope, 200
Red-Throated Loon, 208
red tide, 33
Red-Winged Blackbird, 153
Rhinoptera bonasus, 183
Rhopilema verrilli, 87
Ribbed Mussel, 148–49
Ring-Billed Gull, 89, 207
Rissa tridactyla, 198, 207
rockweeds, 44, 64

rorquals, 188
Rosa rugosa, 103
Roseate Tern, 92, 94
Rose Pogonia, 107
Rough Periwinkle, 48, 168
Roundworms, 164
Ruddy Turnstone, 94, 127
Rugosa Rose, 103
Ruppia maritima, 177, 179, 180, 181
Rynchops niger, 154

S

Salicornia europea, 142
Salicornia virginica, 142
Salsola kali, 103
Salt Marsh Aster, 143
Salt Marsh Cordgrass, 139, 144
Salt Marsh Fleabane, 143
Salt Marsh Hay, 139–40
Salt Marsh Mosquito, 150
Saltmarsh Sharp-Tailed Sparrow,
    153, 154
Salt Meadow Grass, 139–40
Sandbar Shark, 195
Sand Dollars, 85
Sanderling, 94, 127, 206, 214
Sand Fiddler Crab, 146
Sand Jointweed, 103
Sand Lance, 171, 186, 202
sandpipers, 94
Sand Shrimp, 78, 170
sandworms, 164
Sargassum, 96
schooling fish, 186
Scololepis squamata, 74–75
scoters, 208, 209–10
Scup, 133
seabird conservation, 199
seabirds, 196–201
Sea Colander, 67
sea cucumbers, 164
sea ducks, 207–11
Sea Gooseberry, 88
Sea Lettuce, 43, 64
seals, 204–5

Sea Oats, 101
Sea Oxeye, 143
Sea Rocket, 103
Seaside Gerardia, 143
Seaside Goldenrod, 101, 142–43
Seaside Panicum, 103
Seaside Sparrow, 153
Seaside Spurge, 103
sea stars, 61–63
sea turtles, 95–96
sea urchins, 68–69
seaweeds, 26, 42–48
Sei Whale, 187
Semibalanus balanoides, 52
Semipalmated Plover, 93, 94
Semipalmated Sandpiper, 94, 127
shad, 129
sharks, 195–96
Shearwaters, 198
Sheepshead Minnow, 152
Short-Beaked Common Dolphin, 191
Short-Billed Dowitcher, 94
Short-Eared Owl, 206
Sickle-Leaved Golden Aster, 103
silversides, 134, 183
Sipunculid worms, 164
skates, 86, 171
Skeletonema costatum, 113
Smooth Periwinkle, 49
Snail Fur, 84
Snow Bunting, 206, 211, 212
Snowy Egret, 173–75
Snow Geese, 154, 206
Snowy Owl, 206, 213
Soft-Shell Clam, 166–67, 170
Solidago sempervirens, 101, 142–43
Somateria mollissima, 208–9
Sooty Shearwater, 198
Spartina alterniflora, 139
Spartina patens, 103, 139–40
Spatulate-Leaved Sundew, 106
speciation, 8–9
Sperm Whale, 187, 191, 192
spider crabs, 170
Spike Grass, 140–41

Spiny Dogfish, 195–96
Spiranthes cernua, 107
Spisula solidissima, 80
Spot, 78, 183
Squalus acanthias, 195–96
SSO, 109
stalked jellyfish, 87
Stenotomus chrysops, 133
Stercorarius, 198
Sterna antillarum, 92
Sterna hirundo, 91
sticklebacks, 134, 152
Storm Petrel, 198
Striped Bass, 132
Striped Mullet, 133
Strongylocentrotus droebachiensis,
    66, 68
Stylochus ellipticus, 117
Sugar Kelp, 66–67
sulfur bacteria, 137
Summer Flounder, 117, 171, 183
Surf Scoter, 210
swales, 97, 103, 104–6
swash zone, 73–78

T

Tabanus conterminus, 151
Tautoga onitis, 133
Tautogs, 133, 183
Tectura testudinalis, 49
Terebellid Worms, 162
terns, 91–92, 154
thermocline, 15, 32, 112
Thick-Billed Murre, 207
Thunnus thynnus, 194, 195
tide pools, 64–65
tides, 18, 20, 112
Toadfish, 117
toothed whales, 188, 191
Tortoise-Shell Limpet, 49
Toxicodendron radicans, 103
Tri-colored Herons, 173
Trirhabda canadensis, 101
Tubed Weed, 44–45
Tufted Red Weed, 45–46

tuna, 194
Tursiops truncatus, 191
Typha angustifolia, 143

U
Uca minax, 146, 147
Uca pugilator, 46
Uca pugnax, 146, 147
Ulorchestia, 148
Ulva lactuca, 43
Uniola paniculata, 101
urchin barrens, 68–69
Urosalpinx cinerea, 56–58, 117

V
Vaccinium macrocarpon, 106
Virginian Region, 2

W
wading birds, 173
wasting disease, 180
water jellies, 87
waves, 17–18
Wax-Myrtle, 102
Wedge Clam, 75–76

whales, 187–94
whelks, 85–86, 181
White-Footed Mouse, 157
White Mullet, 78
White-Winged Scoter, 210
Widgeon Grass, 177, 179, 180, 181
Willet, 153, 154
Wilson's Storm Petrel, 198
winds, 16–17, 97
Winter Flounder, 132–33, 171
worms, 162–65
Wormwood, 103
wrack line, 78–88

X
Xanthium strumarium, 103

Y
Yellow-Crowned Night Heron, 173

Z
zoea larvae, 122
zooplankton, 31, 186
Zostera marina, 176, 177–81, 182, 183, 184